Saving the Pound? Britain's Road to Monetary Union

We work with leading authors to develop the
strongest educational materials in politics,
bringing cutting-edge thinking and best learning
practice to a global market.

Under a range of well-known imprints, including
Prentice Hall, we craft high quality print and
electronic publications which help
readers to understand and apply their content,
whether studying or at work.

To find out more about the complete range of our
publishing, please visit us on the World Wide Web at:
www.pearsoneduc.com

Saving the Pound?
Britain's Road to Monetary Union

Alasdair Blair
Coventry University

An imprint of **Pearson Education**

London · New York · Toronto · Sydney · Tokyo · Singapore · Hong Kong · Cape Town
New Delhi · Madrid · Paris · Amsterdam · Munich · Milan · Stockholm

Pearson Education Limited
Edinburgh Gate
Harlow
Essex CM20 2JE

and Associated Companies throughout the world

Visit us on the World Wide Web at:
www.pearsoneduc.com

First published 2002

ISBN 0 582 47290 3

British Library Cataloguing-in-Publication Data
A catalogue record for this book is available from the British Library

Library of Congress Cataloging-in-Publication Data
Blair, Alasdair, 1971–
    Saving the pound : Britain's road to monetary union / Alasdair Blair.
        p. cm.
    Includes bibliographical references and index.
    ISBN 0-582-47290-3
    1. Monetary unions—Great Britain. 2. Monetary policy—Great Britain. 3. Currency question—Great Britain. 4. European Union—Great Britain. I. Title.
    HG939.5 .B53 2002
    332.4'941—dc21   2001052377

10   9   8   7   6   5   4   3   2   1
05   04   03   02

Typeset in 10/12pt Sabon by 35
Printed in Malaysia, LSP

Contents

Boxes and tables

Abbreviations

BAG	Business Advisory Group
BBQ	British budget question
Benelux	Benelux Economic Union (Belgium, the Netherlands and Luxembourg)
BIEC	British Invisible Exports Council
BoE	Bank of England
BSE	Bovine spongiform encephalopathy
CAP	Common Agricultural Policy
CBI	Confederation of British Industry
CFSP	Common Foreign and Security Policy
COREPER	Committee of Permanent Representatives: member states' ambassadors to the EC. Coreper I consists of Deputy Permanent Representatives, while Coreper II consists of Permanent Representatives
DTI	Department of Trade and Industry
EC	European Community
ECB	European Central Bank
ECJ	European Court of Justice
Ecofin	EC Economic and Financial Committee
ECSC	European Coal and Steel Community
ECU	European Currency Unit
EDC	European Defence Community
EEA	European Economic Area
EEC	European Economic Community
EFTA	European Free Trade Association
EIB	European Investment Bank
EMCF	European Monetary Cooperation Fund
EMF	European Monetary Federation
EMI	European Monetary Institute
EMS	European Monetary System
EMU	Economic and Monetary Union

EMS	European Monetary System
EPC	European Political Community/Cooperation
ERDF	European Regional Development Fund
ERM	Exchange Rate Mechanism
ESCB	European System of Central Banks
ETUC	European Trade Union Confederation
EU	European Union
Euratom	European Atomic Energy Committee
FCO	Foreign and Commonwealth Office
FTA	Free Trade Area
GATT	General Agreement on Tariffs and Trade
GDP	gross domestic product
GNP	gross national product
IGC	intergovernmental conference
IMF	International Monetary Fund
IoD	Institute of Directors
MEP	Member of the European Parliament
MP	Member of Parliament
MPC	Monetary Policy Committee
MU	monetary union
NAFTA	North American Free Trade Agreement
NATO	North Atlantic Treaty Organisation
OECD	Organisation for Economic Cooperation and Development
OEEC	Organisation for European Economic Cooperation
PermRep	permanent representation
QMV	qualified majority voting
SEA	Single European Act
SEM	Single European Market
TEU	Treaty on European Union
UK	United Kingdom
UNICE	Union des Industries de la Communauté européenne (EC equivalent of CBI)
USA	United States of America
VAT	value added tax
VSTF	very short-term financing
WEU	Western European Union
The Six	Belgium, France, Germany, Italy, Luxembourg, Netherlands
The Nine	Belgium, Denmark, France, Germany, Ireland, Italy, Luxembourg, Netherlands, United Kingdom
The Ten	Belgium, Denmark, France, Germany, Greece, Ireland, Italy, Luxembourg, Netherlands, United Kingdom

The Twelve   Belgium, Denmark, France, Germany, Greece, Ireland,
              Italy, Luxembourg, Netherlands, Portugal, Spain, United
              Kingdom

The Fifteen   Austria, Belgium, Denmark, Finland, France, Germany, Greece,
              Ireland, Italy, Luxembourg, Netherlands, Portugal, Spain,
              Sweden, United Kingdom

Author's acknowledgements

The research for this book draws on a range of sources, including official documentation, speeches, interviews and memoirs. A detailed bibliography at the end of the book provides a list of sources that will be of further assistance to the reader. In conducting the research for this book I owe a great deal of debt to the numerous British government officials and ministers who helped to clarify my thoughts on the subject of Britain and Europe. Numerous academics have talked to me over the last few years about Britain's relationship with the European Union. In particular, Philip Lynch, John Young, Kevin Featherstone and Anthony Forster have influenced my thinking on the Thatcher and Major governments. Some of the material contained in this book draws on research that was also conducted for a co-authored book with Anthony Forster, *The Making of Britain's European Foreign Policy* (Longman, 2002), and I would specifically like to thank him for his insights on this subject matter. I would also particularly like to thank Philip Lynch and John Young for commenting on the draft manuscript. But I must also thank Peter Gowan, David Edye and Mary Farrell with whom I worked at the University of North London, David Baker and John Leopold from Nottingham Trent University, and Michael Smith, David Allen, Helen Drake, Linda Hantrais, Paul Byrne and Phil Saddler, colleagues from Loughborough University. At Coventry University I have had the fortune of being surrounded by a group of individuals interested in international and European affairs. Particular thanks are owed to Steven Curtis and Brian Hocking, while Catherine Hoskyns and Roy May were a great help in assisting with my transition to a new university. Stuart Philip's contribution to teaching European Studies at Coventry was of considerable assistance in freeing up time to complete this manuscript.

Special thanks are also due to the financial support of the Department of European Studies and the Faculty of Social Sciences and Humanities at Loughborough University and the History, International Relations and Politics Subject Group at Coventry. I am also grateful for the kind help and assistance that I received from the staff in the Pilkington Library at Loughborough University, especially Laurie McGarry. The library staff at Coventry University, especially Geoffrey Stratford, have been of immense help in acclimatising me to the workings of a new library. I am further indebted to the kind advice of Tim Stanton and Simon Kear. My thanks also to Emma Mitchell and the staff at Longman for their help in bringing the project to fruition; to two anonymous reviewers whose generous comments improved this piece of work; and to my wife Katherine, who ensured that I maintained other interests outside of university life. I hardly need say that none of these individuals bears the slightest responsibility for the book's remaining deficiencies.

Alasdair Blair
Thornton
June 2001

Publisher's acknowledgements

We are grateful to the following for permission to reproduce copyright material:

Box 3.2 from *European Monetary Integration*, 2nd edn, Pearson Education Ltd (Gros, D. and Thygesen, N., 1998); Table 5.1 and Table 8.4 from *Economic Trends*, Annual Supplement, HMSO, 1995; Table 8.2 from *62nd Annual Report*, Bank for International Settlements.

HarperCollins Publishers Limited for permission to reproduce extracts from *John Major: The Autobiography* by John Major.

In some instances we have been unable to trace the owners of copyright material, and we would appreciate any information that would enable us to do so.

Endorsement

At last an author has produced a well-written, exceptionally well-illustrated and above all properly historically informed work on this vital issue in UK–EU relations.

Blair's thesis is sustained by a clear and cogent analysis of the various negotiating positions adopted by successive UK authorities on the question of monetary union. In the process he highlights the peculiar and evolving nature of British attitudes towards European monetary integration and shows that this was always coloured by wider linkages to the USA.

This is a well-illustrated and clearly argued text which students and practitioners alike will find of great assistance in understanding and unravelling this minefield of technical issues, negotiating strategies and downright political intrigue.

Dr David Baker
University of Warwick

Introduction

Since the end of the Second World War successive British governments have debated the question of whether the nation's destiny has rested in closer co-operation with European states. The fact that this question is still being debated sheds light on the nature of Britain's relationship with the European Union and the perception held by the government (and public) as to the role that Britain should adopt. Of the issues that Britain currently faces, one of the most important is the question of whether (or when) the nation will participate in economic and monetary union. This is a particularly emotive subject, where the facts surrounding membership have often been clouded by more popular perceptions. Political duelling within the House of Commons has often been concerned with the negative effects of British non-participation in the single currency (Labour Party) and the negative effects of Britain participating in the single currency (Conservative Party). It is extremely rare for discussion to be framed in terms of the potential advantages of membership.

That this is true is reflective of the traditional reluctance of successive governments willingly to advocate and defend the benefits of Britain's participation in the European club. In this context, Britain's applications to join the European Community (after it was evident that it could no longer forge an independent policy) had a tendency to emphasise the negative effects of not participating, such as the detrimental impact on the economy. This concept of 'what will happen if we are outwith the Community' has been a near constant factor in framing British policy. By contrast, government has been less clear in stating the benefits of membership. This book offers a new contribution to the debate by both charting the positions taken by successive British governments towards monetary union and examining the implications of monetary union. In examining British policy objectives, this book has three key aims. The first is to examine the reasons for the traditional reluctance of British governments to accept monetary union. The second is to explain the implications of monetary union. The third is to determine the factors and influences that have shaped Britain's policy in this subject area.

This book examines Britain's position on monetary union through an examination of how negotiating positions evolved within government and provides a micro-history of Britain's negotiating stance on this important subject. In examining Britain's membership of the European Union and its negotiating position towards monetary union, a number of important issues are examined. First, what are the reasons for Britain's traditional reluctance to play a full part in policy developments at the EU level? Second, to what extent has there been a merging of the traditional division between domestic policy-making and foreign policy? Third, what are the main influences in determining Britain's negotiating position on monetary union? Fourth, what factors were responsible for advancing the cause of monetary union at the EU level? For instance, do theories of European integration provide an adequate explanation of events? Finally, what are the implications of Britain's negotiating strategy within the EU and more particularly on monetary union?

The organisation of this book is both chronological and thematic. The book makes use of a considerable number of reference boxes and tables so as to provide an easily accessible source of information. It should be emphasised that the book is not an economic study of the implications of monetary union for Britain. However, it makes use of economic data and presents this in the context of a political history of British policy towards monetary union. The book is divided into three parts that examine the context of monetary union, the historical development of monetary union and the implications of monetary union. Within the first part, Chapter 1 provides a historical review of British policy towards Europe. It specifically demonstrates the extent to which the policies that were followed by government were influenced by the historical development of the British economy. Key factors, such as the maintenance of close linkages with the United States of America, were influential in the shaping of foreign policy objectives. This prioritisation accordingly meant that the fostering of closer ties with Europe took place within a framework of existing economic and security linkages. Such competing pressures were consequently illustrative of the reasons for the discomfort that British governments have had towards further commitment to the European Union. Chapter 2 examines the key influences that have shaped the construction of British policy towards monetary union. Particular attention is attached to the influence of the Treasury as well as the role of non-elected policy advisers. Chapter 3 provides an overview of the development of monetary union and examines relevant theoretical approaches. Chapter 4 explains the core features of monetary union and sets out the main costs and benefits of a single currency.

Part II charts in detail the specific policies of British governments towards monetary union. Chapter 5 pays particular attention to British policy towards the Exchange Rate Mechanism (ERM) in the 1980s and shows how key government ministers, particularly the Prime Minister, refused to accept the case for Britain joining the ERM. Chapter 6 demonstrates the factors that were of importance in advancing monetary union in the latter years of the 1980s, paying attention to international events as well as the role of key individuals.

Having provided this background information, Chapter 7 takes an in-depth look at the negotiation of monetary union throughout 1991 as part of the inter-governmental conference (IGC) negotiations that resulted in the Maastricht Treaty on European Union (TEU). Chapters 8 and 9 review some of the difficulties that beset British governments for most of the 1990s. This includes an examination of Britain's exit from the ERM and the splits that beset the then Conservative government on the issue of Europe. In contrast to the more Eurosceptical approach of the Conservative government, the Labour government that was elected to office in May 1997 (and re-elected in June 2001) has provided a more pro-European strategy. This positive approach is analysed in Chapter 10.

The third and final part is concerned with providing an assessment of monetary union. This includes focus on some of the theoretical approaches and the implications of a single currency for the future of European integration. Chapter 11 additionally provides an overview of the way British policy has developed and the extent to which reluctance to accept the cause of monetary union has impacted on British positions in other policy areas that are dealt with at the EU level.

PART I

The context of monetary union

CHAPTER 1

Britain's long road to Europe

Objectives

- Provide an overview of British policy towards European integration in the post-1945 period.
- Highlight the policy options that have influenced the decisions taken by British governments.
- Set European integration against Britain's wider international commitments.
- Compare the role of different Prime Ministers in shaping British policy.

Introduction

When Britain joined the European Economic Community (EEC) in 1973, the issue of membership had been at the forefront of domestic politics for some time; there had already been two previous applications in 1961 and 1967 under a Conservative and Labour government respectively. In the years after 1973 the issue of membership did not fade into the backwaters of British politics, but instead increasingly dominated the political arena. This included the Labour Party's immediate response of renegotiation and referendum in 1974 and 1975, Mrs Thatcher's renegotiation of the budgetary contributions at Fontainebleau in 1984, and the current debate over whether the country should participate in a European single currency. Contemporary debates do, in fact, have much in common with those associated with Britain's first attempts at membership, as both have straddled the common ground of whether the nation is better off inside or outside of Europe. This chapter puts these developments in a historical setting through an examination of the negotiating position of successive British governments in the post-1945 period (see Box 1.1). It specifically demonstrates the policy options which influenced British decision-makers in the post-1945

BOX 1.1

Timeline of Britain and Europe

1947   Britain and France pledged mutual support in the Treaty of Dunkirk.

1951   Belgium, the Federal Republic of Germany, France, Italy, Luxembourg and the Netherlands (the Six) signed the Treaty of Paris which established the European Coal and Steel Community (ECSC).

1952   The six countries which were part of the ECSC also signed the European Defence Community (EDC) Treaty. A treaty of association was signed with Britain.

1954   Collapse of the EDC Treaty. Western European Union (WEU) was established as a response to this development.

1957   Treaties of Rome established the European Economic Community (EEC) and the European Atomic Energy Community (Euratom). Commenced operation in 1958.

1959   The European Free Trade Area (EFTA) was established. It comprised Austria, Denmark, Norway, Portugal, Sweden, Switzerland and Britain.

1961   British application for EEC membership in August.

1963   Collapse of first British application for EEC membership in January.

1965   Signing of treaty which merged the ECSC, EEC and Euratom into the European Community.

1967   Britain advanced its second application for EEC membership. However, the negotiations came to an end in December 1967. Such an outcome was influenced by domestic economic difficulties, illustrated by a 14.3% devaluation of the pound in November.

1968   Completion of EC Customs Union.

1969   Georges Pompidou succeeded General de Gaulle as President of France.

1970   Renewal of British application to join the European Communities. Denmark, Ireland and Norway advanced applications at the same time.

1973   Britain, Denmark and Ireland joined the European Communities.

1974   Renegotiation of Britain's terms of membership. They were eventually finished at the March 1975 Dublin European Council.

1975   British referendum on EEC membership, in which 57% voted in favour of membership.

1979   Start of European Monetary System (EMS) in March.

1981   Greece joined the EC.

1984   Settlement of British budget dispute at Fontainebleau European Council.

1985   Single European Act was passed.

1986   Portugal and Spain joined the EC.

1987   Single European Act (SEA) took effect.

1988   Prime Minister Thatcher attacked the desire of the European Commission to further deepen European integration in her Bruges speech.

1990   Stage 1 of EMU began on 1 July. Britain joined the Exchange Rate Mechanism on 8 October.

1991   Agreement on the Treaty on European Union, with British opt-outs on EMU and Social Chapter.

1993   Treaty on European Union entered into force.

BOX 1.1 (CONTINUED)

1994   Stage 2 of EMU began on 1 January.
1995   Austria, Sweden and Finland joined the EU.
1997   Britain accepted the Social Chapter at the Treaty of Amsterdam, thereby
        overturning the opt-out negotiated at the December 1991 Maastricht
        European Council.
1998   Britain signed a joint European defence initiative with France.
1999   Stage 3 of EMU began. Commencement of the changeover to the euro
        currency in eleven member states, though Britain opted out.
2002   Circulation of euro banknotes and coins in euro-zone countries (not Britain),
        whilst national banknotes and coins are withdrawn.

---

period, chronicles the factors which pushed Britain towards membership of the Community, and outlines the reasons why British governments have clashed with European policy initiatives, especially since the 1980s. An underlying theme throughout this chapter (and indeed the book) is that British governments have attached greater significance to short-term domestic political objectives than to adopting a long-term approach to negotiations within the European Union.

The post-war years

Since the end of the Second World War successive British governments have faced the problem of deciding whether the nation's destiny lay in Europe or not. In those early years, Britain's relations with European states were part of a wider network that included the Empire (subsequently Commonwealth) and a special relationship with the United States of America (USA), the latter being perceived as the more important. This state of affairs reflected Britain's status as a vibrant trading nation with global interests – half of the world's trade and financial transactions were completed in sterling in 1945. In 1946 the total value of British foreign trade was 45.4% of that of Western Europe, while in 1950 it was still 32.6% (Milward, 1984: 335). British steel production after 1945 was more than two-thirds that of other European nations, while its output of coal was nearly equal to that of other European states (Urwin, 1991: 28; Young, 1998: 7). At that time Britain's commitments to Europe merely extended to security ties such as the Dunkirk Treaty of March 1947 and the Brussels Treaty[1] of 17 March 1948, and did not include joining the negotiations between May and June 1950 that led to the European Coal and Steel Community (ECSC). This was because the government of the day did not want to sever the more important connections with the Commonwealth, Empire and the USA, primarily because there was a perception within government that 'European unity was just a lot of Continental hot-air' (Nutting, 1960: 4).

Britain therefore maintained a position of association short of full membership with regard to the European Defence Community (EDC)[2] and the Coal and Steel Community.[3] Such a stance was motivated by the implication of shared decision-making in these new bodies, and, as Harold Macmillan stressed: 'One thing is certain, and we may as well face it. Our people will not hand over to any supranation Authority the right to close down our pits or our steelworks' (Kitzinger, 1967: 10).[4] Herbert Morrison, in his capacity as acting Prime Minister in Clement Attlee's absence, stated that 'it's no good. The Durham Miners won't wear it' (Moon, 1985: 6). But the government suggested no alternative, did not make a counter-proposal and 'turned the Schuman Plan down flat on the grounds that its supranationalism would prejudice her national sovereignty' (Nutting, 1960: 31).[5] It seemed that 'at the heart of British policy-making there was a lack of awareness' (Milward, 1984: 249).

A perception of being outside Europe did not change with the return of the Conservative Party to office in October 1951, despite Churchill having advocated a United States of Europe at the University of Zurich in 1946 (see Box 1.2). But the very strength that British ministers perceived the nation to have in international affairs, and ergo the rationale behind an independent stance, was also considered on both sides of the Atlantic to be the very reason why it should play a key role within Europe. According to Jean Monnet (who was the first President of the European Coal and Steel Community), Britain was the major power that could provide 'a nucleus around which a European Community might be formed', while Dean Acheson stated that 'British participation is necessary' (Duchène, 1994: 204).[6] Crucially, however, the integrative approach advocated by Monnet and Schuman did not mirror the British preference for national control of matters of an economic and political nature.[7]

The government, which since 1955 had been led by Anthony Eden following Sir Winston Churchill's resignation, was opposed to the supranational talks that started at Messina in June of that year (see Box 1.3). While Eden was hostile to the concept of a European federation, the Foreign Secretary, Harold Macmillan, argued that the government would be able to exert a greater influence on the talks if it was a full participant and not just an observer. In the event the government sent Russell Bretherton, an official from the Board of

---

BOX 1.2

Biography of Sir Winston Churchill (1874–1965)

While he held a number of key government posts prior to 1940, it was his position as Prime Minister between 1940 and 1945 for which Churchill is most remembered. Although he lost the 1945 election he was subsequently elected Prime Minister between 1951 and 1955. In the post-1945 period Churchill urged the construction of a United States of Europe in 1946, though he did not think that Britain should be part of any integrated European Community.

BOX 1.3

Supranationalism

This is a process of law that is superior to national governments. In this context, the institutions of the EU have autonomy from national governments and EU law has primacy over national law, while decisions can be taken by a majority vote. To this end, supranationalism has an impact on national sovereignty because it imposes certain limitations on member states. Supranationalism can be contrasted with intergovernmentalism, which is an approach that attaches greater emphasis to the role of member states in the decision-making process.

Trade, to the Messina process which had subsequently moved to Brussels. By November 1955 Bretherton was instructed to tell Paul-Henri Spaak (the Belgian Foreign Minister and Chair of the Messina Committee that examined proposals for a European Community) that the government did not want its views taken into consideration. Spaak noted that 'little by little the British attitude changed from one of mildly disdainful scepticism to growing fear' over the outcome of the meeting, while Bretherton later stated that Britain's decision to distance itself from the talks was because the Foreign Office thought 'that nothing would happen' (Spaak, 1971: 232).

Having decided not to partake in these negotiations of a supranational nature, the British government proposed a Free Trade Area (FTA) with other European nations who also preferred domestic policy-making to remain separate.[8] This strategy proved unpalatable to the larger European nations (especially France[9]), who were perfectly happy with the Messina process that led to the signing of the Treaty of Rome on 25 March 1957.[10] This directly resulted in Britain establishing a European Free Trade Area in 1959 with those nations who felt unable to join the EEC.[11] But the absence of major trading nations, such as Germany, Italy and France, consequently meant that EFTA failed to satisfy Britain's needs because it was a less vigorous organisation. The nation's declining economic growth and the reality that its trading links with the EEC were increasing faster than those with EFTA influenced this. Between 1958 and 1964 the percentage of UK trade with the Six increased from 13.8% to 18.2%, while the percentage of UK trade with the Commonwealth decreased from 38.6% to 29.8%.[12] In this context, it was only after the failure of EFTA to offer a real alternative to the Community, and the decline in Britain's economic fortunes, that the government reappraised its policy of isolation.[13] As one commentator has noted, 'the prospect of EEC membership had come to represent the least worst outcome, the opportunity to assert British influence in a new sphere as the colonies retreated and the Atlantic axis wobbled' (Porter, 1995: 22).

Despite the growing reality that Britain's future lay in Europe (the Commonwealth had begun to fragment and the Empire largely ceased to exist), its first application of 9 August 1961 to join the Community failed.[14] This was because of the January 1963 press statement by French President Charles de Gaulle, which noted the difficulties surrounding British membership (Heath, 1998: 225–35).[15] Just as Britain was not yet ready to join the Community, neither was the Community ready for British membership. We have to remember that the Community was still a fledgling organisation, barely four years old, and one that had yet to define its own objectives, let alone embark on an expansion of membership. As Hugo Young notes, the Community was 'not ready for the easy accession of a country that had variously spurned and tried to spoil it' (Young, 1998: 130).

In the following years the entry torch was taken up by the new Labour Prime Minister, Harold Wilson, with the 1967 application having fewer reservations than the terms advanced by Harold Macmillan in 1961. The openness of the second application reflected the general feeling that a further failure could not be

---

BOX 1.4

Biography of Charles de Gaulle (1890–1970)

Although de Gaulle was the London-based leader of the free French during the Second World War, his influence on European affairs stems from his position as the first leader of the French Fifth Republic in 1958, a post he maintained until 1969. Throughout his period as President, de Gaulle attached great emphasis to French influence over European affairs and sought to distance the input that the USA had on European policy. While committed to European integration, he was nevertheless a champion of the influence that member states should maintain over the future direction of Europe (1966 Luxembourg compromise). He also managed to act as block to British membership of the Community on the grounds that Britain was not ready for membership and that the USA would be able to influence policy through Britain. But his tactics were also based on a desire to maintain French influence over the direction of Europe, and he did not wish to see that challenged by another state such as Britain.

BOX 1.5

Biography of Harold Macmillan (1894–1986)

Served as Prime Minister from January 1957 until October 1963. Previous posts included Chancellor of the Exchequer (1955–57). During his period as Prime Minister he attempted to position Britain closer to Europe and in 1961 announced that he would seek membership of the European Community. The application proved to be unsuccessful, with Charles de Gaulle considering that Britain would act as a 'Trojan horse' for the USA inside the Community. Nevertheless, the application did reflect the changed economic circumstances in which Britain now found itself, with existing trading links to EFTA proving not to be sufficiently vigorous.

risked, being illustrative of support from the government, opposition parties, business and the general public.[16] Between 1958 and 1968 the gross national product (GNP) of the Six had increased twice as fast as Britain's, while between 1958 and 1969 the production of the Six all but doubled. By contrast, Britain's production increased by approximately 50%.[17] But just as he had opposed the first application, de Gaulle vetoed the second one at a press conference on 27 November 1967. Of the reasons for this, specific mention was made of the weakness of the British economy, which was itself highlighted by the 14.3% devaluation of the pound in relation to the dollar in November 1967.[18] (Although the 1967 application did not succeed, the British government did not withdraw the application and instead left it on the table.)

Pragmatic economic reasoning thus determined Macmillan's and Wilson's applications to the EEC in 1961 and 1967 respectively. There was in effect no middle path for the nation to pursue.[19] A decline in economic strength meant that Britain could no longer influence world events to the same extent as it had in the 1940s and 1950s. This was markedly evidenced by the Suez crisis when Britain was forced by US financial pressure to withdraw from Egypt and consequently to give up any attempt to regain control of the Suez Canal in the wake of its nationalisation by Nasser. In this way, Suez was 'a revelation of British strategic and economic weakness' and 'disclosed the precariousness of Anglo-American ties' (Goodwin, 1972: 44). There was consequently a significant alteration of focus towards Europe and away from the Commonwealth, Empire and the USA. In doing so there was a realisation within and outwith government that Britain's economic interests were best served by being in Europe, demonstrated by the applications being principally motivated by the fear of being left out of Europe, rather than the benefits of joining a European economic and political space. In effect the government was searching for a new

---

BOX 1.6

UK Prime Ministers

May 1945: Winston Churchill, Conservative Party
July 1945: Clement Attlee, Labour Party
October 1951: Sir Winston Churchill, Conservative Party
April 1955: Sir Anthony Eden, Conservative Party
January 1957: Harold Macmillan, Conservative Party
October 1963: Sir Alec Douglas-Home, Conservative Party
October 1964: Harold Wilson, Labour Party
June 1970: Edward Heath, Conservative Party
March 1974: Harold Wilson, Labour Party
April 1976: James Callaghan, Labour Party
May 1979: Margaret Thatcher, Conservative Party
November 1990: John Major, Conservative Party
May 1997: Tony Blair, Labour Party

function and, as Dean Acheson noted, 'Britain has lost an empire and not yet found a role' (Kitzinger, 1968: 19).

Into Europe

It would not be an overstatement to say that the options open to Britain by 1970 were relatively few. 'The crux of the matter was whether Britain, both politically and economically, could afford to be left in something of a backwater in the face of a Western Europe which was becoming economically much stronger than Britain, and was now more firmly set politically, in the light of the Hague Declaration of December 1969, on a course towards closer political unity' (Goodwin, 1972: 49). Thus, while there remained the possibility of staying within EFTA, successive governments, in conjunction with business leaders, had advocated that EEC membership was necessary, both on economic and political grounds. The crucial fact was that neither the Commonwealth nor EFTA offered the advantages of market access and increased status that the Community did. As Lynch notes, 'EC membership was necessary if Britain were to be economically competitive and politically influential' (Lynch, 1999: 30). Edward Heath's election as Prime Minister proved to be a watershed in terms of the impression that Britain gave to the Six, due to the government's serious-ness of securing membership (Heath, 1998: 363–77). Unlike his predecessors, Heath saw membership as something desirable, not the lesser of two or more evils. A belief in the overarching importance of Europe was such that, 'in con-trast to all other post-war British Prime Ministers, Heath's Europeanism even led him to distance himself from the US' (Young, 2000: 100).

In seeking once again to enter the Community,[20] with negotiations beginning in earnest on 30 June 1970, Britain benefited from the replacement of French President Charles de Gaulle by Georges Pompidou. The latter was less worried about the effect of British membership than de Gaulle, who had been con-cerned that Britain would challenge the pre-eminent position of France within the Community, while at the same time permeating American interests into this European body. As in previous applications, sovereignty was a key issue in the negotiations, with the 1971 White Paper stating that 'There is no ques-tion of any erosion of essential national sovereignty',[21] while one Member of Parliament noted that 'If we enter this union we shall lose control over our whole national life as we have known it up to the present day' (Pryce, 1973: 52). But the necessity of membership on economic and political grounds meant that the details of this application were quickly settled, with membership becoming effective from 1 January 1973.[22]

Yet, as soon as entry was obtained, its very nature was questioned when Harold Wilson entered Downing Street in March 1974 for his second period as Labour Prime Minister. At this point, Britain had only been a member of the European Economic Community for 14 months. But despite this brief

BOX 1.7

Biography of Edward Heath (1916–)

Served as Prime Minister from June 1970 until 1974. A committed pro-European, Heath was in charge of Britain's first application to the Community under the government that was led by Harold Macmillan. During his premiership Britain eventually managed to secure entry to the Community by following through the second application for membership which had remained on the negotiating table since 1967. Success on the foreign front was, however, not matched at the domestic level, with his period as Prime Minister being marred by industrial unrest that in the end resulted in electoral defeat and the election of a Labour government in March 1974.

period of membership, Wilson was committed to renegotiate the terms of entry obtained by Heath.[23] (The February 1974 Labour Party manifesto was particularly critical of the entry terms.) Wilson was himself actually in favour of membership, but the groundswell of opinion within the Labour Party favoured tough talking with Britain's new European colleagues. And although the government accepted the renegotiated terms obtained at the March 1975 Dublin European Council[24] (the biannual meetings of heads of state and government), the desire to renegotiate affected Britain's status within the Community, as 'our unconcerned readiness to tear up our treaty commitment to the Community merely to meet the internal political problems of the Labour Party had produced a profound shock' (Henderson, 1994: 66). As the former British ambassador to Germany, Nicholas Henderson, commented, Wilson 'did not seem to see himself in any creative political role. He was quite frank . . . about his main objective, which was to keep all the clashing balls of the Labour Party in the air at the same time' (Henderson, 1994: 72). It was in this context that a referendum on membership of the Community took place a few months later in June 1975. And while the 17.3 million people who voted in favour of membership outstripped the 8.4 million who voted against, the whole process seriously strained Britain's commitment to the Community and proved to be a deeply divisive issue within the Labour Party (Jeffreys, 1993: 85–93; Jenkins, 1991: 399–418). Indeed, domestic politics seemed to have taken precedence in determining the European agenda.[25]

These developments nevertheless failed to settle the question of British membership, since the renegotiated terms did not remove all of the problems surrounding Britain's budget contribution. (The then government estimated that Britain would be the largest net contributor to the Community budget by 1978, while being only ranked fifth in terms of its share of the Community's gross domestic product.) This was reflected in the budget question becoming a prominent topic at the domestic and EC level in the latter years of the Callaghan Labour government (1976–79), while it was noticeable that the May 1979 election of Margaret Thatcher as Prime Minister immediately raised the tempo of this issue at the Community level. These developments certainly did not add to

---

BOX 1.8

Fontainebleau European Council

The June 1984 Fontainebleau European Council produced agreement on a budgetary rebate for Britain, with this being an issue that had particularly dominated Margaret Thatcher's period as Prime Minister. She considered that Britain was contributing too much to the Community in relation to its overall wealth. The Fontainebleau meeting reached agreement on the annual correction method for Britain's rebate from 1985, as well as an increase in the resources of the Community from January 1986 by raising the VAT percentage from 1% to 1.4%. For 1984 Britain received a compensation lump sum of 1000 million ECU and in subsequent years it was to receive two-thirds of the difference between what it paid in VAT and what it received from the Community.

Britain's status within the Community, and if anything advanced its position as 'an awkward partner' and reduced the availability of negotiating capital (George, 1998). Prime Minister Thatcher seemed to thrive on the combative nature of the EC debate, partly because the clubbable image of the Community did not sit well with her reformist zeal, while she was also hostile to its integrative instincts.

Her period in office from 1979 to 1990 was nevertheless a mixed record, with the thorny issue of the British budget question[26] dominating the early years of the administration; she famously demanded 'our money back' at the November 1979 Dublin European Council. The previous month in Luxembourg she had claimed that Britain could not accept the existing situation on the Community budget because it was 'demonstrably unjust' (Riddell, 1983: 206). And while this issue was resolved at the June 1984 Fontainebleau European Council,[27] with a 66% rebate for Britain of the difference between what it paid to the Community and what it received from it, Thatcher had adopted a combative style that did not sit well with her fellow European leaders (see Box 1.8). A former member of her Cabinet noted that this action 'only united them more firmly than ever' (Prior, 1986: 144). Thus, while the attainment of the rebate was right for Britain in fiscal terms, the diplomatic methods used in obtaining it caused friction within the European club, this being a particular concern of the Foreign and Commonwealth Office. But this development was not lost on Thatcher, who portrayed the budget issue in the domestic context as a victory for Britain, although the negotiating methods proved to be counter-productive in the longer term with the government becoming more isolated within the Community. This abrasive manner would be more commonplace in later years, producing hostility from Britain's European partners (see Box 1.9). John Major, Thatcher's successor as Prime Minister, commented that 'I had been shocked at my early European Councils to discover that Margaret's strength of will, so admired at home, was used against us abroad. It was the butt of sly little jokes. Most of the other leaders utterly disagreed with her' (Major, 1999: 265).

BOX 1.9

Britain and Europe under the Thatcher governments, 1979–1990[28]

Margaret Thatcher succeeded James Callaghan as Prime Minister in 1979 when the Conservative Party won the general election of that year, and she maintained that position until 1990. In examining her time in office it is possible to divide it into three periods:

1. Between 1979 and 1984 the British budgetary question was a dominant issue. Prime Minister Thatcher was isolated within Europe and obstructed policy, refusing to play by the 'rules of the game'. She rejected a compromise until the 1984 Fontainebleau settlement on the British rebate. By then, Thatcher feared being left behind by France and Germany and consequently promoted the vision of a free market within Europe. This also reflected British domestic interests of a liberal trade environment.

2. From 1984 to 1988 Britain played a more constructive role in EC policy-making, notably on the Single European Market. Yet, Britain was still 'an awkward partner' on the questions of institutional reform, Economic and Monetary Union and social affairs. Thatcher saw the SEM as an end in itself, which fulfilled the Treaty of Rome's potential as the 'charter for economic liberty'. Cabinet disputes began to surface over the Exchange Rate Mechanism.

3. From 1988 to 1990 Britain became increasingly isolated as other member states urged 'positive integration' and 'ever closer union', such as the Delors Report on EMU and the Social Charter. Thatcher's 1988 Bruges speech looked to a Europe based on 'willing and active co-operation between independent sovereign states'. In 1989, Foreign Secretary Geoffrey Howe and Chancellor of the Exchequer Nigel Lawson made Thatcher set conditions for British entry into the ERM at the Madrid European Council. The division of opinion within the Conservative Party was highlighted by the Cabinet resignations of Nigel Lawson, Nicholas Ridley and Geoffrey Howe. The end product of this was for Thatcher to become increasingly isolated on both the European and domestic fronts, by means of her dogmatism and rejection of the Delors Report.

The resolution of the budget issue did nevertheless provide greater freedom for other policy developments at European meetings, evidenced by the subsequent drive towards the Single European Market. This momentum actually came from the Fontainebleau meeting,[29] while the task of drawing up a detailed plan for the establishment of the single market was given to the British European Commissioner, Lord Cockfield. The ensuing White Paper, *Completing the Internal Market*, was presented at the Milan European Council of 1985. Developments subsequently moved at pace, negotiations resulting in agreement on a Single European Act (SEA) at the Luxembourg Council of December that year.[30] The significance of this agreement was the creation of new policy objectives, including the Single European Market and reform of the Community's institutions.[31] A liberalisation of trade policies obviously sat well with the free market ideology that dominated Conservative government thinking. This achievement did, nevertheless, result in the government having to acquiesce to an expansion of the European Parliament's powers and a widening of the policy areas where qualified majority voting could be used in Community decision-making. And while Thatcher would later claim to have been misled by the Foreign and Commonwealth Office in granting these extra competencies to the European Parliament, and in deepening the path of integration, she had been fully briefed by officials as to the likely implications of these changes.[32]

A change of direction

At this time Britain was part of a European Community that had renewed vigour, which was itself partly the result of the dynamic leadership of the European Commission by its new President, Jacques Delors.[33] In Thatcher's eyes it was imperative to water down the integrative policies that were soon being advanced, including Economic and Monetary Union (EMU).[34] However, as far as Delors was concerned, Britain was increasingly out of step with the other members of the Community who did not share the Prime Minister's view that institutional reform was not part of the single market programme. But her position did not sit well with many of her Cabinet colleagues, as many of them considered that Britain should play a central role in the European arena and one that included taking part in European policies. This included membership of the Exchange Rate Mechanism (ERM) (Major, 1999: 138 and 153). Yet, Thatcher continued to lead and dominate government policy and in Bruges on 20 September 1988 she attacked the European Commission for wanting to regulate the internal market through the creation of common rules that she considered would raise employment costs (see Box 1.10).[35]

The Bruges speech, while originally a product of her private secretary, Charles Powell, and John Kerr (an assistant under-secretary of state at the Foreign and Commonwealth Office with responsibility for European affairs), ended up in the second rewrite being dominated by Powell, as it was 'a far harsher exposition of the Thatcherite views on Europe' (Dickie, 1992: 281). Significantly, Foreign Secretary Sir Geoffrey Howe had been unable to tame the speech and 'had given up the struggle and gone off to Africa' (Dickie, 1992: 282). For Thatcher, the speech reflected the point that 'the time had come to strike out against what I saw as the erosion of democracy by centralisation and bureaucracy, and to set out an alternative view of Europe's future' (Thatcher, 1993: 742). But crucially the speech did not represent the views of Cabinet, Geoffrey Howe noting that it was 'sheer fantasy' (Howe, 1994: 537). He was aware that 'the Prime Minister had progressively curtailed Cabinet debate and cut herself off from private discussion with her principal ministers' (Howe, 1994: 539). Howe, though one of the most senior members of the Cabinet, had been increasingly isolated

BOX 1.10

Extract of Bruges speech delivered by Margaret Thatcher, 20 September 1988

My first guiding principle is this: willing and active co-operation between independent sovereign states is the best way to build a successful European Community. To try to suppress nationhood and concentrate power at the centre of a European conglomerate would be highly damaging and would jeopardise the objectives we seek to achieve. Europe will be stronger precisely because it has France as France, Spain as Spain, Britain as Britain, each with its own customs, traditions and identity. It would be folly to try to fit them into some sort of identikit European personality ... We have not successfully rolled back the frontiers of the state in Britain, only to see them reimposed at a European level, with a European superstate exercising a new dominance from Brussels. Certainly we want to see Europe more united and with a greater sense of common purpose. But it must be in a way which preserves the different traditions, Parliamentary powers and sense of national pride in one's own country; for these have been the source of Europe's vitality through the centuries.

My second guiding principle is this: Community policies must tackle present problems in a practical way, however difficult that may be. If we cannot reform those Community policies which are patently wrong or ineffective and which are rightly causing public disquiet, then we shall not get the public's support for the Community's future development.

My third guiding principle is the need for Community policies which encourage enterprise. If Europe is to flourish and create the jobs of the future, enterprise is the key ... Our aim should not be more and more detailed regulation from the centre: it should be to deregulate and to remove the constraints on trade. Britain has been in the lead in opening its markets to others. The City of London has long welcomed financial institutions from all over the world, which is why it is the biggest and most successful financial centre in Europe.

My fourth guiding principle is that Europe should not be protectionist. The expansion of the world economy requires us to continue the process of removing barriers to trade and to do so in the multilateral negotiations in the GATT. It would be a betrayal if, while breaking down constraints on trade within Europe, the Community were to erect greater external protection. We must ensure that our approach to world trade is consistent with the liberalisation we preach at home.

My last guiding principle concerns the most fundamental issue, the European countries' role in defence. Europe must continue to maintain a sure defence through NATO. There can be no question of relaxing our efforts even though it means taking difficult decisions and meeting heavy costs.

Source: May (1988, document 14, pp. 115–16)

from the decision-making inner circle, as he had not been included in the team that drew up the new Cabinet after the 1987 general election victory.

But while Thatcher considered her style of leadership to be one of strength, a tendency to bypass senior ministers from policy-making proved to be a critical error of judgement. To be sure, division over European policy within government was especially evident at this time, but tension between the Prime Minister and ministers was evident on other policy areas, such as the poll tax. The fundamental problem was therefore that Thatcher was foolhardy in regarding herself to be unassailable and did not recognise the full extent to which she depended on support from Cabinet Ministers and other influential policy-makers. As will become evident in the following chapters, by the end of the 1980s there were significant differences of opinion between the Prime Minister and many of her senior colleagues that proved too great to resolve. In this context the lack of support within Cabinet for some of the Prime Minister's sceptical policies, and the consideration that they were harming Britain's position within Europe (a view also held by the business community[36]), was reflective of the wider lack of consensus on all areas of policy-making (Major, 1999: 169).[37] Prime Minister Thatcher may have concluded that 'the Foreign Office was almost imperceptibly moving to compromise with these new European friends' (Thatcher, 1993: 559), but the true reason for her downfall was not divisions over European policy, but rather 'because she failed to recognise her dependency on colleagues within the core executive' (Smith, 1999: 97). Thatcher therefore became increasingly vulnerable to attack from an unsympathetic Cabinet that realised her policies no longer reflected the majority of public opinion. Thus, the 'Iron Lady' appeared to be out of touch. This situation directly influenced Michael Heseltine's decision to challenge Thatcher for the leadership of the Conservative Party.[38] But by 1990 Heseltine had been out of the inner core of government for nearly five years, following his Cabinet resignation in 1986 over the question of whether Britain should build military helicopters under licence from American or European suppliers. Ever the committed European, he had favoured the latter option. Such commitment to Europe, and the fact that he had openly challenged Thatcher's position in 1986 and again in 1990, meant that it would be unlikely for him to receive support from all quarters of the Conservative Party.[39] The effect of this was for the leadership prize to go to the relatively unknown John Major.[40]

A character that was more pragmatic than Thatcher's influenced John Major's election to office. He regarded himself to be 'a pragmatist about the European Community' (see Box 1.11) (Major, 1999: 265). His future Chancellor, Norman Lamont, thought he 'was inclined to sympathise with those who felt a more emollient, constructive negotiating style would be more productive' (Lamont, 1999: 111). To this end, Prime Minister Major sought to cultivate closer relationships with other European nations. This was most markedly demonstrated by the friendship that Major developed with the German Chancellor, Helmut Kohl,[41] and evidenced by John Major's March 1991 commitment for Britain to be at the 'heart of Europe'.[42] Such overtures were nevertheless based on the pragmatic basis that the government was relatively isolated within the EU, and that if it was to be successful in obtaining some of its objectives at the European level then it would have to be supported by other member states. Government strategy was consequently based on the need to satisfy short-term objectives rather than demonstrating a sea-change in the construction and orientation of

---

BOX 1.11

Britain and Europe under the Major governments, 1990–1997

John Major succeeded Margaret Thatcher as Prime Minister in 1990 and continued in that office until 1997. His time in office can be divided into two periods:

1. Between 1990 and 1992 John Major sought to restore British credibility to the EC and ensure that London had influence over the monetary union and political union intergovernmental conferences. He said that Britain should be 'at the heart of Europe', since national interests are best protected by an active role in EC negotiations. Major obtained an EMU opt-out at Maastricht, as well as a Social Chapter Protocol exclusion, and separate 'pillars' rather than a 'federal vocation'. However, significant compromises over institutional reform were made, including a greater role for the European Parliament (co-decision), while he also accepted that the third stage of EMU was 'irrevocable'. Nevertheless, Major claimed that Maastricht and subsidiarity marked the end of the centralisation of EC power. But the reality was that deeper tensions emerged within the Conservative Party.

2. Between 1992 and 1997 there was a growing unease within the Conservative government over European issues. The uncertainty after the Danish referendum resulted in Major pursuing a vision of a more flexible, enlarged EU based on intergovernmental cooperation and 'variable geometry'. The key themes advanced were:

    (I) The need for flexibility in an enlarged Europe, whereby states could proceed at their own pace and stay out of certain policies such as EMU. This rejected the 'hard core' concept, as all states must agree on the future of the EU. This has been criticised as *à la carte* Europe.

    (II) Europe of nation-states with separate pillars, national veto, subsidiarity and a streamlined Commission. Wanted minimalist reforms at 1996–97 IGC.

    (III) Flexible labour markets and reduced social costs.

    (IV) Global free trade and economic deregulation.

    (V) Stressed the need for convergence on EMU and a refusal to rejoin the ERM.

Major noted the need for keeping the EMU option open, though refused to commit Britain either way. This became known as the 'wait and see' approach, being viewed as pragmatic.

British European foreign policy. In this context, there remained no overall sense of direction or commitment to Britain's European policy despite public appearances suggesting otherwise.

Thus, in practice, Major's lack of conviction on Europe meant that he did not always offer a clear lead to Britain's European policy. Some considered that Major was 'too much of a weather-vane on the subject' (Dyson and Featherstone, 1999: 575). Welcomed at home, his appointment was greeted as a positive development among his fellow European leaders, not least because he represented a more consensual style of government.[43] This was immediately put to the test in the intergovernmental conferences on monetary union and political union, which began in December 1990 and culminated in agreement at Maastricht in December 1991. Agreement was, however, not easy for Major. He had to manage the interests of his new colleagues at Cabinet meetings, where he 'chose consensus in policy-making' (Major, 1999: 209). During these discussions it was clear that Major did not want (and was not able) to dominate Cabinet in the manner that Thatcher had.

The immediate effect of this was to ensure that the Foreign Secretary, Douglas Hurd, and the FCO, had a stronger voice in the construction of British European policy. One of the reasons for this was Major's trust in Hurd's capabilities, but it was also because the new Prime Minister was reliant on the support of his fellow ministers. And as Major gave more scope to Cabinet decision-making, there was more scope for government departments to influence policy-making within Cabinet. This sharply contrasted with the decision-making procedures during the last few years of Margaret Thatcher's government, whereby her reliance on private policy advisers for advice on foreign affairs reduced the ability of the Foreign Office to influence the shaping of government policy.

Major's status as first among equals influenced his decision-taking on European (and domestic) affairs. This included having to pander to the interests of an increasingly vocal Eurosceptic element of the party. On European issues, Major knew from the outset that he 'was standing astride a deep and widening fissure in the party' (Major, 1999: 202). It was therefore not a surprise that the resulting agreement on a Treaty on European Union at the Maastricht European Council of December 1991 included the provision for Britain to opt out of the agreement on monetary union, while the Social Chapter was removed from the treaty and replaced by a social protocol that allowed the other 11 member states to proceed without Britain.

While these developments were greeted as a success at home, they also sowed the seeds of discord on the domestic and European fronts. Cabinet Ministers became increasingly disloyal, particularly after the April 1992 general election which brought the Conservative Party an unexpected fourth successive victory, albeit with a reduced majority of 21. Party management was especially problematic, influenced by a growing Euroscepticism that had been stirred by Britain's exit from the Exchange Rate Mechanism (ERM) in September 1992. (Then Chancellor of the Exchequer Major had backed entry in October 1990.) The resulting effect was to hinder the ratification of the Maastricht Treaty in the Commons because of the growing divisions within the government and Cabinet. Major even referred to some of his Eurosceptic colleagues as 'bastards'. Hindered at home from effective government, Prime Minister Major was increasingly isolated on the European front. This included having to do a U-turn in March 1994 over the extension of qualified majority voting.[44] He subsequently vetoed the candidature of the Belgian Prime Minister Jean-Luc Dehaene to succeed Delors as President of the Commission, instead backing the clubbable Prime

---

BOX 1.12

Conservative Party policy on Europe, 1997–

The Conservative Party defeat at the 1997 general election brought with it the resignation of John Major and the election of William Hague as leader of the Conservative Party. This signalled a sceptical outlook on Europe and suggested that the Eurosceptics had won the battle for supremacy within the party, as the Euro-enthusiast, Kenneth Clarke, was defeated in the leadership campaign. During the 1997–2001 Parliament, the shadow Conservative Cabinet had a strong Eurosceptic flavour. Indeed, the predominant issue that the Conservative Party championed in the June 2001 general election was opposition to the euro. This did not, however, galvanise the support of the electorate, and as a consequence the Conservative Party failed to make any progress in reducing the Labour Party's majority within Parliament. The poor outcome of the election for the Conservative Party, and the lack of public support for William Hague, were the key factors that influenced Hague's decision to step down as leader of the party in the immediate aftermath of the June 2001 election. For the Conservative Party as a whole, one key implication of the election defeat has been the need to establish a broader set of policies on education, health and law and order rather than be solely reliant on a Eurosceptical approach. Moreover, having attempted to use Mrs Thatcher as a rallying point in the election campaign (but with no success), such ties with Thatcherism are likely to be greatly reduced.

Minister of Luxembourg, Jacques Santer. But, like John Major himself, Santer was more of a consensus seeker than leader. His appointment did, of course, directly lead to the collapse of the European Commission in 1999.

By the spring of 1997 Major had clung onto power for five years, which was the last possible date for a general election. Defeat for the Conservative Party was inevitable, with Major's decision to hold out to the very last minute having provided even greater time for divisions within the party to develop (see Box 1.12). The Labour Party consequently entered power with a majority of 179 nearly 20 years after the Conservative Party had ejected them from office. And just as Major had brought hope to the European stage in late 1990, so did Tony Blair in 1997. In comparison to Major, Tony Blair exercised a more dominant control over his party and the government, with Labour having undergone a metamorphic modernising change in the preceding years, denoted by the prefix of *New* Labour. These changes, and the cushion of a large parliamentary majority, enabled Prime Minister Blair to adopt a positive tone during the intergovernmental conference that had started at Turin in March 1996 and culminated in agreement at Amsterdam in June 1997 (see Box 1.13). That treaty did not, however, resolve key institutional questions, including the reform of voting in the Council of Ministers and the extension of majority voting. But Britain did exercise a more positive tone, reflected in acceptance of the Social Chapter (which John Major had opposed at Maastricht) and enthusiasm for the creation of the new Employment Chapter.

BOX 1.13

Britain and Europe under the Blair government, 1997–

The election of Tony Blair as Prime Minister in May 1997 had an immediate impact on the construction of British policy towards Europe. Government policy was no longer dictated by domestic splits, as the new Prime Minister achieved a majority of 179 in the general election (44.4% of the vote). The Labour leader, Tony Blair, also became the youngest Prime Minister since 1812. This youth and vitality was especially apparent at the June 1997 Amsterdam European Council, when the Prime Minister accepted the Social Chapter that John Major had opposed at the December 1991 Maastricht European Council. On his return from the Amsterdam meeting, Prime Minister Blair appeared triumphant and this mirrored the view taken by John Major on his return from Maastricht. But just as Major had not resolved all of the issues within the Conservative Party, it became apparent that Blair also did not tackle key issues, especially Economic and Monetary Union.

The government has nevertheless been more constructive and proactive in forging relationships with other European states. Significantly, the government supported the idea of an EU defence capability at a Franco-British meeting in Saint Malo on 4 December 1998, which overturned the traditional British hesitancy to support a European identity. This position was determined by the need to have greater influence in EU policy-making, especially as the government refused to offer any outright commitment to EMU. In the 2001 general election the Labour Party was re-elected with a 167 majority and as such Tony Blair was the first Labour leader to deliver a full second term. In the wake of the general election victory, Blair embarked on a wholescale reshuffle of government posts, the most notable of which was the demotion of Robin Cook from the FCO to Leader of the House of Commons, with the former Home Secretary, Jack Straw, replacing Cook as Foreign Secretary. Among the reasons for this change, Blair was apparently concerned that Jack Straw would be a more convincing advocate of British entry to the single currency, not least because his own views had traditionally been more sceptical on the subject. At another level, the installation of Straw in the FCO was reflective of the shift to a Blairite government.

Within the Labour government a key debate which dominated its first term of office from 1997 to 2001 was the question of Britain's membership of EMU. This was despite the fact that in many respects Labour had taken a more positive approach on the subject than the previous Conservative government by actually outlining the criteria for membership. In examining the EMU debate, a crucial relationship centred on the linkage between Prime Minister Tony Blair and Chancellor of the Exchequer Gordon Brown, with the latter exercising a dominant control over economic policy and favouring a more cautious approach to EMU in comparison with Blair. As Chancellor, Gordon Brown proved to be one of the most dominant Chancellors of recent years and his reach extended far beyond the ability of the Treasury to influence fiscal and monetary policy. But while Labour established the criteria for EMU membership they were at the same time unwilling to extend a positive endorsement for membership.

Conclusion

This brief overview of Britain's relationship with the European Union has highlighted some of the key developments that have influenced the fashioning of government policy. The following chapters pay particular attention to the construction of British policy towards the Exchange Rate Mechanism (ERM) and Economic and Monetary Union (EMU). These two policies became intertwined in the late 1980s and early 1990s, with both the Thatcher and Major governments finding it difficult to fashion a negotiating policy that was acceptable to MPs. This became a more difficult task after Britain's exit from the ERM in the autumn of 1992 proved to be a shattering blow to the formation of a constructive European policy. The effect of this was that the remaining years of the Major government were dogged by splits over European questions. And although those divisions concerned matters other than EMU, it nevertheless remained (and remains) the key policy in determining Britain's relationship with the European Union. Whilst the first Labour government set down the criteria for EMU membership, it did not formally commit itself (in public at least) to EMU and this reflected the scepticism that some members of the government had towards this policy and the difficulty that the government considered it had in selling such a policy to the British electorate. Nevertheless, having been re-elected by a landslide majority in the June 2001 general election, the Labour government will more than likely hold a referendum on EMU in the immediate future.[45] The subsequent chapters review the construction of British negotiation objectives in this policy field, mapping the role of key policy-makers and evaluating the influence that Britain has brought to bear in this policy arena.

Key points

- British foreign policy in the early years after 1945 was not solely focused on Europe. Relations with European states were part of a broader policy that included the Empire (subsequently Commonwealth) and the United States of America.

- While Britain did not fully participate in the talks that led to the establishment of the European Economic Community, only four years after the founding of the EEC the British government of Harold Macmillan applied for membership.

- In the late 1950s and throughout the 1960s it was clear that EEC countries were enjoying faster economic growth than that of Britain.

- Britain eventually joined the EEC in 1973, but only after two previous applications had failed. This was primarily because of the views of the

French President, Charles de Gaulle, who blocked Britain's applications. Of the reasons for this, de Gaulle considered that Britain was not fully committed to the Community, though British membership would also have had an impact on French dominance of the Community.

- Since becoming a member Britain has often been perceived as an awkward or reluctant member of the Community.

Key terms

- **Council of Ministers** The Council of Ministers represents the member states' governments. As the main decision-making body of the EU, the Council of Ministers is comprised of ministers from member states, with the composition dependent on the subject under discussion: for instance, agriculture or fisheries. Broader issues are discussed by heads of state or government who meet two or three times a year as the European Council.

- **directives** The Council and the Commission can issue directives, which are binding in terms of the result to be achieved by the member states to which they are directed. In this context, member states are able to decide on the method and form of implementation, thereby creating the possibility of distinctions arising between member states in terms of the scope and coverage of the directive.

- **Economic and Monetary Union** EMU refers to the zone of countries within the EU that have the same currency and monetary policy. EMU commenced in January 1999 when the euro became a legal currency.

- **European Commission** As the executive body of the EU and the guardian of the treaties, the European Commission initiates EU legislation, implements policies that have been agreed on, and has the job of negotiating on behalf of the EU on trade matters and in relation to third countries. It is also the job of the European Commission to ensure that agreed policies have been implemented by member states. Where implementation has not taken place, the Commission can refer such matters to the European Court of Justice.

- **European Council** The European Council is a special meeting of the Council of Ministers when the representatives are the political heads of government. While the European Council was formally established in 1974, its existence was only legally recognised in the 1987 Single European Act.

- **European Court of Justice** Based in Luxembourg, the court acts as the final arbiter of all legal issues, including the settling of disputes between member states, between member states and the EU institutions, and between EU institutions and firms or individuals. The rulings that the court makes are directly applicable to all member states concerned.

- **European Parliament** Comprising 626 members (MEPs) who are directly elected for a five-year term from each member state, the Parliament has in recent years had a more prominent role in EU policy. This includes appointments to the European Commission requiring approval from the European Parliament. The creation of the co-decision procedure in the Maastricht Treaty provided the Parliament with greater powers, while the scope of coverage of the co-decision process was widened in the Treaty of Amsterdam.

- **federalism** A political system where power is divided constitutionally between different levels of government, such as in the USA. In terms of the EU, federalism refers to the relationship between the EU and the member states being ordered in a clear and constitutional manner.

- **multi-speed Europe** Recent changes to the European Union include an expansion in membership and a deepening of the policy areas covered by the EU, while further enlargement and internal reform will take place in the future. Such changes have resulted in some member states, including Germany and France, advocating a faster pace of reform. However, other countries, particularly Denmark and Britain, have traditionally been reluctant to support such rapid changes, and they instead have tended to want to reduce the pace of integration. As a response to these tensions, the idea of a multi-speed or variable geometry Europe has been suggested. In such a scenario, core member states would make further advances in EU political and economic integration, while other member states would have reduced involvement in the particular policy areas.

- **regulations** EU regulations can be made by the Council and the Commission. The regulations are applicable in all member states and are binding in their entirety.

- **sovereignty** This term refers to the ability of nation-states to take decisions by exercising their own authority. For instance, it applies to the competence of a state to have sovereign control over the setting of legislation and its ability to have law-making powers. In addition to these internal powers, sovereignty also relates to the ability of a nation-state to exercise its role as an international actor. Membership of the European Union has had an impact on the ability of member states to exercise absolute sovereignty, as they are influenced by rules and decisions which limit their room to make individual policies.

- **subsidiarity** This term refers to the situation whereby the EU should only perform those tasks that cannot be carried out by member states, or those tasks that are better carried out at the EU level. The provision was introduced in the Maastricht Treaty (Article 3b).

Questions

1. What factors explain Britain's initial lack of enthusiasm towards European integration?

2. Why did the Wilson Cabinet decide to explore the possibility of European Community membership in 1966–67?

3. 'Britain made its second attempt to enter the EEC primarily because there was no alternative if the country wished to remain a major power.' Discuss.

4. Assess the significance of Edward Heath to Britain's eventual entry to the European Community.

5. Why, and with what success, did Margaret Thatcher seek to reduce Britain's net payment to the European Community, 1979–84?

6. To what extent can traditional British reticence about deeper European integration since 1945 be explained by a continued desire to play a 'world role'?

7. Is it correct to consider that, from Heath to Blair, the United Kingdom has remained an unwilling partner of the EC/EU rather than a committed member state?

8. Are there particular reasons why Britain has had an uneasy relationship with closer European integration?

9. Does Britain still have a special relationship with the USA?

10. Do you think that Britain should continue to punch above its weight in international affairs?

Further reading

Bulmer, Simon (2001) 'Britain and European Integration', in Bill Jones et al. (eds.) *Politics UK*, 4th edn, Harlow: Longman, pp. 653–78.

Denman, Roy (1996) *Missed Chances*, London: Indigo.

Forster, Anthony and Blair, Alasdair (2002) *The Making of Britain's European Foreign Policy*, Harlow: Longman.

George, Stephen (1998) *An Awkward Partner: Britain in the European Community*, 3rd edn, Oxford: Oxford University Press.

George, Stephen and Bache, Ian (2001) *Politics in the European Union*, Oxford: Oxford University Press, Chapter 16.

Gowland, David and Turner, Arthur (2000) *Reluctant Europeans: Britain and European Integration, 1945–1998*, Harlow: Longman.

Kavanagh, Dennis (2000) *British Politics: Continuities and Change*, 4th edn, Oxford: Oxford University Press, Chapter 4.

May, Alex (1999) *Britain and Europe since 1945*, Harlow: Longman.

Sanders, David (1990) *Losing an Empire, Finding a Role: British Foreign Policy since 1945*, Basingstoke: Macmillan.

Young, Hugo (1998) *This Blessed Plot: Britain and Europe from Churchill to Major*, Basingstoke: Macmillan.

Young, John W. (2000) *Britain and European Unity, 1945–1999*, 2nd edn, Basingstoke: Macmillan.

Notes

[1] The signatories of the treaty were France, Belgium, the Netherlands, Luxembourg and Britain. It constituted a 50-year alliance against attack in Europe, and provided for economic, social and military cooperation.

[2] The need for the EDC arose from US pressure to rearm West Germany during the Korean War so as to ensure that there were enough troops to secure the defence of Western Europe against a possible attack from Eastern Europe. The initial US proposal favoured the re-creation of the West German army, which created fears in Europe, notably in France, but also in West Germany itself. The solution was to create a defence community composed of national armies under the authority of a supranational command.

[3] In August 1952 the High Authority was formally established in Luxembourg with a British diplomatic representative attached to it. An agreement of association followed on 11 December 1954 which was signed in London ten days later by Duncan Sandys and Jean Monnet and was ratified by the House of Commons in February 1955. This provided for a Council of Association meeting alternately in London or Luxembourg made up of four representatives from each side with a provision for subsidiary committees. The Council provided for exchanges of information and consultation and joint action on such matters as pricing, raw material supplies, research and safety relating to both coal and steel. Provision was made for Britain to meet ECSC ministers if necessary, and representatives of the Six could sit on the Council of Association as observers (or even as participants if a state's special interests were affected).

[4] The British position with regard to the Schuman Plan was highlighted in the government command paper 'Anglo-French Discussions regarding French Proposals for the Western European Coal, Iron and Steel Industries, May–June, 1950'. The creators of the plan believed that for a peaceful and united Europe to prosper there was a need to get rid of the traditional antagonism between France and West Germany and the method of accomplishing this task was by placing French and West German coal and steel production under a common authority. The reasoning behind the Schuman Declaration was displayed in a memorandum sent by Jean Monnet to Robert Schuman and Georges Bidault on 4 May 1950. See Vaughan, 1976: 51–6.

[5] Nutting also stated: 'I am convinced that Great Britain's rejection of the Schuman Plan marked the most vital turning point in Anglo-European relations since the Second World War. This was the opportunity for Great Britain to get into the business of rebuilding Europe' (Nutting, 1960: 34).

[6] Anthony Nutting also noted that Britain 'could have had the leadership of Europe on any terms which she cared to name. If we had offered our hand it would have been grasped without question or condition' (Nutting, 1960: 3).

[7] This policy was highlighted in *European Unity*, an official Labour Party pamphlet that was published in May 1950. It argued that it was not necessary to have close economic or political cooperation with Europe as the economies were not complementary. The text of the document is reproduced in Kitzinger, 1968: 59–79, especially 65.

[8] The FTA proposal of November 1956 only referred to industrial goods and was to include as many members of the OEEC as possible, as well as all members of the EEC. It would have allowed Britain to import foodstuffs at low or zero tariffs without any accompanying measures, while being able to give preferences to Commonwealth countries and keep Britain together with the Six.

[9] France walked out of the Maudling Committee on 14 November 1958. The committee had been established in August 1957 to thrash out the case for a FTA link, and that action effectively brought FTA negotiations to an end. France believed that the FTA proposal was a weak alternative to the EEC because it lacked the strength and rigour that the Treaty of Rome placed on its members.

[10] The Treaty of Rome provided for a common market and on the same day the Euratom Treaty was signed.

[11] EFTA comprised Austria, Switzerland, Denmark, Norway, Portugal, Sweden and Britain. EFTA's objective was to establish a free market between its members through the abolition of tariffs and other obstacles to trade in industrial products. The reduction of tariffs was to be progressive over a number of years (same as the EEC) and the convention was that this period would be ten years, unless a decision was taken to make it shorter.

[12] *If Britain Joins. The Economic Effects of Membership of the Common Market*, London: The Economist Intelligence Unit, December 1957, p. 8.

[13] All quantitative restrictions on industrial goods had been removed within the Community by the end of 1961. *Britain and the European Communities. Background to the Negotiations*, London: HMSO, 1962, p. 12. With regard to the integration of the Six, see *The First Stage of the Common Market. Report on the Execution of the Treaty January 1958–January 1962*, Brussels: Commission of the European Economic Community, July 1962.

[14] The Lord Privy Seal, Edward Heath, outlined the government's position as to membership of the EEC at a meeting of the European Economic Community in Paris on 10 October 1961. This statement was subsequently published as a government White Paper, Cmnd. 1565, London: HMSO, 29 November 1961.

[15] De Gaulle stated: 'England is insular, maritime, linked by trade, markets and food supply to very different and often distant lands.' Source: De Gaulle, press conference, 14 January 1963. Taken from *The Annual Register*, 1963.

[16] *The Times*, 7 June 1966.

[17] *Factsheets on Britain and Europe*, No. 4: *Industry and the Common Market*, London: HMSO, April 1971, p. 2. The weakness of the British economy is examined by Porter, 1995: 18–21.

[18] A communiqué issued by the Council of Ministers on 19 December 1967 referred to the need for the British economy to be strengthened before it would be possible for membership to take place. The text of the press conference and communiqué is reproduced in Kitzinger, 1968: 311–19. With regard to the issue of de Gaulle emphasising economic rather than political reasons, see Camps, 1969: 213.

[19] A 1977 report of the Central Policy Review Staff stated that Britain's share of the total GDP of OECD countries had fallen by one-quarter in the past 20 years. See Central Policy Review Staff, *Review of Overseas Representation*, London: HMSO, 1977. An example of the decline in the importance of Britain was that when fighting broke out between India and Pakistan in April and September 1965 the conflict was settled not by Britain, but by Russia at Tashkent.

[20] *The United Kingdom and the European Communities*, Cmnd. 4715, London: HMSO, July 1971. For a short version of the government's White Paper see *Britain and Europe*, London: HMSO, July 1971.

[21] Ibid., p. 8.

[22] See treaty concerning the accession of Denmark, Ireland, Norway and the United Kingdom to the EEC, 22 January 1972, Cmnd. 4862-I, London: HMSO.

[23] The four issues that dominated the negotiations were the reform of the Common Agricultural Policy, the Commonwealth, state aid to industry and the regions, and the budget.

[24] The European Council has the job of being a political decision-making body, while also providing the impetus to the development of the EU by setting priorities.

[25] *The Times*, 28th January 1977.

[26] The budget question was important because it had been estimated that Britain would be the largest net contributor to the Community budget by the end of the transitionary period in January 1978, while at the same time being ranked only fifth in terms of its average share of the Community's gross domestic product (GDP). See Commission document COM(79) 462, Reference Paper on Budgetary Questions, 12 September 1979. It was similarly clear that by the 1980s Britain would have had a deficit under the CAP. This was because British farmers tended to be more efficient than continental farmers, as well as concentrating in areas such as sheep farming that were not as generously subsidised by the CAP, which meant that Britain received little benefit from the agricultural programmes which comprised the majority of the Community budget. Also see *Survey of Current Affairs*, Vol. 10, No. 3, London: HMSO, March 1980, pp. 71–2.

[27] The agreement reached at Fontainebleau involved an increase in VAT revenues to be paid to the EC from 1% to 1.4%, while Britain got a 66% rebate of the gap between what it paid to the EC and what it received from it. With regard to the 1984 budget see *Statement on the 1984 Community Budget*, Cmnd. 9174, London: HMSO, March 1984.

[28] *The Economist*, 24 November 1990, pp. 19–26.

[29] Two committees were established at Fontainebleau, viz.: the ad hoc committee on a people's Europe (later called the Adonnino Committee) which received a mandate to examine aspects of the Community that were directly visible to the common citizen, and the ad hoc committee for institutional affairs (renamed the Dooge Committee) which examined institutional, political and economic reform.

[30] *Survey of Current Affairs*, Vol. 16, No. 1, London: HMSO, January 1986, p. 6.

[31] The SEA codified the role of the European Council whereby the institution had developed over the years from the European summits, thereby making the European Council meetings part of the institutional machinery of the European Community.

[32] Interview: Foreign and Commonwealth Office official.

[33] Delors' predecessor, Gaston Thorn (1981–85), had not dominated the Commission but instead had been party to a Commission that had been driven by the Commissioners. Similarly, Roy Jenkins (1977–81) had been President of a Commission that had not been dominated by one person but instead by numerous Commissioners, despite his personal role in the launch of the EMS.

[34] Margaret Thatcher noted that 'I had witnessed a profound shift in how European policy was conducted – and therefore in the kind of Europe that was taking shape. A Franco-German bloc with its own agenda had re-emerged to set the direction of the Community' (Thatcher, 1993: 558–9). Also see Dyson and Featherstone, 1999: 3–4.

[35] *The Times*, 21 September 1988, pp. 1 and 24. Prime Minister Thatcher gave five guiding principles for the future development of the Community. The first concerned the concentration of power and the suppression of nationhood, as she believed that willing and active cooperation between states was the best way to build a successful Community. The second issue concerned the need to tackle problems such as CAP before the Community progressed any further, while the third mentioned the need for the Community to develop policies that fostered enterprise. The fourth stated that Europe should not develop into a protectionist grouping of states, while the fifth and last point was her concern over the role of NATO, which she believed was still the bedrock of a sound European defence system. See *The Times*, 21 September 1988, p. 7, and *Survey of Current Affairs*, Vol. 18, No. 10, London: HMSO, October 1988, pp. 336–40.

[36] *The Economist*, 21 July 1990, p. 25.

[37] John Major reflected that 'too often she [Thatcher] conducted government by gut instinct; conviction, some said admiringly, but at any rate without mature, detached examination of the issues. She lost her political agility; the Poll Tax and crude anti-Europeanism were the policies that resulted.'

[38] *The Economist*, 10 November 1990, p. 36 and *Financial Times*, 20 November 1990, p. 21.

[39] *The Economist*, 17 November 1990, pp. 37–8.

[40] See *Survey of Current Affairs*, Vol. 20, No. 12, London: HMSO, December 1989, *The Economist*, 1 December 1990, pp. 33–9, and *Financial Times*, 28 November 1990, p. 6.

[41] *The Economist*, 16 February 1991, p. 34 and 9 March 1991, pp. 27–8.

[42] John Major, *The Evolution of Europe*, speech to the Konrad Adenauer Foundation, London: Conservative Political Centre, 11 March 1991.

[43] *The Guardian*, 30 November 1990, p. 23 and 7 December 1990, p. 8.

[44] The enlargement of the European Union to include the applicant states of Austria, Finland, Norway and Sweden resulted in disagreement among member states as to the necessary institutional adjustment to accommodate a larger EU. The main source of debate concerned the weighting for qualified majority voting (QMV), particularly the number of votes required in the Council of Ministers to form a blocking majority which can veto a Council decision on a proposal from the European Commission.

[45] *The Guardian*, 1 May 2001, p. 18.

Constructing Britain's monetary policy

CHAPTER 2

Objectives

- Highlight the factors that influence the construction of Britain's position on monetary union.
- Evaluate the role of the Treasury.
- Demonstrate the changing role of the Bank of England.

Introduction

The previous chapter provided a broad political history of Britain's engagement in European integration in the post-1945 period. Particular emphasis was attached to demonstrating the manner by which the options for British policy-makers have increasingly focused on the European Union. Having provided this general background information, the rest of this book is specifically concerned with analysing Britain's engagement in the policy area of monetary union and the implications for the nation of the policies taken by successive governments. The manner by which different governments have responded to integration in the field of monetary policy is chronicled in Part II of the book (Chapters 5 to 10). But prior to that information, the next three chapters examine the forces that have shaped this debate and the economic and political implications of monetary union. In accordance with this aim, this chapter focuses attention on the main factors that have shaped the construction of British policy towards monetary integration, paying attention to the role of key government departments and the involvement of individual ministers.

Context

In the construction of a British position on European matters, it might appear that the Foreign and Commonwealth Office (FCO) is the leading department in terms of establishing a British negotiating position. But the fact of the matter is that the British system of policy coordination places a great deal of emphasis on policy being constructed from a neutral position. To this end, the Cabinet Office[1] European Secretariat is entrusted with the task of establishing the priorities for British negotiating tactics (Box 2.1). This strategy is reflective of the fact that all of the departments within government are invariably affected by European policy, from Agriculture to the Treasury, and Social Security to the Home Office.

European affairs therefore do not just fall under the responsibility of the FCO. Instead, issues of a policy-making and policy-implementing nature pervade the wider body of domestic government departments. In such a scenario it is evident that so-called domestic departments are involved in regular (sometimes daily) contact with their counterparts in the member states and institutions of the

---

BOX 2.1

Cabinet and Cabinet Office

Policy decisions in the UK tend to be taken by Cabinet, and then approved by Parliament. Within Cabinet each minister tends to fight their departmental rights and in matters of public expenditure it is the case that the Chancellor of the Exchequer and the Chief Secretary to the Treasury play important roles. At times smaller groups of ministers, on the grounds of efficiency or because of the need for confidentiality or speed, take decisions. The Cabinet Office serves the Cabinet, but also the Prime Minister. The office, while being small, has traditionally been the closest the Prime Minister has to a department. The Cabinet Office can order and control Cabinet business. The Cabinet Office exercises strong control over international economic negotiations, especially EU policy through the European Secretariat of the Cabinet Office.

Margaret Thatcher was regarded as a dominant force within Cabinet, while John Major attached emphasis to a method of decision-making that was based on consensus. In contrast, Tony Blair, like Thatcher, has taken a strong grip on government and reduced the relative importance of Cabinet as a method of decision-making. More and more business is now channelled outside of Cabinet, either through Cabinet committees or informal meetings between ministers (especially the Chancellor and the Prime Minister). A further important trend under the Blair premiership has been the dramatic expansion in the number of officials who staff his own private office of No. 10 Downing Street. This is in conjunction with the relative strengthening of the Cabinet Office as a supporting department to the Prime Minister, thereby increasing the resources available to Tony Blair, and resulting in some commentators referring to his style of leadership as more presidential than prime ministerial.

EU. Thus, the importance of British negotiating tactics being established in a neutral and non-departmental arena is that the final decision can be more easily accepted by departments than if it had been purely constructed by the FCO.

But while this method of policy coordination is true for issues of a political nature, questions concerning monetary union are generally not subjected to such a widespread process of coordination throughout Whitehall (Blair, A., 1998a: 166). One of the reasons for this is that monetary policy falls within the remit of a more select group, including the Treasury,[2] Foreign Office,[3] Cabinet Office,[4] Bank of England[5] and Department of Trade and Industry (DTI).[6] Nevertheless, it is the Treasury that has traditionally occupied a central role, not least because of the expertise that its officials and ministers have on these matters. This is obtained both at the domestic level and also from interaction with colleagues in other member states and the institutions of the EU, such as at meetings of European Finance Ministers (Ecofin). To this end, it is the Treasury that tends to have its ear closest to the European debate on financial matters. Such knowledge is a source of strength to the Treasury, as it is for the Bank of England.

As has already been mentioned, other government departments do have a direct interest in monetary policy. The most prominent of these is the FCO. This does, of course, stem from its experience of EU negotiations and ergo the expertise of its officials on these matters, whilst the Foreign Secretary is responsible for introducing EU policy at meetings of Cabinet and also chairs the key Cabinet committee that deals with European policy. The Foreign Secretary additionally attends key EU meetings, including the European Council and the General Affairs Council. Moreover, the FCO is directly responsible for Britain's permanent representation to the European Union (UKRep), which is the frontline base in terms of Britain's negotiations within the EU. Its staff come from a wide range of domestic government departments, including Agriculture, Employment, Home Office, Transport, and Trade and Industry, and are therefore representative of the different areas of EU negotiations which they take part in.

It is additionally evident that questions of a monetary nature impact on other matters of EU policy. Thus, in contrast to all other government departments, the FCO has a broad overview of all EU policies and can therefore place monetary union within the wider parameters of Britain's European foreign policy. Of the other government departments that have an involvement in these matters, the DTI does exercise some influence. This partly flows from its own degree of expertise on EU policy, being for instance at the forefront of the transposition of EU legislation into British law. On the specific question of monetary union, the DTI's input is directly related to the interests of the business community, with whom it naturally has close contacts. In this context, while the DTI is rarely (if at all) involved in the nuts and bolts of policy-making on monetary union at the EU level, it does play an important role at the domestic level by informing (and obtaining information from) business as to the issues concerning the single currency. For instance, in recent years the business community has expressed particular concern over the detrimental impact that an over-valued pound has been having on manufacturing competitiveness.[7]

When examining the influence that the Treasury, DTI and FCO bring to bear on monetary policy it is important to be fully aware of the influences and beliefs that often shape their negotiating viewpoints. In a nutshell, this has meant that whereas the Treasury has been concerned with the technical aspects of monetary union, such as the nature of the convergence criteria and institutional dynamics, these concerns are not always shared by the DTI and FCO. They, by contrast, have tended to be concerned with the impact that Britain's strategy on monetary union has related to wider EU negotiating tactics and the extent to which policy options on monetary union relate to the practicalities of business competitiveness. Somewhat inevitably these differing viewpoints have not always sat easily together.

The Prime Minister additionally plays a significant role in this policy field, and this is of course evidenced by the office-holder being 'the First Lord of the Treasury'. In day-to-day matters the power of the Prime Minister is apparent in terms of departmental supervision and also by means of attendance at European Council meetings, where matters of a monetary nature are often discussed. As will become apparent in the chapters which follow, Margaret Thatcher was a particularly dominant Prime Minister and acted as a brake on the wishes of some Cabinet Ministers, especially Nigel Lawson and Sir Geoffrey Howe, for Britain to become actively engaged in discussions on monetary union. John Major adopted a more consensual style of decision-making, though one which fundamentally failed to establish cohesiveness within the Conservative government (Blair, A., 1999b: 35–6). Tony Blair's style of governance has attached greater emphasis to the strong prime ministerial mould of Thatcher, with a greater amount of business conducted outside Cabinet, often involving a small number of individuals, whilst he has additionally greatly strengthened the support provided within No. 10 Downing Street (Rawnsley, 2001: 50).[8] In essence, 'The power structure of economic policy in Britain is very much in favour of a determined Prime Minister and Chancellor . . . And the key decisions are made either by the Chancellor and the Prime Minister, or by a Cabinet Committee which they can nominate to suit themselves' (Keegan, 1984: 14).

It is therefore evident that there are broadly two different styles of government, namely one which centres on Cabinet government and one which centres on prime ministerial government. In this sense the Prime Minister is either referred to as being 'first among equals' or someone who is more powerful than anyone else. In general terms it is apparent that a Prime Minister has considerably greater power than was the case in the early part of the 19th century when power tended to lie in the hands of Parliament. Of the factors that have influenced this change, it is possible to point to the Prime Minister's position as leader of the governing political party, combined with a more rigid party system. But it is also evident that the growing influence of the media and the personalisation of politics has added to this influence, as well as the increase in international summits that a Prime Minister has to attend. In domestic matters, the Prime Minister's strength is also apparent by being head of the civil service.

Finally, monetary policy (and EU policy more generally) is also subject to influence from a myriad of different pressure groups, including the Confederation of British Industry (CBI), the Institute of Directors (IoD), the Trades Union Congress (TUC) and a number of more specific pro- and anti-euro pressure groups. Those of a more Eurosceptic nature include the 'Business for Sterling' campaign and the 'New Europe' movement, while pro-Europe groups include the 'Britain in Europe' campaign. Of the less issue-specific pressure groups, the CBI and TUC have generally adopted positive positions towards British participation in the EU and membership of the single currency, whilst the IoD tends to be less supportive of further integration at the EU level, and ergo the transfer of policy-making capacity from Britain to Brussels, and is particularly hostile towards the single currency. The IoD does not, however, reflect the broad interests of the business community in the sense that the CBI does.

Shaping monetary policy

Although many government departments might have an interest in monetary policy, it is the Treasury that sits at the heart of British policy on EMU, whilst also playing an important role on EU policy in general. The debate over Britain's budget contributions that dominated the early years of the Thatcher administration, combined with moves towards EMU, helped to place the Treasury in the front line of European developments. At a domestic level it is also true that the Treasury has a commanding role over all other government departments. Its interests touch on every government department through its responsibility for taxation and public spending,[9] the latter of which means that the Chancellor is involved in every area of government activity as a result of the allocation of funding to government departments. At the same time the Treasury has had success in sending its officials into other government departments, thereby ensuring that it 'has had a significant impact over the general direction of policy' (Smith et al., 1993: 587). The reality of this situation, combined with the sheer number of Cabinet Committees that the Chancellor sits on, means that he has an ability to influence the construction of policies in other government departments. As Nigel Lawson, himself a former Chancellor, has commented: 'the Chancellor has his finger in pretty well every pie in government' (Lawson, 1992: 273). In this sense the Chancellor's viewpoints carry greater weight than virtually every other Cabinet position (apart from the Prime Minister). This state of affairs is itself demonstrated by government ministers who wish to put a paper to Cabinet having in the first instance to submit the proposal to the Treasury. In specific terms, the Chancellor sits below the Prime Minister in the Whitehall pyramid of power and influence, after which come the Foreign Secretary and the Lord Chancellor. Where a Deputy Prime Minister has been appointed, as

---

BOX 2.2

Treasury power and influence

The Treasury is essentially the most powerful department within Whitehall. The main responsibility is 'to assist Ministers in the formulation and implementation of the Government's economic policy'.[10] Although there are other important government departments, such as the Foreign and Commonwealth Office and the Department of Trade and Industry, the Treasury has the advantage of perspective over all government departments. This is because the Treasury is able to obtain an understanding of the wider picture of what is happening in government through its allotted role as expenditure controller. Not only does this give the Treasury, particularly the Chancellor of the Exchequer and Chief Secretary, an ability to shape the basic priorities of government spending across government, but it also means that they are able to gain an understanding of the operation of specific government departments. This is something that is not true for any other government department. Indeed, the very fact that the Chancellor has responsibility for public expenditure and taxation differs from the situation in many other countries. For instance, in the US, the Treasury Secretary is responsible for tax, the Office of Management and the Budget is responsible for public expenditure, and the Chairman of the Federal Reserve for monetary policy.[11] And while UK Chancellors have in the past combined all three roles, the 1997 decision to give the Monetary Policy Committee the responsibility for setting interest rates removed one element of the Chancellor's power.

---

in the case of John Prescott, it is he who is second in command to the Prime Minister on operational matters, such as in the event of a crisis, though it is the Chancellor who is nearly always the second most powerful minister in government (see Box 2.2). The Chancellor and the Treasury accordingly occupy a core role within government.

This state of affairs is the result of the Chancellor's office of the Treasury being involved in virtually all aspects of government policy-making, purely from its role of allocating funding to all government departments. But apart from this distributive function, the Treasury is staffed with some of the ablest officials in government, who are able to command a great many of the resources behind specific projects. So, for instance, if the Chancellor considers a particular policy to be in the national interest, it is often difficult for other ministers to challenge that viewpoint because they generally do not have the same degree of detailed information to hand. Moreover, the Chancellor and his colleagues (both official and ministerial) sit on a whole range of government committees and are therefore able to get their viewpoint across in a way that a more minor department, such as Culture, is not. Nigel Lawson has also pointed out that the Treasury has the ability to vet any new proposal before it enters the Cabinet system. An ability to mobilise resources to advance or counter policy proposals has been a central element in determining the degree of British involvement in making policy. Thus, Nigel Lawson was able to exert considerable influence on other colleagues to the view that Exchange Rate Mechanism (ERM) entry was of importance.

It is thus possible to summarise that the power of the Treasury is influenced by certain key factors. At the heart of these points is the fact that the Treasury generally has a superior access to, and an ability to control, the supply of economic information. Secondly, because the Treasury has contacts with every government department through its responsibility for public spending, it therefore has an unparalleled understanding of the organisation of government. This means that it has a full understanding of the decision-making process of government, with such knowledge greatly increasing the power of the Treasury. The third factor concerns the procedural practice whereby government ministers have to submit any proposal to the Treasury before it can go before Cabinet, thereby bolstering Treasury power.

This strength, combined with the historical reluctance of the Treasury towards Europe, has provided it with an ability to act as a barrier to the pro-European instincts of other government departments. One of the reasons for this is that the Treasury has for the most part not responded as positively to European integration as other government departments for whom closer involvement with Europe has provided new opportunities, as in the case of the DTI and the FCO. The Treasury, by contrast, has had a stronger domestic policy outlook than many other government departments, with the Chancellor being responsible for domestically orientated policies of taxation and spending. Moreover, as the Treasury has essentially been the dominant domestic government department, its officials and ministers have not been used to the same degree of bargaining, the skills of which are crucial in European negotiations. The Treasury has also often been concerned with the technical aspects of negotiations when it has been involved in EU negotiations rather than the broader political implications of membership. The overall effect of these policy developments has been that the dominance of the Treasury at the domestic level has impacted on its general unwillingness to enter into compromises and engage in bargaining at the European level. Britain's opt-out from the single currency has further cemented this state of affairs as Treasury officials and ministers have been isolated from key debates at the European level. Gavyn Davies has reflected that a 'two tier decision system may develop in the European Union where those inside the single currency have a disproportionately large impact on the decisions of the Union compared to those outside'.[12] The overall picture is therefore one where the Treasury has not had the same level of involvement in EU policy-making, which has had a knock-on effect of cultivating a more sceptical position within the Treasury which would, after all, lose a significant degree of power and influence with the adoption of the euro.

Yet while the Treasury, in particular the Chancellor, may want to pursue a particular policy, this is generally dependent on the agreement of the Prime Minister. In this context, the connection between Prime Minister and Chancellor is a core axis upon which government sits as both individuals carry such considerable power and influence. As Philip Stephens has noted, 'the relationship between Prime Minister and Chancellor is the essential hinge of effective government. When it snaps . . . the consequences are momentous' (Stephens, 2001: 205). Thus, the breakdown in the relationship between Margaret Thatcher and Nigel Lawson, because of the desire of the latter for Britain to enter the ERM, severely disrupted the effective running of government policy. In the end, Lawson and the Foreign Secretary, Sir Geoffrey Howe, resigned from Cabinet at the expense of further weakening Thatcher's status and position within government.

The strength of the Chancellor is, of course, greatly determined by the personality and relative power and influence of the person who occupies the office. To this end, the high status that Nigel Lawson had within the Conservative Party and government meant that Prime Minister Margaret Thatcher could not ignore her Chancellor, though she became increasingly reliant on Alan Walters (her economic adviser). In a similar vein, John Major could not ignore the pro-European views of Kenneth Clarke because of his standing within government. In such situations it is the ability of the Chancellor to block policy proposals that is particularly noticeable. So while the Chancellor might not be able to override the Prime Minister on specific policy decisions, he can nevertheless play a blocking role on all areas of policy. As outlined in Chapter 9, Clarke was not prepared to accept a shift to a Eurosceptic position favoured by the Cabinet and a great deal of the Conservative Party. But whereas Clarke and Lawson can be portrayed as dominant Chancellors, the same cannot be said for Norman Lamont who occupied that office from 1990 to 1993.

In contrast to the influence that Lawson and Clarke were able to exert, they did not enjoy the same dominant role within government that Gordon Brown has occupied since his appointment as Chancellor in May 1997. Indeed, upon election to office in 1997 Gordon Brown had already shadowed the post of Chancellor for some five years and was therefore more prepared and knowledgeable for his new post than any Chancellor has been in recent years. This even differed from Tony Blair who took up the post of leader only after the death of John Smith in 1994 (the then leader of the Labour Party). In appointing a leader after the untimely death of Smith, Brown and Blair agreed on a deal that saw Blair appointed leader but left Brown in sole charge of economic policy-making. When in government this would see Brown exercise influence over all areas of government policy-making, from social policy to the welfare to work programme.[13] Evidence of the key role to be played by Brown was his appointment as chair of the most important economic Cabinet Committee, namely Economic Affairs (EA). This meant that Blair was the first Prime Minister since the 1960s not to chair this key Cabinet Committee (Hennessy, 1998: 14). Gordon Brown's consolation prize for not challenging Blair for the leadership was therefore the consolidation of his own power base. In essence, Brown was given a free rein to get involved in all aspects of policy-making of an economic nature, while Blair focused his attentions on foreign and defence policy, Northern Ireland, and other domestic policies that included health and education. In government, this has basically meant that 'Brown's control of the economic agenda

extended well beyond the narrow boundaries of fiscal and monetary policy'
(Stephens, 2001: 188).

The net outcome of this state of affairs was that the Treasury emerged as
a significant (and essentially the dominant) government department during
the first Labour administration of 1997–2001. However, as many commentators have pointed out, the perceived power of the Treasury was the product
of Brown's own personal involvement in policy decisions and did not mean
that the Treasury as a department had had its powers significantly augmented.
Indeed, some powers, such as decisions over interest rates, were transferred
out of the Treasury's competence. If anything, Brown's own personal style
of decision-making, based on support from his own close advisers such as
Ed Balls – who were not Treasury officials – meant that the vast majority of
decisions were taken outside of the reach of the Treasury. This meant that
the task of the latter was merely 'to implement not question them [the deci-
sions]' (Stephens, 2001: 187). We can therefore see that while the Treasury has
become more actively involved in the work of all government departments,
many key decisions are taken by the Chancellor's inner group of personal
advisers. Such use of individual policy advisers, a practice that was also true of
Blair, clearly had significant implications for the ability of the wider echelons
of government and moreover Parliament[14] to have influence over key areas of
government policy.

But while Chancellor Brown's control of macroeconomic policy was subject
to little or no outside involvement, the same cannot be said for matters
concerning the single currency, where both the Prime Minister and Foreign
Secretary exercised considerable influence. As Foreign Secretary in the first
Labour government of 1997–2001, Robin Cook took up a position that
advocated entry and one which was radically different from his own initial
scepticism towards Europe. Such a positive approach increasingly appeared
to be at odds with the more prudent and cautious approach of Chancellor
Brown on the single currency.[15] Indeed, throughout the 1997–2001 Parliament
it appeared that Brown's scepticism on the subject grew deeper. In many
respects this was influenced by his own lukewarm views on European politics,
whereby he appeared to prefer visits to Washington DC rather than the
monthly Ecofin meetings. He was also hostile to EU attempts to make further
inroads into policy areas that he regarded as domestic matters, notably taxation and public spending.[16]

On the question of the single currency, Brown's more sceptical approach
was based on the fact that he knew that no decision on entry would be taken
in the 1997–2001 Parliament. In any case Brown based the case for entry on
economic grounds by establishing a series of economic tests that would establish when the conditions would be right for entry. For the Chancellor, the
significance of the setting of such economic tests was a means of providing the
government with enough time to prepare for a referendum on the subject. In
this sense, although the establishment of economic conditions might have
appeared as a means of diluting the need to campaign for the political case for

entry, as economics would be the determining factor, it was nonetheless a highly political decision. In addition to this strategic handling of the subject – so as to reduce divisions within the Labour government – the economic conditions also meant that any decision on the single currency would be determinant on the views of Gordon Brown. This was a move which had essentially 'given him a veto over if and when the government recommended entry' (Stephens, 2001: 202).

As Prime Minister, Tony Blair too put reliance on the economic case for Britain's participation in the single currency, though he was also fully conscious of the importance that membership of the euro would bring to positioning Britain in the front line of European states. Nevertheless, for Blair the economic case was the core issue and he was fully conscious of the divisions that had emerged within the Conservative Party on the issue of the single currency and consequently did not wish to see the Labour Party similarly divided. In contrast to the positions of Blair and Brown, Robin Cook adopted a more positive approach and sought to advance the case for entry from his position as Foreign Secretary.[17] However, his more public approach, combined with the division between himself and Brown on the subject, essentially cost Cook his job in the June 2001 Cabinet reshuffle. For some time before that change in office, Tony Blair had in any case sought to dampen down Cook's enthusiasm for the single currency so as to reduce division within government.[18]

The significance of the replacement of Cook as Foreign Secretary by the more naturally Eurosceptic Jack Straw is the manner by which the FCO's naturally pro-European instincts have been sidelined.[19] This was further demonstrated by the appointment of a whole new team of ministers in the FCO, with, for instance, the new Minister for Europe, Peter Hain, being equally cautious on the euro, with this more careful approach being made clear at the Gothenburg European Council of June 2001.

For Prime Minister Blair, it appears that there were various strategic reasons for this Cabinet reshuffle, which was clearly centred on Britain's negotiating strategy towards the euro. In the first instance, it has to be emphasised that the replacement of Robin Cook was completely unexpected by media observers, as well as by himself, as he had spent the previous days preparing for a forthcoming European summit in Gothenburg. While his grasp of his portfolio appeared less sure-footed in the early stages of the Blair administration, by the end of the 1997–2001 Parliament Cook had become a highly respected Foreign Secretary.[20] Prime Minister Blair was, however, clear that the lack of cohesiveness within government on the euro, particularly between the Foreign Secretary and Chancellor, was a major cause of concern and he therefore appreciated the need to establish a united policy. The appointment of Straw (a staunch ally of Tony Blair) was therefore perceived as a means of rectifying any divisions and reducing tension between the FCO and the Treasury.

More significantly, the change of ministerial team at the FCO was also part of Blair's strategy to exercise control over foreign affairs from No. 10. At the same time it was also a means of ensuring that the key debate on the single currency remained one between the Prime Minister and the Chancellor. That this is so is reflective of Tony Blair's desire to act as a powerful Prime Minister, which, as some commentators have noted, has resulted in 'overbearing prime-ministerial government' (Hennessy, 1998: 14). As will become apparent in subsequent chapters, a desire to take control of policy was inevitably influenced by John Major's inability to exercise control over the Conservative Party in the 1992–97 Parliament. The net effect of this desire by Prime Minister Blair to take a leading role was immediately apparent in the strengthening of his own private office in No. 10 Downing Street (Hennessy, 2000; Burch and Holliday, 2000).

Bank of England

In addition to this input from Whitehall, monetary policy has also been the concern of central banks, which played an important role in the construction of the European Central Bank, while central bank governors also participated in the drafting of the Delors Report. The latter was a particularly contentious issue within Britain, as Prime Minister Thatcher considered that the Governor of the Bank of England should have done more to limit the prescription for monetary union contained in the report. But as Chapter 6 makes clear, the Governor considered that the purpose of the Delors Committee was not to answer whether monetary union was preferable, but rather how it could be achieved.[21] Yet, the fact that Thatcher thought that she could 'instruct' the Governor to adopt a particular negotiating position demonstrated the reality that the Bank of England was the least independent of the EU central banks (Box 2.3). In this

---

BOX 2.3

Bank of England

Established in 1694, the Bank of England is the central bank of the United Kingdom, and plays an important role in the formation of monetary policy and the overall stability of the financial system. It plays a key function in the fight against inflation by making changes to the interest rate, though the decisions on that rate are taken by the Monetary Policy Committee (on which the Bank of England is represented). Decisions on interest rates have only been taken in this way since the government gave the responsibility for the setting of interest rates to the Monetary Policy Committee of the Bank in May 1997. These decisions were previously taken by the Chancellor after consultation with the Governor of the Bank of England. As far as Economic and Monetary Union is concerned, the Bank of England was involved in the technical preparations for the single currency and its institutional framework, while the Bank continues to play an important role in assisting British business (especially the City of London) with preparations for the introduction of the euro.

context, the Bank of England did not possess the constitutional independence of the German Bundesbank or the US Federal Reserve. It was, by contrast, essentially a servant of the Treasury and therefore subject to its control.

The existence of political linkage between Whitehall and the Bank of England ensured that government controlled a particular lever of economic policy, namely monetary control (Lawson, 1992: 83–4). This specifically provided the government with an ability to have a direct input on interest rates and exchange rates rather than letting the Bank of England have control over this policy area. The status of this relationship had, in fact, been true for many years, although the 1946 Bank of England Act gave status to the system, whereby 'although operationally and institutionally distinct from Government, the Bank accepted Treasury control over policy'.[22] As Nigel Lawson himself commented, 'We [the Treasury] take the decisions but they [the Bank of England] do the work.'[23] Lawson had earlier reflected that 'When I think they [interest rates] ought to go up they go up and when I think they should come down they come down.'[24] This relationship was therefore characterised by a situation where the Treasury has taken the decision as to what policy should be adopted, while the Bank has had a degree of operational autonomy in the execution of that policy (Wallace, 1975: 42). In this context, the Bank of England has therefore been accountable to the Treasury, particularly the Chancellor of the Exchequer, for its actions.

The reality of Treasury dominance in its relationship with the Bank of England has been particularly noticeable during periods when monetary policy was central to government objectives. Nigel Lawson considered that the 'Bank of England was essentially the executive arm of the Treasury in the financial markets' (Lawson, 1992: 383). Treasury dominance was especially noticeable during the 1980s when the Thatcher government placed greater emphasis on monetary policy than had been evident for much of the post-war period, the effect of which was a decline in the relative power of the Bank of England. This was emphasised by Thatcher's refusal in 1983 to renew Gordon Richardson's term as Governor, replacing him with Robin Leigh-Pemberton, who she thought would pose less of a conflict in the pursuit of the government's monetary policy objectives. And while Leigh-Pemberton did not contradict government policy outright, the Bank notably argued that British participation in the Exchange Rate Mechanism would provide a more stable monetary environment, resulting in lower inflation rates. The Chancellor of the Exchequer, Nigel Lawson, equally supported this option, while also favouring the granting of independence to the Bank of England, though one where there would continue to be a degree of accountability rather than control (Lawson, 1992: 272). Prime Minister Thatcher was nevertheless opposed to this objective, as was her successor, John Major (Major, 1999: 675). Yet the case for independence became stronger in the wake of the Maastricht Treaty, which established a timetable for monetary union that involved a move away from national control of monetary policy.

BOX 2.4

Monetary Policy Committee (MPC)

The MPC was created as the new body with the responsibility for setting British interest rates. The MPC consists of the Governor of the Bank of England, the two Deputy Governors and six other members. Meetings take place every month, with the interest rate decision being immediately announced after each meeting. The establishment of the MPC was a result of the decision on 6 May 1997 by the Chancellor of the Exchequer, Gordon Brown, to grant the Bank of England operational responsibility for setting interest rates. While interest rates are set by the MPC, legislation ensures that it is possible for the government to instruct the Bank of England to set a particular rate, though this can only be achieved for a limited period. The MPC meets every month, with decisions taken by a committee vote of one person, one vote. In the case of there being no majority vote, then the Governor of the Bank of England is entrusted with a casting vote.

From the above discussion it is clear that one of the main cases for devolving monetary policy to the Bank of England was the argument that an independent Bank would be more likely to pursue long-term economic goals rather than short-term policies in support of political objectives. Such an argument was supported by the experience of the American, German and Swiss central banks, which all enjoyed a notable degree of independence and had a good track record in the delivery of stable monetary policy. But in addition to this evidence, the case for granting the Bank of England independence was further bolstered by the question that remained over the Treasury's competency to conduct monetary policy in the wake of sterling's exit from the Exchange Rate Mechanism in September 1992. The reality at that time was that the separation between the Treasury's policy formulation role and the Bank's policy implementation role produced a rather disjointed response at a time of severe economic tension. It is in this context that one of the first actions of the New Labour government in 1997 was to grant independence to the Bank of England, with interest rates to be determined by a new Monetary Policy Committee (Box 2.4).

Conclusion

The significance of the separation of monetary policy from government was that it removed a potential source of conflict between Whitehall and the Bank of England in this area. More importantly it took away a further hurdle to British participation in monetary union because it could no longer be argued that a single currency would result in a loss of monetary control by government over interest rates, as this had already taken place.[25] In the wake of this development the primary tensions on monetary union have been between the Treasury, the FCO and the Prime Minister (though the debate today is essentially between the Treasury and the Prime Minister). This triangle of competing forces has been central to establishing Britain's negotiating positions on monetary union and before that its entry to the Exchange Rate Mechanism (ERM). The chapters that follow demonstrate the role of such key government departments and the involvement of the ministers within them.

Key points

- After the Prime Minister, the Chancellor of the Exchequer is the most powerful government minister.

- The Treasury and the Chancellor of the Exchequer are able to exert a great deal of influence over other government departments and ministers primarily through having control over government expenditure.

- Although the Treasury and the Chancellor have a great deal of involvement with EU policies, they have tended to have a more domestic focus than other government departments.

- The opt-out negotiated by Britain from monetary union has meant that the Treasury has been somewhat isolated from key debates on the single currency at the European level.

- The granting of independence to the Bank of England in 1997, with interest rates being determined by a Monetary Policy Committee, has removed government control over the setting of interest rates. The importance of this development is that it has taken away a further hurdle to Britain's participation in monetary union.

- The re-election of the Labour government in June 2001 increases the likelihood of a referendum on monetary union in the immediate future. Despite the reservations of Gordon Brown on the single currency, Prime Minister Blair is in a more commanding position, having been the first Labour Prime Minister to have been re-elected for a full term of office. Moreover, the Labour Party's majority within Parliament is substantially greater than that obtained by Margaret Thatcher in 1983 for her second term of office.

- The replacement of Robin Cook as Foreign Secretary by Jack Straw has ensured that the key debate on monetary union is between the Chancellor (Gordon Brown) and the Prime Minister (Tony Blair).

Questions

1. To what extent has the British government been Europeanised as a result of membership of the EU?

2. What are the main factors that have resulted in the Treasury being the most powerful government department?

3. In the construction of Britain's negotiating position on monetary union, which government departments have the greatest influence?

4. What were the main reasons behind the decision to grant the Bank of England independence from government interference?

5. What were the implications of granting independence to the Bank of England and the creation of a Monetary Policy Committee for Britain's negotiating position on monetary union?

6. To what extent can the Treasury act as a barrier to the more pro-European interests of the Foreign and Commonwealth Office?

7. 'The Cabinet has essentially been isolated from key decisions on monetary union.' Discuss.

8. To what extent has the Bank of England been sidelined by successive governments' discussions on monetary union?

9. 'Deputy Prime Minister in all but name': is this a correct assessment of Gordon Brown's position within the Labour government?

10. For what reasons has the Labour government adopted a more cautious approach towards the euro?

Further reading

Blair, Alasdair (1998) 'UK Policy Coordination during the 1990–91 Intergovernmental Conference', *Diplomacy and Statecraft*, Vol. 9, No. 2, pp. 160–83.

Bulmer, Simon and Burch, Martin (1998) 'Organizing for Europe: Whitehall, the British State and European Union', *Public Administration*, Vol. 76, Winter, pp. 601–28.

Bulmer, Simon and Burch, Martin (2000) 'The Europeanisation of British Central Government', in R. A. W. Rhodes, *Transforming British Government*, Vol. 1: *Changing Institutions*, Basingstoke: Macmillan, pp. 46–62.

Dyson, Kenneth (2000) 'EMU as Europeanization: Convergence, Diversity and Contingency', *Journal of Common Market Studies*, Vol. 38, No. 4, pp. 645–66.

Dyson, Kenneth (2000) 'Europeanization, Whitehall Culture and the Treasury as Institutional Veto Player: A Constructivist Approach to Economic and Monetary Union', *Public Administration*, Vol. 78, No. 4, pp. 897–914.

Forster, Anthony and Blair, Alasdair (2002) *The Making of Britain's European Foreign Policy*, Harlow: Longman, Chapters 3 and 6.

Kassim, Hussein (2000) 'The United Kingdom', in Hussein Kassim, B. Guy Peters and Vincent Wright (eds.) *The National Co-ordination of EU Policy: The Domestic Level*, Oxford: Oxford University Press, pp. 22–53.

Kavanagh, Dennis (2000) *British Politics: Continuities and Change*, 4th edn, Oxford: Oxford University Press, Chapters 10–13.

Stephens, Philip (2001) 'The Treasury under Labour', in Anthony Seldon (ed.) *The Blair Effect*, London: Little, Brown, pp. 185–207.

Notes

[1] The Cabinet Office serves the Cabinet, but also the Prime Minister. Although small, the office is the closest the Prime Minister has to a department. The Cabinet Office can order and control Cabinet business.

[2] http://www.hm-treasury.gov.uk/pub/html/docs/emu/main.html

[3] http://www.fco.gov.uk/news/keythemehome.asp?19

[4] http://www.cabinet-office.gov.uk/cabsec/2000/guide/euro.htm

[5] http://www.bankofengland.co.uk/euro/

[6] http://www.dti.gov.uk/europe/pagea.html

[7] *The Guardian*, 26 May 2001, p. 26.

[8] *The Times*, 27 November 1998, p. 14.

[9] The Chief Secretary to the Treasury has particular responsibility for this area.

[10] Cm. 2217, *Departmental Report of the Chancellor of the Exchequer's Departments: The Government's Expenditure Plans 1993–94 to 1995–96*, London: HMSO, February 1993.

[11] *Financial Times*, 22 September 2000, World Economy Survey, pp. II and IV respectively.

[12] Gavyn Davies, in House of Lords, 1995–96, Q. 126, pp. 35–6.

[13] *The Times*, 10 January 1998, p. 21.

[14] *Daily Telegraph*, 19 February 1999, p. 10.

[15] *The Times*, 16 September 1999, p. 15.

[16] *The Guardian*, 8 May 2001, p. 18.

[17] *The Times*, 6 September 1999, p. 2.

[18] *The Guardian*, 8 July 2000, p. 5.

[19] *The Guardian*, 12 June 2001, p. 1.

[20] *The Guardian*, 16 March 1999, p. 8, and *Financial Times*, 16 April 1999, p. 11.

[21] Private information. Also *Financial Times*, 25 June 1990, p. 40.

[22] 'The Role of the Bank of England', First Report, Vol. 1, *Treasury and Civil Service Committee*, House of Commons, Session 1993–94, para. 15.

[23] Nigel Lawson, 'Fourth Report from the Committee', *The 1988 Budget*, House of Commons, 1987–88, para. 400, Q. 251.

[24] Nigel Lawson, 'First Report from the Committee', *The Government's Economic Policy: Autumn Statement*, House of Commons, 1987–88, para. 197, Q. 139.

[25] *Financial Times*, 6 May 1999, p. 14.

The history of
monetary union

Objectives

- Provide an overview of progress towards monetary union.
- Demonstrate how economic and political difficulties hampered progress towards monetary union in the 1970s.
- Highlight the forces that pushed monetary union back on to the agenda of the Community in the 1980s.
- Demonstrate the factors that have shaped the monetary debate in the 1990s.
- Outline theoretical approaches that seek to explain the outcomes of monetary union.

Introduction

Whereas the previous chapter focused on the factors that have influenced Britain's negotiating position on monetary integration, the next two chapters examine both the history and implications of monetary union. In focusing on the history of monetary union, this chapter examines key policy developments and identifies the factors that have shaped the progress of monetary union.

Overview

One of the constant factors of European integration in the post-1945 period has been a desire to deepen the economic and political linkages between nation-states. In the early years of the European Economic Community (EEC), its interests were primarily directed towards assisting core industries such as agriculture, coal and steel. At the same time, a common external tariff was also created. Today, the competence of the now European Union (EU) extends into many aspects of economic and political affairs which were previously considered to be the purely domestic interest of member states. Central to the development and progress of the EU has been the creation of a single internal market that has permitted the free movement of people, goods, services and capital. Progress towards the single market in the 1980s represented a significant achievement in overcoming national barriers to economic integration. The very creation of the single market and the renewed interest in European integration that dominated the second half of the 1980s additionally played a significant part in advancing the cause of monetary integration. As Amy Verdun has commented, 'the launching of the internal market campaign contributed importantly to the renewed desire for an EMU in Europe' (Verdun, 1999: 310).

Whilst we may consider that the momentum towards monetary union is the product of recent years, proposals for monetary cooperation were evident in the immediate post-1945 period. Of the reasons for such interest in cooperation on monetary matters, the primary motivation was to expand the process of intra-European trade. With this in mind a European Payments Union (EPU) was established in 1950 to assist with the removal of exchange and trade restrictions through movement away from an emphasis on bilateralism. The EPU system basically ensured that trading relations among European countries could be conducted in a multilateral framework whereby a country could, for instance, be able to offset a deficit with one country by a surplus with another. In this sense the EPU acted as a vehicle for promoting trade liberalisation, something which it continued to do until it ceased operating in 1958.

But despite this early attempt to coordinate monetary policy, no substantial progress towards monetary union was made in the immediate post-war period. Indeed, when examining the origins of the current progression towards monetary union it is perfectly evident that it does not have its birthplace in the Treaty of Rome. That treaty made no direct reference to the coordination of monetary policy or the creation of a single currency. But despite the absence of any such commitment, there grew an interest among member states in the 1960s in the possible benefits to be obtained from the coordination of currencies. With this in mind, the Barre Report of February 1969 advocated that economic policies should be coordinated and that closer monetary cooperation should be advanced. This initiative helped to give impetus to member states deciding at The Hague summit of December 1969 that Economic and Monetary Union (EMU) would be recognised as an official goal of European integration.[1] The primary driving force behind this initiative was the then German Chancellor, Willy Brandt, who suggested that member states should formulate medium-term objectives for the creation of a monetary union, including the harmonisation of short-term policies. The ambitious nature of Brandt's plan also envisaged the establishment of a monetary union of permanently fixed exchange rates.

BOX 3.1

The Werner Report

At The Hague summit of December 1969, heads of state and government set up a High Level Group under the Luxembourg Prime Minister, Pierre Werner, to report on how Economic and Monetary Union could be achieved by 1980. The final report of the 'Werner Group' was submitted in October 1970 and set a three-stage process for the achievement of a complete EMU within a ten-year period. This included the objective of the irrevocable conversion of member states' currencies, free movement of capital, the permanent locking of exchange rates and the possibility of replacing member states' currencies with a single currency. The specific recommendations of the report were:

- the strengthening of economic policy coordination in parallel with the narrowing of exchange rate fluctuations;

- decisions on interest rates, exchange rates and the management of reserves were to be taken at Community level;

- it would be necessary to have fiscal harmonisation and for cooperation in structural and regional policies to take place;

- in terms of institutional building, the report vaguely called for the creation of 'the centre of decision for economic policy' and of 'the Community system for the central banks'.

France was equally in favour of some type of monetary cooperation, though its preference was for a form of balance of payments cooperation.

The end product of these positions was that member states agreed at The Hague meeting of December 1969 to the commissioning of a major study on how the goal of EMU could be realised by 1980, to be chaired by the then Luxembourg Prime Minister, Pierre Werner (Box 3.1). Some ten months later, the October 1970 Werner Report contained an early blueprint for monetary union that could be attained in stages by 1980 (Werner et al., 1970). This gradual approach to monetary union attached emphasis to the coordination of national monetary policies and a reduction in exchange rate fluctuations. Ultimately, the final goal would be the full liberalisation of capital movements, the irrevocable fixing of parities and the creation of a single currency. As the report stressed, monetary union would involve 'the total and irreversible fixing of parity rates and the complete liberation of movements of capital' (Werner et al., 1970: ch. 3, para 10). The recommendations of the report were adopted in March 1971 at the Council of Finance Ministers meeting (Ecofin), and thus the report helped to inspire such initiatives as the 1972 European currency management system (the snake) and the 1972 heads of government commitment to the creation of a single currency by 1980 (Box 3.2).

The Werner Report was, of course, an ambitious plan and necessitated a greater commitment to European integration than member states were able

BOX 3.2

Chronological history of the snake

1972

24 April	Basle Agreement entered into force. Participants were: Belgium, France, Germany, Italy, Luxembourg, the Netherlands.
1 May	The United Kingdom and Denmark joined the system.
23 May	Norway became associated.
23 June	UK withdrew from the system.
27 June	Denmark withdrew from the system.
10 Oct.	Denmark returned to the system.

1973

13 Feb.	Italy withdrew from the system.
19 March	Transition to the joint float: interventions to maintain fixed margins against the dollar ('tunnel') were discontinued.
19 March	Sweden became associated.
19 March	The Deutschmark was revalued by 3%.
3 April	Establishment of a European Monetary Cooperation Fund was approved.
29 June	The Deutschmark was revalued by 5.5%.
17 Sept.	The Dutch guilder was revalued by 5%.
16 Nov.	The Norwegian krone was revalued by 5%.

1974

19 Jan.	France withdrew from the system.

1975

10 July	France returned to the system.

1976

15 Mar.	France withdrew from the system.
17 Oct.	Agreement on exchange rate adjustment ('Frankfurt realignment'): the Danish krone was devalued by 6%, the Dutch guilder and the Belgian franc by 2%, and the Norwegian and the Swedish kroner by 3%.

1977

1 April	Swedish krona was devalued by 6%, Danish and Norwegian kroner were devalued by 5%.
28 Aug.	Sweden withdrew from the system. The Danish and Norwegian kroner were devalued by 5%.

1978

13 Feb.	Norwegian krone was devalued by 8%.

BOX 3.2 (CONTINUED)

---

17 Oct.   Deutschmark was revalued by 4%, and the Dutch guilder and Belgian
             franc by 2%.

12 Dec.   Norway announced its decision to withdraw from the system.

1979

13 Mar.   European Monetary System became operational.

Source: Gros and Thygesen (1998: 17).

---

to offer at the time and in subsequent years. Of the reasons for the lack of commitment, member states were generally reluctant to give up their independence to set macroeconomic policy objectives at a time of increasing turbulence in the international economy. At the same time the 1973 enlargement of the Community posed the further difficulty of having to integrate greater numbers of countries. But despite these difficulties, member states nevertheless did agree in March 1972 to restrict currency fluctuations in an effort to establish some form of harmony among European economies, though crucially this did not involve any path towards monetary union. Known as the 'snake', this system of cooperation restricted fluctuations in exchange rates between member countries to +/−2.25%. However, the absence of stable currencies meant that the objective of monetary integration became less likely (see Box 3.3). For instance, within two months of the launching of the snake sterling was set free to float on 23 June 1972 and Denmark withdrew on 27 June. France left in January 1974 and its attempt to return was short-lived as it only lasted between July 1975 and March 1976. The net effect of this was that only Germany, Denmark and the Benelux nations remained in the snake by 1977. These events essentially meant that this early objective of European monetary integration was put on hold.

We can therefore see that the economic difficulties (oil price increases and unemployment) which beset much of the industrialised world throughout the

---

BOX 3.3

The snake in the tunnel

The 'snake' was the common name for a March 1972 agreement that limited the fluctuation of European currencies by creating the 'snake in the tunnel'. This was a mechanism to permit a managed floating of currencies (the snake) within a slim band of fluctuation against the US dollar at a rate of 1.25% on either side (the tunnel). The subsequent oil crisis of the 1970s reduced the momentum behind this project, with the majority of the snake's members leaving within two years. By 1976 the snake was reduced to a 'mark' area that consisted of Germany and the Benelux countries.

1970s had a severe impact on the progression towards monetary union. The reality of this state of affairs was further evidenced by a 1975 Commission report that noted that 'Europe is no nearer to EMU than in 1969. In fact, if there has been any movement, it has been backward' (Marjolin et al., 1975: 1). Failure to move towards monetary union was attributed to various factors, including global economic difficulties, a lack of political will to unite and confront such difficulties, and a lack of analysis on the part of national governments to understand what would be necessary in terms of the pooling of authority to achieve EMU. At the same time, European governments were for the most part not following a path of strict budget discipline and 'ignored the prescriptions of the Werner Report for the harmonization of fiscal and monetary policies and were able to do this because the authorities in Brussels did not have the jurisdiction to press for the necessary adjustments' (Aldcroft and Oliver, 1998: 149). We also have to remind ourselves that the objective of establishing a monetary union was indeed a grand plan, and the Community was hardly 20 years old at this point. A lack of maturity therefore played a part in the stunted progress towards EMU, though it would not be long before Europe awoke from its period of slumber. But despite these difficulties there nevertheless remained a desire for further integration in the field of monetary policy.

European Monetary System

By the end of the 1970s member states were once again thinking about the possibility of some form of monetary cooperation. Much of the impetus behind this proposal came from Roy Jenkins, who upon his appointment as President of the European Commission in January 1977 sought to revive the sluggish progress of the Community which had dominated much of the 1970s. Central to this process for Jenkins was 'reproclaiming the goal of monetary union', which he publicly announced in a speech at the European University Institute in Florence on 27 October 1977 (Jenkins, 1991: 463). Among Community member states, France and Germany were crucial to this further development of monetary integration, and at the April 1978 Copenhagen European Council Helmut Schmidt and Valery Giscard d'Estaing discussed the issue of constructing a new route to EMU in a private meeting with other heads of government. They specifically envisaged a fixed exchange rate that linked European currencies together, and this interest in monetary union crucially reflected a change in the underlying political climate that once again attached emphasis to further integration in this area of policy-making (Ludlow, 1982). Three months later, the Bremen European Council provided the seal of approval to the Franco-German initiative and instructed Finance Ministers to set down the plans for the system. Thereafter, the Brussels European Council of 5–6 December 1978 adopted the conditions of operation for the proposed European Monetary System

---

BOX 3.4

European Monetary System

The EMS was established in 1979 as a 'zone of monetary stability' (stable but adjust-able exchange rates). Exchange rates would be for all intents and purposes stable with a small degree of adjustment. Participants in the system would coordinate exchange rates through the ERM. The technicalities of the system were that currency rates were established in relation to the ECU at meetings of finance ministers, and in the interven-ing period member states supported the agreed value of the currencies within the system by drawing on the resources of the EMCF. The EMS had three key elements:

1. **Exchange Rate Mechanism (ERM).** This was a parity grid whereby currencies were given central value in relation to the ECU. Prior to 1993 states were not allowed to let their currencies diverge from the central valuation by more than 2.25% (Italy, Spain and the UK had 6% bands). Member states had to intervene by means of interest rates and intervention on foreign exchange markets if their currency reached a level of three-quarters of the fluctuation margin.

2. **European Currency Unit (ECU).** A basket currency of weighted amounts of each member currency that acted as the denominator of the ERM.

3. **European Monetary Cooperation Fund (EMCF).** A pool of 20% of each mem-ber's gold and dollar reserves that acted as a credit facility.

(EMS), with the system commencing in March 1979 (see Box 3.4). The EMS began operating on the 13th of that month when the central banks of the Community formed an agreement which established the operating mechanisms and procedures of the EMS. The EMS, which consisted of the European Currency Unit (ECU) and the Exchange Rate Mechanism (ERM), was seen as a way of reducing exchange rate instability and as a means of combating the divergent inflation rates that were prevalent in European economies in the late 1970s. In reality this meant that the German rate of inflation, which was the lowest in the Community, emerged as the target rate for EMS member countries (Levitt and Lord, 2000: 38–41).

Whilst the EMS established the broad framework for the coordination of currencies, the ERM acted as the specific mechanism for reducing currency fluctuations among the participating member states (see Box 3.5). This was based on a currency grid, whereby currencies were allowed to fluctuate within a specified band above or below the nominated central rate of the currency. When the fluctuation bands of a currency were reached, then intervention was required. In such a scenario, the central bank of the strong currency would be required to purchase the weak currency on its foreign exchange market. In addition to this strategy of intervention, the value of currencies could also be realigned through a devaluation or revaluation.

For much of the 1980s the EMS was successful in reducing the fluctuations in the level of exchange rates and in inducing the reduction and convergence of

---

BOX 3.5

Development of the EMS

The EMS can be divided into four periods of development.

1. **1979–83.** During this period the ERM provided a framework of stable, though adjustable exchange rates. There were eight realignments as currencies found a settled parity.

2. **1983–87.** This was the most successful period of the system as states viewed the ERM as the instrument of domestic monetary discipline. Weaker states gained anti-inflationary credibility by tying monetary policies to the Deutschmark which became an anchor currency. This resulted in a minimalisation of exchange rate fluctuations and lower inflation rates, with only four realignments during this period.

3. **1987–93.** During this period the ERM reflected a semi-fixed exchange rate system, though this impacted on the flexibility of the system. This was a period of time when exchange rate controls were removed and the lack of limitations on currency transfers meant that member states were more exposed to currency speculation. Turbulence in the ERM was also caused by German unification, which caused high interest rates across the EU during a recession. But there was no broad realignment of the ERM, with the UK refusing to devalue. The Bundesbank became concerned about ERM rigidity and focused on the domestic economy. In September 1992 the lira and sterling were forced out of the ERM as speculators attacked currencies. In addition, the peseta, escudo and punt were devalued in 1992–93.

4. **1993.** Pressure on the French franc led to the August 1993 decision to widen the ERM bands by 15% for all but the Deutschmark and the guilder. By 1994 many states were informally operating in narrow bands. For EMU purposes 15% bands were accepted as 'normal'. There was a pre-EMU division into strong and weak currencies – the lira was readmitted in 1996, while the peseta and escudo were devalued in 1995.

---

member states' inflation rates. The EMS therefore provided a framework within which member countries were able to pursue counter-inflationary policies at a lesser cost in terms of unemployment and lost output than would have been possible otherwise. But while most governments decided to participate in the ERM, successive British governments declined, as they did not want to be committed to maintaining the value of sterling within a fixed system, though there was not necessarily complete consensus within the British government on this policy (see Chapter 5). This was particularly evident from the mid-1980s onwards when key figures such as Nigel Lawson (Chancellor) and Geoffrey Howe (Foreign Secretary) argued that the ERM would provide a more stable framework for economic policy.

Of the factors that influenced this viewpoint, one of the most important was the lower rates of inflation enjoyed by ERM members. But despite the practical economic benefits associated with membership, Prime Minister Thatcher advocated sterling's independence, not least because of her opposition to closer European integration, and noted that Britain would join when 'the time was right'. Certainly, between 1985 and 1986, it did appear that the time might have been 'right' for British membership, as the rate of inflation in Britain was at a level which was temporarily below the European average. However, as Chapter 5 outlines in more detail, one stumbling block to membership was sterling's role as a petrocurrency, which the government argued meant that membership was unrealistic at a time of significant fluctuations in oil prices. It was therefore because of concerns that the time was not right for membership and Prime Minister Thatcher's own distaste for the system that Britain stayed out of the ERM at this time.

Towards the end of the 1980s the case for British independence from the ERM became harder to defend and Prime Minister Thatcher was increasingly in an isolated domestic position. The net effect of this state of affairs was that Britain finally joined the ERM in October 1990 at a central rate of 2.95 Deutschmarks, with sterling permitted to fluctuate 6% above or below that level. At the domestic level, entry was perceived as a means of reducing inflation so as to provide a more stable economic framework. In terms of Britain's relationship with other member states, the government also viewed ERM entry as a means of demonstrating a commitment to the EU at a time when Britain was perceived to be an isolated member (Davies, 1989).

Developing a single currency

The success of the ERM in providing a framework of monetary stability for much of the 1980s certainly bolstered the belief of some member states that the Community should once again attempt to progress towards monetary union. In attempting to explain the central place of EMU on the Community's agenda in the late 1980s it is possible to identify a number of factors. This list includes the Single European Market (SEM) programme, a convergence of national interests among European member states and the role of supranational bodies.

As far as the SEM was concerned, there was a general consideration that its full benefits could not be realised as long as national currencies remained in place. This was because of the impact that transaction costs and fluctuations in exchange rates had on business competitiveness. This was the economic argument that was advanced by the European Commission, who considered that the benefits of the SEM could not be fully enjoyed without greater macroeconomic coordination. With this in mind, the June 1988 Hanover European Council established a committee to investigate the possibility of economic and monetary union. Being chaired by the then President of the European Commission, Jacques Delors, the committee completed its report in April 1989 and advocated a three-stage route to monetary union:

- Stage 1: Involved completion of financial details of the single market, with, for instance, the establishment of free capital movements among member states. At the same time all member states would participate in the narrow band of the ERM and closer monetary and macroeconomic cooperation between member states and their central banks, whilst usage of the ECU would be further developed.

- Stage 2: Of the three stages, the second was the most vague. It was essentially a transition stage when the new institutions that would be required for the third stage would be developed. It was envisaged that realignments of the ERM would be gradually reduced and in effect the system would become fixed, whilst in line with the goal of establishing a European Central Bank in the third stage the national central banks would become operationally independent.

- Stage 3: The third stage of the Delors Report advocated that exchange rates of member states would be irrevocably fixed and that a European Central Bank would have full authority for establishing economic and monetary policy which would result in the creation of a single currency. At the same time, so as to ensure convergence of national economies, rules would be established governing budget deficits, whilst poorer regions would be given subsidies.

The Delors Report presented EMU as being necessary to achieve effective economic integration through further developing the SEM. In focusing on the importance of the argument that the SEM was a significant factor in advancing the cause of EMU, such an approach could in the first instance be viewed as being reflective of the neo-functionalist idea of spillover (Haas, 1958; Lindberg, 1963; Tranholm-Mikkelsen, 1991). Such an approach emphasised the importance of sector-by-sector expansion of integration, driven by interest group pressure.

Of the economic advantages of monetary union, key factors included the end of transaction costs and exchange rate uncertainty, which would help to stimulate greater cross-border trade and investment and thereby provide conditions for economic growth and jobs. This was certainly a view advocated by the Commission. A second factor was a general view at the time that an independent European Central Bank (ECB) would be committed to low inflation and, crucially, it would not suffer from decisions being taken to reflect political objectives. Third, monetary union was presented as a means of fulfilling the goals of the SEM (see Box 3.6). Fourth, EMU would provide Europe with a major international currency. Finally, monetary union would provide greater monetary sovereignty in light of the fact that nation-states would lose relative monetary sovereignty because of the power of financial markets and the general nature of national interdependence.

Whilst such economic factors help to shed light on the proposed benefits to be obtained from monetary union, they do not provide the sole reason why

---

BOX 3.6

The single market and EMU

One of the factors that influenced the case for a single currency was the need to complete the single market. The latter involved the removal of all non-tariff barriers to the free movement of goods, services, people and capital. In this context, it was evident that it would be difficult to achieve the full benefits of a single market in the absence of a single currency, as the transaction costs involved in converting currencies were relatively high. At the same time, stock exchanges also created the potential for instability. A further point was that some observers, particularly central bankers and economists, considered that national monetary authority was not consistent with the objective of free trade, free capital movements and fixed exchange rates. Thus, there was a genuine belief that a single currency was a necessary element to the completion of the single market.

---

member states agreed to EMU. To obtain a fuller understanding of the factors that influenced the decisions that were taken on EMU it is important to look at other elements, including the role of the European Commission. In the context of monetary union the Commission was particularly active in selling EMU as a necessary component for the completion of the Single European Market. In advancing such a strategy the Commission made use of its various resources, including the provision of economic data, so as to add support to the view that benefits of economic growth would be realised through monetary union. The central role of the Commission was most notably evident through the part that its President, Jacques Delors, had in driving forward the study on monetary union to which he gave his name (Delors Report). But despite the important role played by the Commission, the success of its policy proposals was crucially dependent on the support of member states and it is this third factor which acted as a major mechanism in advancing the cause of monetary union. In this context, whilst some authors may consider that monetary union was shaped by factors outside of government, including the momentum provided by 'spillover' theory and the role of the European Commission, this approach does not give enough attention to the role of national governments. As Levitt and Lord have commented, 'full monetary union only came on to the agenda in response to the political preferences of key member governments, and not through economic necessity' (Levitt and Lord, 2000: 34–5).

A significant factor in the 1980s was therefore a convergence of national interests and economic policies, with many Community member states sharing similar goals such as a commitment to low inflation. France, for instance, abandoned a Keynesian approach to monetary policy in 1983 and thereafter followed a policy of price stability which broadly followed that of Germany. A convergence of economic policy was most notably evident through the operation of the Exchange Rate Mechanism (ERM), which member states looked to as a method of maintaining low inflation in conjunction with independent central banks. This economic convergence of policy interests does, however, only paint half of the picture, as there was additionally a convergence of political will among core member states as to the necessity for a collective approach to monetary union.

A united desire for monetary union among such key states as France and Germany did not mean that they were motivated by the same domestic interests. On the contrary, as the chapters which follow demonstrate, there were notable differences in national interests. France, for instance, was one of the strongest supporters of monetary union. But this policy objective was determined by the fact that policy-makers considered it as the best means of regaining a degree of French influence over monetary policy. This was in light of the dominant influence that the German Bundesbank had over European financial policy and particularly those countries which participated in the ERM. So for France EMU was crucially seen as a means of boosting its influence over monetary policy.

Whereas it is possible to perceive EMU as a means of advancing French influence, it is more difficult to use this objective as a means of understanding German support. Germany, for instance, had no obvious national economic interest in EMU, as the Bundesbank was the dominant force in European financial markets and any move to monetary union would diminish German monetary sovereignty, whilst there could be no guarantee that a single currency would be as strong as the Deutschmark. So, as far as economic issues were concerned, German interests essentially stood opposite to those of France. As the negotiations on the details of monetary union took place under the aegis of the talks which resulted in the Maastricht Treaty, Germany consequently insisted that the mechanics of monetary union would be based on its terms of financial rigour (Sandholtz, 1993). It had, after all, the most to lose and the least to gain in economic terms. So whereas economic factors can identify French policy objectives, the same is not true for Germany. It, by contrast, was largely motivated by broader political concerns, and particularly the view of the then Chancellor, Helmut Kohl, that Europe was central to German foreign policy and that the nation somehow had to be bound to Europe. For Kohl, EMU was such a means of doing this, whilst monetary union was also part of a broader strategy of political union whereby there would not just be a development of new policy objectives such as a single currency, but also the strengthening of the institutional mechanisms which governed the Community. Such distinct interests in monetary union therefore demonstrate that it is important to focus on the factors that shaped national policies in understanding the reasoning behind EMU.

Such national interests came to the fore during the negotiations on the nuts and bolts of monetary union that took place during 1991. These talks were part of a series of agreements in the period after member states accepted the Delors Report at the June 1989 Madrid European Council. At that meeting they decided to establish the first stage of EMU from 1 July 1990, whereby there would be a full liberalisation of capital movements in eight member states.

Subsequently, at the December 1989 Strasbourg European Council, member states agreed on the need to have an intergovernmental conference (IGC) to further investigate the necessary treaty requirements so as to progress to EMU. The IGC was duly launched at Rome in December 1990, by which time member states had also agreed on the need to hold a second IGC to examine the reform of the political aspects of the treaty. Both of these IGCs proceeded in parallel throughout 1991 and eventually resulted in the conclusion, at the Maastricht European Council in December of that year, of a new treaty on European Union.

As far as EMU was concerned, the December 1991 Maastricht European Council produced agreement that during Stage 1 of EMU, which began in July 1990, there would be the completion of the Single Market, with, for instance, the restrictions on capital flows to be abolished. Stage 2 would begin on 1 January 1994 and would act as a transitional phase, when a European Monetary Institute would be established to administer the European Monetary System, coordinate national monetary policy and monitor progress towards convergence. Finally, Stage 3 would involve the irrevocable locking of exchange rates and the adoption of a single currency. The treaty contained a provision for this to start on 1 January 1997 if the Council decided (by QMV) that a majority of states had met the 'convergence criteria'. This proved not to be possible[2] and therefore the deadline date of 1 January 1999 was used for those states that did meet the criteria.

In progressing towards a single currency the treaty attached a great deal of importance to a set of convergence criteria, so as to ensure that member states were economically fit enough to take part. As far as Britain was concerned, the government obtained an opt-out from the single currency at the Maastricht European Council and therefore it was not committed to progress to the final stages of EMU. This did not, however, mean that a future government would not have the option of taking part in the single currency if it so desired. In this sense, Britain was not locked into EMU, rather than being locked out of EMU, and such an outcome reflected the negotiating objectives of the government that was led by John Major.

Whilst the Maastricht Treaty appeared to set a solid path to EMU, for much of the 1990s the monetary project was troubled by a number of significant developments which raised some concern about the viability of the project. Of these developments, the first concerned the tension that dominated the ERM throughout 1992 and 1993, and resulted in the British pound and Italian lira leaving the system in September 1992 because of currency speculation. Pressure continued within the ERM until August 1993 when the remaining currencies within the system were given greater room for fluctuation so that they were able to move 15% either side of their currency parity. For all intents and purposes, this greater room for manoeuvre essentially represented the end of the ERM as a vehicle for effectively managing European currencies.

Over the months and years that followed the events of 1992–93, European governments had to struggle to meet the convergence criteria that would allow

---

BOX 3.7

Stability and growth pact

The Dublin European Council of June 1996 reached agreement on a stability and growth pact, which is of relevance for all member states that will adopt the euro. It specifically requires them to adhere to detailed fiscal and budgetary measures so as to ensure that each member state maintains sound finances, and therefore does not develop a situation that would undermine the stability of the euro economy.

---

them to participate in the single currency. For most governments this proved to be a tricky task, particularly because European economies were suffering from low economic growth and consequently higher levels of unemployment. This accordingly meant it was politically insensitive for governments to reduce levels of public spending at a time when most faced higher spending demands through benefit payments and lower revenue from taxation. Concerns over the extent to which member states would satisfy the criteria for EMU resulted in considerable debate on the extent to which countries should be 'fined' if, having met the convergence criteria, they relaxed their controls over economic management in the period leading up to the adoption of the single currency. This accordingly resulted in the drafting of a stability and growth pact at the Dublin European Council of December 1996, which both reaffirmed German concerns over strict economic management and the concerns of other countries, such as France, for a more flexible approach that took account of particular national circumstances (see Box 3.7).

An awareness of the economic difficulties that many European member states faced at this time resulted in emphasis being attached to programmes which focused on job creation, and accordingly the Amsterdam European Council of June 1997 reached agreement on a growth and employment pact which would supplement the stability and growth pact that had been agreed to at Dublin some six months earlier. The months that followed Amsterdam saw national action plans for tackling unemployment being drawn up, with them being subject to debate at a special 'jobs summit' in November 1997 in Luxembourg. The overall strategy of European governments was therefore focused on reviving the economic performance of European economies and simultaneously ensuring that member states were focused on achieving the requirements of the convergence criteria that had been set at Maastricht.[3] This eventually resulted in Greece being the only country that was excluded from joining the single currency when it came into existence in January 1999 because it had failed to meet the convergence criteria (Greece subsequently joined in 2001). By contrast all 11 other member states that had committed themselves to joining the single currency met the criteria, though not every country did so convincingly. This particularly applied to Italy, which appeared only to have met the requirement concerning national budget deficits through

---

BOX 3.8

Chronology of EMU

1969

Dec.   The Hague summit set goal of EMU by 1980.

1970

Nov.   Werner Report provided the first plans for economic and monetary union.

1972

April   Establishment of 'snake in the tunnel' to coordinate European currencies.
June   British pound withdrew from the 'snake'.

1977

Oct.   Roy Jenkins, as President of the European Commission, called for a
        renewed impetus in EMU.

1978

Dec.   Bremen European Council took the decision to establish the European
        Monetary System (EMS), of which the Exchange Rate Mechanism (ERM)
        was a core aspect.

1979

March   EMS started working.

1985   Single market programme adopted. It provided for the free movement of
        labour, goods, services and capital.

1988

June   Hanover European Council agreed to a proposal put forward by Jacques
        Delors for a new study on EMU, which was published on 12 April 1989.

1989

June   Britain established conditions at the Madrid European Council that would allow
        it to join the ERM, culminating in British entry on 8 October 1990 at a central
        rate against the Deutschmark of 2.95, with the pound being allowed to float
        at 6% either side of its central parity (same rate as the Spanish peseta).
Dec.   Agreement at Strasbourg European Council to assemble an
        intergovernmental conference to draw up a treaty on monetary union on
        the basis of the Delors Report.

1990

July   Stage 1 of EMU formally began, resulting in the Committee of Central Bank
        Governors being able to carry out the technical preparations for the
        Monetary Institute.

BOX 3.8 (CONTINUED)

Oct.   Agreement at Rome European Council that Stage 2 of EMU would
          commence on 1 January 1994.

1991

Dec.   Agreement at Maastricht European Council on a Treaty on European
          Union, incorporating EPU and EMU agreements, and thereby establishing
          a timetable for their implementation. The agreement stressed that a single
          currency would be introduced by 1 January 1999 at the latest. Britain
          obtained an opt-out from the third stage of EMU.

1992

Sept.   British interest rates were increased to 15% in an inadequate effort to
          combat financial speculation, resulting in Britain pulling out of the ERM.
          The EC's Monetary Committee also agreed to the temporary suspension
          of the Italian lira, while the Spanish peseta was devalued by 5%.

1993

Aug.   ERM of the EMS effectively collapsed. Agreement was reached to allow
          currencies to fluctuate within a broad band of 15% either side of their
          central rates, rather than the 2.25% band for strong currencies or 6%
          for Spanish and Portuguese currencies.

1994

Jan.   Stage 2 of EMU began. The European Monetary Institute was established
          in Frankfurt as a precursor to a European Central Bank.

1995

Dec.   Madrid European Council confirmed that the single European currency
          would be introduced from January 1999 and called the currency the euro.

1996

Dec.   Dublin European Council produced agreement on the legal status of the
          euro and currency discipline, the stability and growth pact. Financial
          penalties applied to all member states running a GDP deficit (negative growth)
          of up to 0.75%. EU Finance Ministers were able to exercise discretion to
          apply penalties if GDP fell between 0.75% and 2%. Member states which
          ran an excessive deficit would automatically be exempt from penalties if
          GDP was at least 2% over one year, or in the event of a natural disaster.

1997

Feb.   Member states completed their 1997 statistical reports to decide whether
          they would be able to participate in the single currency. All except Greece

BOX 3.8 (CONTINUED)

	met the convergence criteria, although a strict application meant only Finland, France, Luxembourg and the UK met the debt criterion. Belgium and Italy registered debt in excess of twice the level required (the target was no more than 60% of GDP). The treaty provided flexibility by referring to a 'reference value' of 60% of GDP which should be achieved 'unless the ratio was sufficiently diminishing and approaching the reference value at a satisfactory pace'. Some countries imposed significant changes in economic policy; Italy imposed a special one-off euro tax and Germany discounted large amounts of hospital debt from its budget deficit.
March	European Commission recommended 11 member states adopt the single currency from 1 January 1999: Austria, Belgium, Finland, France, Germany, Ireland, Italy, Luxembourg, the Netherlands, Portugal and Spain. Denmark, Sweden and the UK opted out of joining the euro in the first wave and Greece was not considered to have met the required criteria. A further report by the European Monetary Institute stressed that Belgium and Italy had not made sufficient progress in reducing their debt ratios.
April	The Noordwijk Finance Ministers meeting established agreement on an outline timetable for EMU, and endorsement of the single currency stability pact. Agreement was reached that a special European Council would be held in May 1998 with the task of deciding which countries met the economic criteria for joining EMU. Central bank governors had pushed for the decision on EMU eligibility to be taken at an earlier stage, which would allow more time for southern European states, such as Italy and Spain, to fulfil the criteria. Thus, there would be only eight months for those countries which did not meet the criteria to prepare for the launch of a single currency on 1 January 1997.
	Brussels EMU Council decided that 11 of the 15 EU member states were deemed to have qualified to adopt the single currency on 1 January 1999, namely Austria, Belgium, Finland, France, Germany, Ireland, Italy, Luxembourg, the Netherlands, Portugal and Spain.

1999

Jan.	Start of third stage of EMU with the launch of the single currency (euro). This signalled the start of the transition period that would last until December 2001. Britain, Denmark and Sweden decided not to participate, whilst Greece failed to satisfy the convergence criteria.

2001

Jan.	Greece adopted the single currency.

2002

Jan.	Changeover to the use of euro banknotes and coins and withdrawal of national banknotes and coins.
Feb.	Final withdrawal from use of national banknotes and coins in those states participating in the single currency.

a short-term policy of applying a one-off 'euro tax' to reduce the deficit in the year that applied to the implementation of the criteria. Of the remaining countries, Britain, Denmark and Sweden refused to participate in the single currency despite the fact that they had met the convergence criteria.

Conclusion

The implication of implementing the European single currency (the euro) is one of the most important and hotly debated topics in European politics today, as the implementation of a single currency will have a range of political and economic outcomes. Not least, the euro will have a significant impact in establishing a 'European identity' and will act as a form of glue to the myriad of cultural and social identities that reside within the EU. In examining EMU, it is evident that the Maastricht Treaty finally set in motion the process for the establishment of a single currency that had initially been outlined in the 1970 Werner Report (see Box 3.8). Of the reasons for the renewed interest in EMU, much of the momentum behind this initiative came from France and Germany, who crucially helped to keep the momentum going during the 1990s. Our understanding of the factors that were influential in propelling monetary union forward can be aided by different theoretical approaches, such as the neofunctionalist account. For much of the time period that monetary union was being debated by other member states, successive British governments showed a lack of willingness to commit to the monetary project. Moreover, as the single currency becomes a reality in other member states the case for British participation has grown, not least within the business sector. The chapters that follow provide an examination of the negotiating strategies of successive British governments towards monetary integration. But prior to this historical survey, the next chapter takes a closer look at explaining the implications of monetary union.

Key points

- In December 1969 The Hague summit recognised Economic and Monetary Union as an official goal of European integration.

- In October 1970 the Werner Report outlined a path for EMU to be obtained by 1980.

- In an effort to coordinate European currencies, a system of exchange rate control was introduced in the early 1970s. Known as the 'snake', the system did not prove to be an effective mechanism for coordinating economic policy and essentially collapsed by the mid-1970s.

- The collapse of the snake and the general downturn in European and world economic fortunes throughout the 1970s limited the process of European integration, including the progress towards monetary union.

- By the end of the 1970s the concept of monetary union was raised by Roy Jenkins, who in 1977 called for fresh progress in this policy field. This ultimately influenced the creation of the European Monetary System (EMS) in 1979, which provided a broad framework for economic coordination based on an Exchange Rate Mechanism (ERM).

- The early years of the ERM witnessed a number of revaluations of the participating currencies. By the mid-1980s the system was proving to be more stable and helped to ensure that those member states within the ERM benefited from lower rates of inflation. Britain continued to be outside the ERM, though there were strong debates within government from the 1980s onwards as to the merits of joining.

- The relative success of the ERM combined with moves to establish a Single European Market led to interest among some member states and European institutions in establishing a single currency. The link between the single market and monetary union can be viewed through the neo-functionalist account of European integration.

- In 1988 the then President of the European Commission, Jacques Delors, was given the task of chairing a study group to examine the feasibility of EMU and to outline a possible route to its attainment. This resulted in the publication of the Delors Report in April 1989.

- After the publication of the Delors Report member states decided to establish an intergovernmental conference on EMU to properly examine the case for a single currency. This resulted in the Maastricht Treaty on European Union which set a path for EMU based on three specific stages, whilst it also established strict convergence criteria that member states had to meet to progress towards a single currency. Britain obtained an opt-out from being committed to move towards the single currency.

- In the early part of the 1990s European currencies suffered from instability and Britain was forced to leave the ERM in 1992, having only joined in 1990. Italy also left the ERM at the same time. Fluctuations in European currencies continued throughout 1993 and this instability caused some uncertainty as to the likelihood of a smooth progression towards monetary union.

- The single currency (euro) was eventually launched in 1999, though Britain, Denmark and Sweden declined to participate, whilst Greece did not satisfy the necessary convergence criteria at that time (though it subsequently did in 2001).

Key terms

- **convergence criteria** There are four convergence criteria which act as economic tests that are used to decide whether a member state is ready to participate in monetary union. The four criteria concern price stability, government finances, exchange rates and long-term interest rates. They are specifically: (1) price stability – the inflation rate of a member state must be within 1.5% of the three best-performing countries in terms of price stability; (2) government finances – there must be an absence of excessive government deficit and debt: in specific terms the ratio of gross government debt to GDP must not exceed 60% at the end of the preceding financial year, while the ratio of government deficit to GDP must not exceed 3% at the end of the preceding financial year; (3) exchange rate stability – member states must have participated in the Exchange Rate Mechanism of the EMS without a break for two years prior to the examination of their readiness to participate in monetary union and, moreover, a member state must not have devalued its own currency on its own initiative during this period; (4) long-term interest rates – the nominal long-term interest rate should not be more than 2% above the rates in the three countries with lowest rates of inflation.

- **Ecofin** This is the main decision-making body for macroeconomic policy among the EU member states. The meetings, which are composed of national Finance Ministers, take place every month. With the introduction of EMU, Ecofin will be responsible for general economic guidelines. However, only those Finance Ministers who are part of the euro-zone will be able to vote on the external exchange rate policy of the euro and on the use of sanctions against those member states that are not meeting the fiscal conditions necessary for EMU.

- **European Currency Unit (ECU)** This is the name of a monetary unit whose value was a weighted average of the currencies of the European Community. This is similar to the retail price index, being a weighted average of prices. On 1 January 1999 it was replaced by the euro at the rate of 1 ECU = 1 euro.

- **European Monetary Cooperation Fund (EMCF)** Although the EMCF was established in 1973 as part of the Community's early drive towards monetary union, the lack of progress in this area meant that the EMCF suffered from a lack of use until its 1979 revival when the ECU became part of the European Monetary System. To this end, member states who participated in the EMS reached agreement that they would deposit 20% of their gold and dollar reserves with the EMCF, which in exchange issued ECUs. The EMCF also regulated central bank interventions on the exchange markets of the ERM, while the EMCF could additionally provide short-term financial credits to assist with member states' balance of payments difficulties.

With the firm commitment to monetary union that was established by the Maastricht Treaty, the EMCF's operations finished on 1 January 1994, when its tasks were taken over by the European Monetary Institute (EMI) as part of the second stage of EMU.

- **Exchange Rate Mechanism 2** This refers to the body that has linked the currencies of certain non-participating member states to the euro since 1 January 1999. Membership of ERM 2 is voluntary, although member states outside the euro area are nevertheless expected to participate. The reference currency for the system is the euro, with the central rates and fluctuation bands expressed in euros. It is permissible for a currency's central rate to fluctuate by +/–15% against the euro, though Denmark has operated to a 2.5% limit. Where there is a need for intervention at the margins of the ERM 2, it is intended that this will be automatic and unlimited. This is also true for the availability of financing by means of the Very Short-Term Financing (VSTF) facility. But, in contrast to the ERM, the European Central Bank and those central banks from the countries not participating in the single currency will have the ability to stop this form of intervention if it clashes with the main objective of price stability. Britain has not yet joined the ERM 2, but the Bank of England is nevertheless a signatory of the agreement.

- **Stage 1 of Economic and Monetary Union** This embraced the period from 1 July 1990 to 31 December 1993, with greater attention given to economic convergence while the remaining restrictions on the free movement of capital were lifted.

- **Stage 2 of Economic and Monetary Union** This started on 1 January 1994 and lasted until 31 December 1998. It was during this period that the majority of the arrangements for EMU were made. This included the establishment of the European Monetary Institute, the precursor of the European Central Bank.

- **Stage 3 of Economic and Monetary Union** This started on 1 January 1999 when the conversion rates of national currencies of the 11 participating member states were irrevocably fixed and when the euro became a currency in its own right. On the same date the European System of Central Banks took responsibility for monetary policy in the euro area. At the same time the Exchange Rate Mechanism known as ERM 2 became operational so as to link the currencies of certain 'pre-ins' (see p. 84) to the euro. Finally, the stability and growth pact came into force as an instrument for discouraging member states from allowing excessive deficits in public finances.

- **transitional period** The transitional period started on 1 January 1999, when the euro became the EU's single currency, and terminates on 31 December 2001. The latter is when there will be a release of euro notes and coins and the commencement of the process of withdrawing national currency from circulation. The need for the transitional period is because of the time necessary to print the bank notes and euro coins that will go into circulation.

- **withdrawal of national notes and coins** Those countries participating in the euro-zone have agreed to attempt to remove the majority of their national notes and coins by the end of February 2002. Agreement has also been reached that within the first two weeks of January 2002 it will be possible to make the bulk of cash transactions in euros.

Questions

1. Why did the initiatives to establish closer integration in the field of monetary policy fail in the 1970s?

2. To what extent were developments that took place in the 1970s and 1980s a central factor in the creation of a single currency?

3. Can monetary union be regarded as a spillover from the creation of a Single European Market?

4. 'A single currency is an essential component in completing the Single European Market.' Discuss.

5. Was the progress that was achieved in monetary integration in the 1980s solely because of the influence of the European Commission?

6. 'The key factor in the relaunch of European integration in the 1980s was the convergence of interests among member states.' Discuss.

7. Assess the role of Jacques Delors in advancing the cause of monetary union.

8. For what reasons did France support monetary union?

9. Examine the successes and failures of the European Monetary System since 1979.

10. 'The Deutschmark in all but name': is this a correct assessment of the euro?

Further reading

Aldcroft, Derek H. and Oliver, Michael J. (1998) *Exchange Rate Regimes in the Twentieth Century*, Cheltenham: Edward Elgar, Chapter 6.

Apel, Emmanuel (1998) *European Monetary Integration: 1958–2002*, London: Routledge.

Dyson, Kenneth (1994) *Elusive Union: The Process of Economic and Monetary Union in Europe*, London: Longman.

Dyson, Kenneth and Featherstone, Kevin (1999) *The Road to Maastricht: Negotiating Economic and Monetary Union*, Oxford: Oxford University Press.

George, Stephen and Bache, Ian (2001) *Politics in the European Union*, Oxford: Oxford University Press, Chapter 26.

Gros, Daniel and Thygesen, Niels (1998) *European Monetary Integration*, 2nd edn, Harlow: Longman, Chapter 10.

Johnson, Christopher (ed.) (1991) *ECU: The Currency of Europe*, London: Euromoney Publication.

Levitt, Malcolm and Lord, Christopher (2000) *The Political Economy of Monetary Union*, Basingstoke: Macmillan.

Szász, André (2000) *The Road to European Monetary Union*, Basingstoke: Macmillan.

Notes

[1] 'Hague Communiqué', *Bull. EC*, No. 1, 1970.

[2] *Progress Report on the Preparation of the Changeover to the Single European Currency*, submitted to the European Commission on 10 May 1995, Luxembourg: Office for Official Publications of the European Communities, 1995, p. 4.

[3] *Financial Times*, 26 March 1998, p. 2.

CHAPTER 4

Explaining monetary union

Objectives

- Describe the main features of a monetary union.
- Explain the costs and benefits of monetary union.
- Demonstrate the impact of monetary union on national decision-making procedures.
- Outline the impact of British non-participation.

Introduction

The previous chapter examined the historical development of monetary union, demonstrating how the project was conceived and the forces that were influential in advancing its cause. This chapter focuses on the implications of monetary union by seeking to explain the costs and benefits of monetary union.

What is a monetary union? It is a situation in which the various national currencies of a group of member states are replaced by a single, common currency, which then circulates as legal tender in all participating countries (see Box 4.1). The European Union's progression to monetary union is primarily the product of initiatives that were taken in the 1980s, though the goal of establishing a monetary union in Europe can be traced back to 1969. A monetary union between two or more countries means that those countries agree to maintain the same currency. To this end, the central issue about a monetary union is that those countries that participate in such a system no longer have the ability to pursue independent national policies. Thus, there no longer remains the opportunity to allow national exchange rates to vary between those countries participating in the monetary union.

BOX 4.1

Monetary union

In contrast to an economic union, a monetary union is representative of a situation where there is either a single currency or locked exchange rates, though a single currency is the preferable option to achieve the credibility of the monetary union. It is also important that the monetary union is centrally managed so as to achieve common macroeconomic objectives. For a monetary union to be completely effective it is necessary for financial markets to be integrated, for capital transactions to be liberalised and for there to be flexible labour markets. A monetary union has certain benefits over an economic union. These include the elimination of exchange rate fluctuations between the countries participating in the system, thereby reducing the risks for trade within the European Union. In a similar vein, the existence of one currency creates benefits by reducing transaction costs that would otherwise be incurred through changing one currency for another. Both of these cases are advantageous to investment and trade. A monetary union does, however, involve certain costs, of which a loss of national sovereignty over an area of economic policy is often cited as one of the most important. And because each member of a monetary union is subjected to the same monetary policy, it is possible that some policies will not suit each member of the monetary union. Nevertheless, it is also true that the national economic policies of those countries which are not part of a monetary union often result in policy decisions that are detrimental to some areas of the economy.

One of the main benefits of a monetary union is that it permits a single currency to be used by a greater number of people and over a wider area, though a principal cost is that of not being able to permit variations in the exchange rates against other members of the monetary union. But despite this lack of national control, advocates of a single currency point to the benefits that can be obtained through the removal of transaction costs involved in exchanging one currency to another. While this benefit is patently clear, other benefits are harder to quantify. This does not mean that they are insignificant. For instance, the absence of national exchange rates within a monetary union would ensure that businesses would not be hindered by difficulties of competitiveness because of an unnecessarily high national rate of exchange. A single currency would therefore be more than likely to assist business trade. A further benefit is that of price transparency, as a single currency would make it easier to compare product costs in all participating countries. There are, nevertheless, certain potential problems of joining a monetary union, such as the 'one size fits all' nature of the monetary policy which therefore begs the question as to whether a single monetary policy would be representative of the interests of all who participate in it.

The debate

One of the core questions that is of relevance to any debate on monetary union is the issue of national sovereignty and more specifically the ability to exercise control over a national currency (see Box 4.2). In this context, those who are against a single currency, such as the Conservative Party and the Institute of Directors, consider it to be a further unacceptable erosion of national power and influence in the direction of the creation of a European superstate. At the same time, opponents have also pointed to the fact that there are many other important issues that the EU has to deal with, such as enlargement, and therefore a single currency is somewhat of a distraction from these policies.[1] In contrast to this hostile approach, supporters of a single currency point to its economic and political benefits. These include the ability to further strengthen the EU through closer economic and political integration and also the creation of a currency unit that will challenge the US dollar and Japanese yen as an international currency.

The position of Britain in this debate is further complicated by the strategic alliances that the nation has with countries outside the EU, particularly America, and the fact that further integration at an EU level could constrain the number of international opportunities offered to Britain. Such an approach is, however, forgetful of the fact that over half of Britain's trade is now with the EU[2] and that the further enlargement of the EU will increase this ratio. It is also true that key non-EU countries, notably the US, place a great deal of emphasis on Britain playing an important role in the EU. Such a stance has, in fact, been a key element of American strategic thinking for much of the post-1945 period. Furthermore,

---

BOX 4.2

Sovereignty

This term refers to the claim by a state to be able to govern independently and the recognition of other states of its independence. It therefore concerns the ability of a state to be able to exercise control over a multitude of matters, such as economic policy and political affairs. Nevertheless, it has been demonstrated in recent years that states do not have full economic sovereignty because world financial markets are able to exercise considerable influence on the stability of a state's economic basis. For instance, the ERM crisis of 1992 demonstrated that governments did not have full economic sovereignty because they were unable to stop the selling of their currency by speculators. As far as economic and monetary union is concerned, some people have expressed concern that this will result in an erosion of a state's sovereignty. There is a degree of truth in this because individual countries will no longer be able to vary their exchange rates or control their money supply. But because of the doubt concerning the ability of a state to have full sovereignty, it is not such a clear-cut case that a state has sovereignty to lose.

those advocates of British non-participation in the single currency do not give enough attention to the detrimental impact that it is likely to have on inward investment to Britain, much of which comes from America and Asia.[3] Neverthe-less, it is true that the nature of Britain's more diverse trading links with countries outside of Europe does present specific problems as to the convergence of the British economy with those member states participating in the single currency.

The very adoption of a single currency will result in the removal of national control over monetary policy, though that is not to say that nation-states will have any further erosion of their national sovereignty in other areas. Today, it is widely accepted that the internationalisation of financial affairs has meant that it is virtually impossible to talk about national sovereignty in these matters. There are many reasons for this, not least the existence of a plethora of choices as to the currencies that can be used by businesses and individuals. The effect of this has been that governments basically need to make their national cur-rency as attractive as possible so that it will remain in use. And while EU cur-rencies have generally been stable, it nevertheless means that governments cannot pursue whatever actions they like. Governments are, in fact, constrained in their actions by the need to ensure the stability of their currency, thus demon-strating that complete national sovereignty in financial matters does not exist.

Irrespective of these constraints, it is evident that monetary policy can be exercised at a domestic level. This specifically concerns the setting of interest rates, whereby interest rate increases assist in reducing the level of inflation in the economy. This can be achieved because a rise in interest rates will make saving more attractive than borrowing, while also increasing mortgage repay-ments. This consequently reduces present spending, both on consumption and investment. In a similar vein, changes in interest rates have an immediate effect on other assets, such as housing and stocks and shares. Thus, a relatively low level of interest rates can result in an increase in the number of people who are willing to borrow and spend money, thereby increasing the demand for houses which has a knock-on effect by increasing their value. Correspondingly, an increase in interest rates can have the effect of dampening down the level of borrowing, and ergo the value of housing. Finally, a high level of domestic interest rates can attract foreign capital and consequently lead to an increase in the valuation of the exchange rate. An enhancement in the value of the pound does, however, reduce the competitiveness of domestic manufacturing, as the exportation of goods becomes more difficult. Of course, a high pound does lessen the relative costs of imported goods.

The retention of the ability to make decisions at a national level is never-theless not always the most satisfactory development, particularly when gov-ernments take decisions to achieve political objectives. This was certainly a situation that existed during the 1980s under the Thatcher governments when there were significant differences between the inflation and interest rates in Britain and those in other EU member states. And, as Chapter 5 makes clear, one of the driving factors behind British participation in the Exchange Rate Mechanism was the desire to reduce inflation rates.

The possibility of political interference in the setting of interest rates thus influenced the New Labour government in 1997, in particular Chancellor Gordon Brown, to remove from government the task of setting interest rates. This was instead given to the Bank of England, with the rates being determined by the newly established Monetary Policy Committee.[4] And while one of the main reasons for this strategy was to provide a more stable environment for economic growth, it also removed the link between the elected government and a key tool of economic policy. A distancing of government interference also lessened the argument that participation in monetary union would remove the ability for government to set policy, since there had already been a diminution in this capability.

The argument that a lower level of inflation has been delivered by an independent Bank of England and Monetary Policy Committee can similarly be applied at the European level to an independent European Central Bank. For some countries, such as Greece and Italy, the benefit of the European Central Bank is generally perceived to outweigh any costs. This is because they have not been so successful in maintaining a low level of inflation, though of course for others, such as Germany, the benefits are less clear-cut. So a reduction in inflation rates is one of the core benefits associated with a single currency. An additional and equally important factor is that the European Central Bank will provide all participating member states with an ability to exercise some degree of influence on decisions of a monetary policy nature. This benefit is particularly attractive to smaller countries whose monetary policy was essentially shadowed by other EU nations such as Germany. In this sense, many EU member states considered that monetary union offered an ability to reduce the overall strength of the Bundesbank (and the Deutschmark)[5] in European financial markets and thus provided them with an opportunity to have a voice in the monetary policy debate. This was certainly an argument that was advanced by France.

A third factor to take into consideration is that a single currency will reduce currency transaction costs within the EU. A single currency will eliminate the need to purchase the currency of other foreign nations when travelling within the EU and having to incur the costs associated with currency commission charges. In this context, a single currency will be of benefit to the individual traveller as well as businesses, resulting in savings of both cost and time that are associated with currency transactions, though banks are unlikely to stop charging completely for the cross-border services that they carry out. An absence of national currencies also eliminates the potential for variations in exchange rates within the euro-zone. This will therefore assist those businesses that trade or invest in currencies within the EU because exchange rate changes can upset their plans. Such uncertainties will therefore be removed where trade is conducted within the euro-zone.

As far as business interests are concerned, a single currency offers the greatest potential benefits. In the first instance, monetary union is a further step in the integration of European economies and represents a final segment in the completion of the single market. As Lord Kingsdown (a former Governor of the Bank of England) commented:

> I see it [the single currency] as a logical extension of the single market, the belief that the countries in the single market will be strengthened and will work better through a single currency than through diverse currencies which at the present moment are acknowledged to run the risk of devaluing and throwing out the relationship between the Member countries.[6]

Companies should therefore find it easier to operate in other member states because of the removal of individual national currencies. Leading on from this factor is that an absence of individual currencies will make it easier to compare the prices of goods in all member states and such transparency of costs should have a significant impact in lowering the price of products in some member states.[7]

That Britain has not committed itself to joining the euro does place certain restrictions on business interests. An absence of an outright political commitment by government could have an impact on the traditional dominance of the City of London in European financial markets. In addition to the above points, the case for membership of the euro has been bolstered in recent years by the pound being overvalued by at least 20%, therefore making it more difficult for British manufacturers competitively to export to the continent. In this context, euro membership offers a means of ensuring business competitiveness through stable interest and inflation rates.[8]

The significance of British non-participation in EMU, having gained an opt-out from this policy area in the Maastricht Treaty (along with Denmark) is the degree to which it impacts on further European integration. This is because the single currency makes a crucial distinction between those member states that are committed to it and Britain and Denmark which have an opt-out, as well as making progress to EMU dependent on clear requirements. There is therefore a basic assumption that some member states will proceed to monetary union ahead of others. Non-participants at the same time have not been given a more gradual process of membership, which has in the past been the case for other EU policy initiatives in which every member state has not participated from the outset. Those countries not participating in the single currency will be able to decide whether they will join a revised version of the ERM, whereby they will keep their currencies within certain limits.

EMU is thus representative of a situation where some member states may adopt 'core' EU policies, while others remain outside this policy area. At present this is a situation that is representative of monetary union, but a division between the 'ins' and the 'outs' is likely to become starker as the membership of the EU expands with enlargement and when not every member state is willing or able to adopt each policy initiative.[9] The consequence of British non-participation is that it places the government on the periphery of a core aspect of EU policy.[10] It moreover raises the possibility of isolation from discussions on both EMU and non-EMU policy that might be taken at the margins of euro-zone meetings.

But whilst there are certain tangible and strategic benefits to be obtained from the single currency, it would be false to say that there do not exist certain important factors that have acted as a restraint on government policy in this area. One of the most important potential problems of joining the single currency is the extent to which a single monetary policy would best represent the interests of all those participating in it. This is referred to as the 'one size fits all' problem and there are clearly notable concerns as to whether it would ever be possible to establish a monetary policy that represents the best interests of all member states. Indeed, even within Britain it is often the case that domestic monetary policy does not represent the interests of all areas of the country and the economy. The most notable example of this is the manner in which interest rates have often been increased so as to act as a curb on house price inflation in the south of England, while having a knock-on effect on the ability of manufacturing industry to be competitive in the north of England. So this issue of whether a single monetary policy could best represent the interests of all member states is clearly an important concern of those who are uncertain as to the benefits of a single currency.

A second key area of concern is the question as to whether it would be possible to obtain long-term convergence of the British economy with those member states participating in the single currency (the so-called euro-zone). Of the factors which might act as a potential barrier to possible convergence, it is evident that the British economy is subjected to a wider set of financial pressures than many other EU economies. This includes its greater trading linkages which North America and the continued production of oil and gas in the North Sea, which expose the economy to certain conditions that are not so prevalent in other EU member states.

A third potential concern relates to the provision that membership of the single currency would lead to possible curbs on British budgets by means of the stability and growth pact. This is a particularly real problem, as evidenced by the European Commission's recent concern over the extent to which the Irish economy was maintaining a convergent approach to monetary union and the particular feature of the stability and growth pact that is relevant is the ability of the Commission to fine member states who are not maintaining a stable approach to the single currency. For the Labour government, it is therefore evident that the stability and growth pact could act as a potential barrier to its ability to engage in significant large-scale spending on public services, which would of course be likely to reduce the public opinion ratings of the government. Indeed, the reality of this state of affairs was evidenced by the Commission having already expressed concern at the most recent budget presented by Chancellor Gordon Brown.

A fourth factor that must be considered is the extent to which sterling has been overvalued in recent years, which has meant that the British currency has not been as closely linked to the euro as it should have been, and this overvaluing is a particular concern of the Bank of England and the Treasury. A final potential hurdle to EMU membership is the question as to whether Britain should or must join the Exchange Rate Mechanism (ERM 2) prior to entry to the single currency.

Conclusion

It is evident that any decision by the British government on monetary union will have a major impact on the nation. Before that decision can be taken, both the government and Parliament will have to agree on the case for membership, while the government is committed to seek the agreement of the electorate in a referendum. Both a 'yes' and a 'no' vote will have a major impact on Britain's position within the EU, with any decision not to join likely to have a significant and lasting detrimental impact on the nation. As Chapter 1 makes clear, successive British governments have had difficulty in committing the nation to a united Europe.[11] While such hesitancy was once based on an assumption that Britain could play a meaningful role in international affairs outside the European club, the reality today is that the nation is fully intertwined with EU member states in terms of trade, culture, society and education. Many of the concerns and interests of Britain are shared by other EU nations, from the environment to security and defence policy. British participation in the single currency would thus cement its commitment to the EU, while non-participation lays open the possibility of the further erosion of the nation's status within Europe. At the same time, however, there are a number of important hurdles which need to be passed before membership could take place and in this sense the case for and against entry is quite finely balanced. But whatever decision is taken, it is nevertheless the case that British firms who want to trade with the euro-zone will have to adapt to using the euro, including the giving of quotations, issuing invoices and marketing.[12] The complexity of these matters and the difficulty that successive governments have had in orchestrating a coherent policy on them is analysed in the chapters that follow.

Key points

- One of the core debates concerning the adoption of the euro concerns national sovereignty. Certainly, participation in the single currency will reduce a national government's ability to exercise control over certain aspects of monetary policy. For instance, decisions on interest rates will no longer be taken at a national level.

- Despite a concern over the loss of sovereignty through participation in the single currency, the fact of the matter is that governments are not able to exercise full sovereign control over the national economy. There are many factors that impinge on national policy-making, including the role of currency speculators. For instance, Britain's exit from the Exchange Rate Mechanism (ERM) in September 1992 demonstrated the inability of government to control sterling. So concerns over sovereignty have to be based on the understanding that national government is not fully able to exercise control over all aspects of financial policy in the first place.

- The granting of independence to the Bank of England in 1997 and the creation of a Monetary Policy Committee to establish interest rate levels meant that government was no longer able to interfere in decisions in this policy area. The significance of this development was that it removed a hurdle towards Britain's participation in the single currency, as it could no longer be argued that the government would be giving up control over the setting of interest rates. However, it is true that a major worry is the extent to which a European single interest rate will be suitable for all member states by taking into account particular national concerns.

- A core benefit of a single currency is a reduction in currency transaction costs and this will have a significant benefit on both individual travellers and business competitiveness by reducing costs.

Key terms

- **banking sector** The banking sector plays a central role in the introduction of the euro as the single currency. Although the European Central Bank issues euro notes and coins, banks facilitate the increasing number of automated transactions, including loans, securities and payment by cheque and bankcard. And because national currencies will be replaced by the euro, banks have to ensure that all transactions can operate in euros.

- **central banks** National central banks will continue to exist and play an important role under EMU. Along with the European Central Bank (ECB), they form the European System of Central Banks (ESCB). National central banks will retain operational responsibility for the policy that is determined by the governing council of the ECB. If it is required, national central banks will also intervene in foreign exchange markets.

- **Committee of Central Bank Governors** This refers to the Committee of Central Bank Governors that was established in 1964 to assist with the cooperation of EU central banks. The progress towards monetary union increased the work of the committee, resulting in the formation of various sub-committees and working groups to tackle specific areas of policy, such as monetary policy and banking supervision. The Maastricht Treaty made provision for central bank governors to play a key role in EMU as it merged with the European Monetary Cooperation Fund (EMCF) in 1994 to form the European Monetary Institute (EMI). At the end of Stage 2 of EMU, the EMI became the European Central Bank.

- **common currency area** This is a term often used to describe the operation of a single currency. There are various economic arguments to support a common currency area. In the first instance, interest rates can be equalised with the removal of the possibility of currency movements. Second, in a

common currency area there is no likelihood of an individual country trying to solve problems by means of inflation. Finally, an absence of exchange
rates means that business and trade can prosper because of the removal of
transaction costs.

- **Council of Economics and Finance Ministers** Responsible for defining the
  broad guidelines of economic policy of EMU. It can apply pressure on
  participating countries to meet budgetary commitments.

- **cross-border transactions** This refers not just to the exchange of currencies,
  but also a shift from one payment system to another. Prior to the introduction of the euro, the domestic payments system in each member state did
  not inter-operate, the effect of which was to increase the costs associated
  with transactions. The introduction of the euro as a single currency will
  therefore result in a reduction in costs. This is because the euro will no
  longer involve foreign exchange transactions, and thus many of the associated costs, such as commission charges on exchanging currency, will no
  longer exist. In a similar sense, card transactions will also benefit because a
  fixed conversion rate will apply. A second benefit will be an acceleration in
  the processing of payments because there will be a reduction in payment
  delays with an absence of currency exchange transactions.

- **definitive conversion rate** This term refers to the definitive conversion
  between each of the currencies participating in the euro. The rate was fixed
  by the European Council on 1 January 1999.

- **dual circulation of currencies** This refers to the situation that will take place
  for a short period immediately after the introduction of euro notes and
  coins on 1 January 2002. At this point both euros and national currency
  notes and coins will be in circulation within each member state in the euro-
  zone. By 30 June 2002, old national banknotes and coins will be withdrawn
  from circulation.

- **Economic and Financial Committee** This committee was established by
  virtue of Article 109c(2) of the Maastricht Treaty and came into existence
  at the start of Stage 3 of EMU, at which point it assumed the role and
  responsibilities of the Monetary Committee (which was abolished at the
  start of Stage 3). The committee will replace the rather secretive EU monetary committee that prepared Ecofin meetings, but it will continue to be
  composed of central bankers, national treasury officials, and two members
  of the European Commission.

- **Economic and Monetary Union institutions** EMU is built on the Council
  of Economics and Finance Ministers (to assist with the coordination of
  economic policies) and the ESCB (an independent monetary institution).

- **economic convergence** This refers to the process whereby the economies of
  all the member states in the euro-zone needed to converge so that when they
  adopted the euro on 1 January 1999 they were broadly performing on the

same lines. In this context the Treaty on European Union specifically set convergence criteria for member states to meet.

- **economic union** This refers to an area where there are no barriers to trade or payments, or for that matter to the movement of capital and labour. Thus, the single market programme made a significant contribution to the achievement of a European economic union. It is possible for an economic union to exist with (or without) a monetary union. The main benefit of an economic union over a monetary union is for nations to be able to determine economic policy. But at the same time, the economic union does not deliver the trade and investment benefits associated with a monetary union, which are generally perceived to outweigh the loss of national sovereignty with regard to the control of economic policy.

- **euro** This is the name for the single currency to be used in most EU member states after 2002, represented by the € symbol. The euro is the legal currency for EMU and will become legal tender from 1 January 2002. There will be seven banknotes in denominations of 5, 10, 20, 50, 100, 200 and 500 euros and eight coins in denominations of 1 cent, 2 cents, 5 cents, 10 cents, 20 cents, 50 cents, 1 euro and 2 euros. From January 2002 national currency coins and notes will start to be withdrawn, being legal tender in the nations concerned for a further six months. Thereafter the euro will be used.

- **excessive deficit procedure** The excessive deficit introduced in the Treaty on European Union as one of the convergence criteria under the provisions of monetary union. The treaty specifically stated that member states should not have excessive government deficits, being defined as a budget deficit not exceeding 3% of GDP and a public debt not exceeding 60% of GDP (Article 104c and the protocol on the excessive deficit procedure). The treaty did, however, make reference to 'gross errors' in Article 104c(2), and this ensured that the excessive deficit procedure would only come into use occasionally rather than as the norm. This was because cyclical developments would be taken into consideration when making calculations. An emphasis on a flexible interpretation was additionally highlighted by Article 104c, noting that allowance could be made if a country's deficit had 'declined substantially and continuously' or 'is only exceptional and temporary'. In this context the convergence criteria were both tough and flexible.

- **inflation** This term refers to an increase in the amount of money that is in circulation and is demonstrated by an increase in prices and depreciation in value.

- **Monetary Committee** Established by Article 109c of the Maastricht Treaty, its main purpose was to monitor the budgetary performance and monetary situation of member states. Having advisory status only, it was composed of two representatives from each member state and delivered opinions to the Council and Commission on its own initiative, or by their request, and at least once a year. It was replaced by the Economic and Financial Committee at the start of Stage 3 of EMU.

- **monetary policy** Monetary policy is concerned with the value, supply and cost of money in the economy. The monetary policy for the euro-zone is conducted by the European System of Central Banks. The latter is composed of the European Central Bank and national central banks. Monetary policy is the primary means of obtaining price stability (low inflation), which is the ESCB's main objective as set out in the Maastricht Treaty. The main instruments of monetary policy are changes in short-term interest rates.

- **no bail out** This refers to a situation whereby the EU and its member states are not allowed to be liable or take responsibility for the commitments of a member state, as set out in the Maastricht Treaty (Article 104b). Thus, a nation that is not able to cope with its debts cannot be 'bailed out' by means of a transfer of funds. By contrast, the nation concerned has to accept the sanctions that are imposed by the financial markets, which might include the imposition of higher interest rates.

- **no compulsion, no prohibition** This term refers to the principle that defines the usage of the euro during the transition period from 1 January 1999 to 1 January 2002. This basically means that while it is possible to have transactions in euros (if both parties agree) there is no legal requirement to use the euro during the transition period. Nevertheless, there is an exception to this rule whereby if payment is made through a bank account in euros, then the bank of the creditor is required to convert the sum into the currency where the account of the creditor is based.

- **pre-in countries ('pre-ins')** This term refers to the four member states that did not participate in the adoption of the euro and a single monetary policy on 1 January 1999, namely Denmark, Greece, Sweden and the UK. Although Greece adopted the euro in 2001, the Danish referendum of September 2000 resulted in a negative vote against the single currency. Sweden is additionally expected to hold a referendum on the subject in 2002. Britain has also committed itself to holding a referendum on the euro before it is adopted, although it does have an 'opt-out' at present.

- **price convergence** It is anticipated that the introduction of the euro will result in the narrowing of price differentials between member states for the same product. This is because it will be simpler for comparisons to be made between member states.

- **price stability** This is a key objective of the EU's economic policy, with the aim being to establish the lowest possible rate of inflation. This is because there is an understanding that inflation has a negative impact on economic stability, and particularly affects investment.

- **single currency** The single currency of the member states participating in the euro area is the euro. The European System of Central Banks operates the single monetary policy for the euro. There are a number of benefits to a single currency. In the first instance there will be an elimination of transaction costs caused by the conversion of one currency into another. There will also be a transparency of prices because goods and services will be priced in the one currency. A single currency is further likely to provide a clear identity to the EU, with the currency competing against the US dollar and the Japanese yen.

- **stability and growth pact** So as to ensure the proper application of the excessive deficit procedure of the Maastricht Treaty, regulations were set out in the stability and growth pact. The first regulation establishes the medium-term goal of a balanced budget or a budget that is in surplus, as well as a system to identify and rectify any slippage at an early stage. The second regulation establishes the timetable and details of sanctions for countries with regular excessive deficits. Sanctions do, however, only apply for euro-zone countries and are on a sliding scale of between 0.2% and 0.5% of GDP depending on the extent to which the 3% reference value has been exceeded. In the first instance, sanctions are embodied by a refundable deposit, that is converted into a definitive fine after two years if the situation is not corrected. The pact was agreed at the Amsterdam European Council in June 1997.

Questions

1. What are the main features of a monetary union?

2. 'The most important economic benefit in the creation of a single currency is the removal of currency transaction costs.' Discuss.

3. To what extent does a monetary union differ from an economic union?

4. Explain the main benefits of a single currency.

5. 'Governments which choose not to participate in a single currency will have full sovereign control over their own national currency.' Discuss.

6. 'The main factor which influenced the decision of governments to accept the single currency was the prospect of challenging the dominance of the US dollar in international currency markets.' Discuss.

7. To what extent will the member states not participating in the single currency be frozen out from key decisions on monetary matters and others concerning the future of European integration?

8. Review the arguments for and against membership of the single currency.

9. To what extent has membership of the EU impacted upon British sovereignty?

10. What are the implications of British non-participation in the euro for business interests?

Further reading

Dyson, Kenneth (1994) *Elusive Union: The Process of Economic and Monetary Union in Europe*, London: Longman.

Eijffinger, Sylvester C. W. and De Haan, Jakob (2000) *European Monetary and Fiscal Policy*, Oxford: Oxford University Press, Chapter 1.

Gros, Daniel and Thygesen, Niels (1998) *European Monetary Integration*, 2nd edn, Harlow: Longman, Chapters 7 and 8.

Levitt, Malcolm and Lord, Christopher (2000) *The Political Economy of Monetary Union*, Basingstoke: Macmillan, Chapter 2.

Notes

[1] Sir Samuel Brittan, House of Lords Select Committee on the European Communities, *An EMU of 'Ins' and 'Outs'*, Vol. II – Evidence, HL86-I, Session 1995–96, Q. 495, p. 171.

[2] http://www.dti.gov.uk/intrade/index.htm

[3] For a review of the impact of inward investment in Britain, see Andrew Fraser, 'Case Study: Inward Investment in the UK', Paper presented at *Industrialisation and Globalisation in the 21st Century: Impact and Consequences for Asia and Korea*, East–West Centre, 2–3 August 1999. http://www.invest.uk.com/students/pdf/ History_of_Inward_ investment.pdf. Also *The Guardian*, 1 July 2000, p. 24.

[4] *The Guardian*, 7 April 1998, p. 19.

[5] *The Times*, 20 June 1998, p. 13.

[6] Lord Kingsdown, 'Stage Three of Economic and Monetary Union: Minutes of Evidence', *Treasury Committee*, House of Commons, Session 1995–96, 6 March 1996, para. 82.

[7] *The Observer*, 28 June 1998, p. 6, and *Financial Times*, 21 April 1998, p. 29.

[8] *The Guardian*, 6 April 2000, p. 22.

[9] For an overview of the aspects surrounding this issue see House of Lords, op. cit., 1995–96.

[10] This point was raised by Lord Kingsdown, in ibid., Vol. II – Evidence, HL86-I, Q. 249, p. 68, and Sir Samuel Brittan, Q. 496, p. 171.

[11] *The Guardian*, 14 December 1999, p. 16.

[12] *The Times*, 8 April 1998, p. 30.

PART II

Creating monetary union

CHAPTER 5

Chasing the ERM: 1985–1990

Objectives

- Chronicle the development of the Exchange Rate Mechanism and its working methods.
- Outline the reasons for British non-participation in the ERM in the 1980s.
- Demonstrate the influence that key individuals had on British negotiating objectives.
- Outline the case for British membership of the ERM in the mid-1980s and make comparisons with 1990.
- Highlight the extent to which Britain's eventual entry to the ERM was influenced more by political factors than economic conditions.

Introduction

The dramatic announcement on 5 October 1990 by the British government that it would join the Exchange Rate Mechanism of the European Monetary System ended more than a decade of indecision and argument over British participation (Currie and Dicks, 1990). Prior to that statement there had been many debates within government as to the merits of and hindrances to membership, of which the views of those who were inclined to be more sceptical had held sway. Of those individuals, the principal campaigner against membership was the then Prime Minister, Margaret Thatcher. But by 1990 it was clear that she was no longer the dominant force in Cabinet that she had once been. That is not to say her impending removal from office in November 1990 was widely predicted. Of the reasons that influenced Britain's entry into the ERM, one of the most important was the view that entry would provide sterling with greater stability. Sterling had, for instance, fallen from $2.1225 in 1979 to $1.5158 in

1983 and \$1.3364 in 1984, while it reached \$1.093 during the sterling crisis of January and February 1985.[1] An additional factor to that of currency stability was the perception that entry would provide Britain with a stronger voice when matters of a monetary nature were discussed at European meetings. To put it bluntly, many government officials and some ministers considered that any British proposals on monetary policy at the European level would be adversely affected by non-participation in the ERM. This was a view particularly held by the Foreign and Commonwealth Office, though the Treasury was also aware of the need to engage in constructive discussions. So the motivation for entry was a culmination of factors, with the end product being that sterling was set at a central rate against the Deutschmark of 2.95. In doing this, the government opted for the maximum amount of flexibility that the system offered, with sterling being permitted to float at 6% either side of its central parity, which was the same rate as the Spanish peseta. This was a wider band than the 2.5% margin of flexibility afforded to other nations, such as France and Germany. Britain's participation therefore meant that it was no longer isolated from the ERM club, by which stage the only EC nations that remained outside were Portugal and Greece.

The events that led up to Britain's entry to the ERM are chronicled in this chapter. Particular attention is attached to the debates within government over the merits of membership, including the pressure exerted upon Prime Minister Thatcher by the Chancellor of the Exchequer, Nigel Lawson and the Foreign Secretary, Geoffrey Howe.[2] The chapter also stresses the importance attached to membership by business groups in the latter half of the 1980s. This was a time when the ERM was providing a stable mechanism for economic growth. Nevertheless, the underlying theme of the chapter is the lack of consensus within government over ERM entry, especially within Cabinet. As will become clear in Chapter 6, the necessity of participation was accentuated by the drive towards monetary union by other member states after 1988. These two policies, ERM and EMU, while being separate, became linked, with the resulting effect that Britain's position on the ERM was increasingly dictated by political considerations rather than economic benefits.

Overview

Britain's participation in the ERM ended years of aloofness since the system had entered operation in March 1979[3] with a view to creating a 'zone of monetary stability' in Europe (Box 5.1). Its very creation was a response to the lack of success associated with its predecessor, the 'snake',[4] and the lack of economic stability within the Community in the latter part of the 1970s (see Chapter 3). In addition to a perceived need to provide a framework of economic stability, movement towards the ERM was also viewed as a means of strengthening the

---

BOX 5.1

Operational workings of the ERM of the EMS

1. The ERM established a currency grid – a set of all bilateral exchange rates between participating countries with a nominated central rate for each and a permissible band of fluctuation. A currency's central rate was re-expressed in terms of the European Currency Unit (ECU). The essence of the ERM was the obligation to maintain bilateral exchange rates within the permitted bands of fluctuation. Before the August 1992 decision of European Finance Ministers to allow ERM currencies to float within a margin of +/−15%, the size of this band was set at +/−2.25% for the majority of the participating currencies.

2. Intervention in participating currencies was compulsory when the intervention limits were reached. The central bank of the strong currency was required to purchase the weak currency on its foreign exchange market, while the central bank of the weak currency sold the strong currency. Members might also take pre-emptive action, intervening before the limit was reached. This was known as intra-marginal intervention. Members might also act together in a collective show of support for a currency in the form of concerted intervention.

3. The formal devaluation or revaluation of currencies took place at realignment (normally conducted by the EC Monetary Committee on behalf of Finance Ministers and central bank governors).

Provisions of the EMS

1. Set of provisions regarding exchange rates.
2. Set of provisions regarding access to credit facilities.
3. Common currency of denomination, namely the ECU.
4. Special provision for a divergence indicator. This was to impose a symmetrical adjustment process.

Community vis-à-vis the USA. This viewpoint was influenced by the dominance that the USA exerted on world financial policy and the desire of the Community to water down this influence. This was a position held by the French President, Valery Giscard d'Estaing, and the German Chancellor, Helmut Schmidt. It was in this context that they proposed a joint initiative for the creation of a European Monetary System (EMS) with an ERM on 7 April 1978 at the Copenhagen European Council. To this end the Bremen European Council, three months later, gave its seal of approval to the Franco-German initiative and instructed the Ministers of Finance to elaborate a system based on the ECU, provided with rules as strict as the snake's, and endowed with substantial financial means by the pooling of part of the reserves. Later, at the Brussels European Council of 5–6 December 1978, member states adopted the conditions of operation of the EMS. The three aims of the EMS were in the first instance to improve trade through creating a zone of monetary stability in the Community and, second, to coordinate monetary and exchange rate policies of member states with regard to the rest of the world. Finally, the EMS hoped to create a route for the establishment of a European Monetary Federation (EMF) and to promote the use of the European Currency Unit (ECU) as a reserve currency. Somewhat predictably the then British government was uncertain about participating in the new system, noting that: 'the government cannot yet reach its own conclusion on whether it would be in the best interests of the United Kingdom to join the exchange rate regime of the EMS as it finally emerges from the negotiations'.[5]

That Britain was hesitant to participate in the ERM was partly because of the recent experience of the renegotiation and referendum on the question of Community membership (see Chapter 1). This had resulted in a degree of uncertainty towards participation in further Community policies, while it was also evident that the government had been taken by surprise by the desire of other member states to pursue the Giscard–Schmidt initiative (Dyson and Featherstone, 1999: 540). (A decade later the Conservative government of Margaret Thatcher would equally be taken by surprise as to the desire of other member states to pursue monetary union.) In addition to these political factors, hesitancy towards participation was influenced by a consideration by government that sterling was subject to a different set of external pressures from those experienced by other EC member states (Dyson and Featherstone, 1999: 538–43). Of these, the most important was sterling's sensitivity to oil price movements and its importance in trading and financial relationships with non-EC countries, such as the Commonwealth. Moreover, there was also a significant concern among Cabinet Ministers that the participation of sterling in the ERM would result in it being dominated by the Deutschmark, which was the key currency within the system.[6] These various viewpoints resulted in the conclusion that the exchange rate should continue to be managed domestically.

A preference for floating rather than tied exchange rates was principally because it enabled sterling's rate to be determined by market conditions and was therefore a 'softer' and often more 'painless' option than being committed to a fixed-rate system. In this context, the government and the Bank of England were not committed to keeping sterling within a certain parity vis-à-vis other currencies. That is not to say that they did not intervene to maintain a preferred rate for sterling, because they often did just that. But they were fundamentally not bound by a formal commitment to maintain sterling's value within a fixed exchange rate band. A knock-on effect of this was that an absence of commitment meant the government was not tied to further political and economic cooperation with other member states. Thus, on the one hand floating exchange rates allowed domestic independence, and hence isolation from difficult cooperation with our European partners, while on the other hand they provided the government with the ability to generate economic growth by manipulating the internal money supply. This scenario was particularly true for Britain because monetary policy was determined by the Treasury and not the Bank of England (see Chapter 2). Yet, while the desire to float was based upon political and economic considerations, one effect of such a policy was that businesses

---

BOX 5.2

Biography of Geoffrey Howe (Lord Howe of Aberavon) (1926–)

Served as Chancellor of the Exchequer from 1979 until 1983 and then Foreign Secretary until 1989. A committed pro-European, his views often clashed with Prime Minister Thatcher, particularly on the question of Britain's membership of the ERM. Thatcher's disapproval of his leanings towards Europe resulted in his dismissal as Foreign Secretary in 1989 and appointment as Leader of the House of Commons and Deputy Prime Minister, a position he maintained until 1990. His own frustration with government policy towards Europe influenced his decision to resign in November 1990 and his resignation speech greatly harmed Thatcher's command over the Conservative Party and directly led to her downfall as Prime Minister.

---

were hampered in their ability to expand by not being able to adequately project what the future exchange rate would be. And it would be this question of business interest that would play a vital role in influencing (though not determining) policy-making in future years.

The effect of these developments was that throughout the 1980s there was a dispute between (as well as within) the government, Bank of England, industry and academic circles over whether Britain should join the ERM (Thatcher, 1993: 691–3). While the first Thatcher government of 1979 to 1983 initially decided not join the system, the issue of membership was evaluated at a series of meetings involving Thatcher, key ministers and the Governor of the Bank of England in October 1979, March 1980 and January 1982 (Thatcher, 1993: 691–2). At that time there was unanimous consensus that sterling should join 'when the time was right', and everyone with the exception of the Foreign and Commonwealth Office considered that the time was not right (Howe, 1994: 275–6).

Within government, the Chancellor of the Exchequer, Nigel Lawson, had been converted as early as 1981 to the concept that the ERM would provide a better 'anchor' for monetary policy (Lawson, 1992: 111–13). However, it was not until 1985 that the issue of membership began to influence the government's agenda, with Lawson having decided during the 1984–85 Christmas and New Year break that it was time to think seriously about joining, though he still thought Thatcher was against membership (Dyson and Featherstone, 1999: 544–8; Lawson, 1992: 484–5).[7] While not advocating membership outright, Lawson essentially stated that there was merit in joining. This was a point that had been previously raised in a 1983 House of Lords Select Committee report on the European Communities, noting that 'participation in the ERM is desirable' and that 'the balance of advantage lies in early, though not immediate entry'.[8]

The viewpoint held by the majority of the House of Lords Committee was influenced by reports suggesting Britain should enter the ERM, especially in light of the lack of government intervention during the July 1984 and January

---

BOX 5.3

Biography of Nigel Lawson (Lord Lawson of Blaby) (1932–)

Served as Secretary of State for Energy from 1981 to 1983 and Chancellor of the Exchequer from 1983 to 1989. As Chancellor he was an advocate of British membership of the ERM (but not monetary union) and his views were often different from those of Margaret Thatcher. A desire to demonstrate the benefits of ERM membership resulted in Lawson 'unofficially' shadowing the Deutschmark in 1987–88. His actions irked Thatcher, who became increasingly reliant on advice from advisers such as Sir Alan Walters. The end product was a series of dramatic clashes between the Chancellor and the Prime Minister over the conduct of economic policy, leading to Lawson's resignation as Chancellor in October 1989.

1985 sterling crises (partly due to low reserves[9]). At that time, the inability of the Conservative government to tackle the situation led to speculative attacks that affected the value of sterling. Consequently, an argument in favour of entry was that it would provide a barrier against further speculation.[10] But the committee's conclusion that entry was favourable was not reflected in all circles. It was, for instance, notable that the Confederation of British Industry (CBI) considered that 'membership could impose undue constraints' and that there was little chance that 'membership would improve the stability of sterling's exchange rate'.[11] It is therefore clear that while there was increasing momentum behind the cause for entry, there was by no means unanimity outwith government (never mind within government) over whether Britain's participation in the ERM was justifiable. In hindsight, it is also evident that the ERM had at that stage failed to deliver the currency stability that it managed in subsequent years. There were, for instance, seven realignments by 1983.

Differing opinions

As already noted, Lawson was one of the few individuals in government who favoured ERM entry, principally as a means of providing greater economic stability. The fact that his opinions were not shared by a majority of his colleagues influenced his decision to resolve these differences by calling a meeting of his Treasury ministerial colleagues and officials on 11 January 1985 to examine the possibility of membership. At the meeting, Sir Terence Burns (government chief economic adviser), Sir Peter Middleton (permanent secretary) and Ian Stewart (economic secretary) were all opposed to entry, but Lawson was himself a supporter of Britain's participation in the system. Because of this, and his dominant position as Chancellor, he was able to ensure that his view was the

---

BOX 5.4

Arguments in favour of ERM membership in 1985

1. One of the key issues concerning membership was that the domestic economic fortunes within Britain were not as conducive to economic growth as those evident in ERM member countries. The ERM fixed exchange rate system therefore provided a means of ensuring financial discipline and low inflation.

2. The ERM had established a track record of success by 1985, while also demonstrating a degree of flexibility. Sterling would therefore be participating in a system that was stable enough to provide a framework for economic growth, while one that was also flexible enough to allow for realignments. It was therefore a semi-fixed exchange rate system.

3. ERM membership would provide a more stable exchange rate in comparison to the unpredictability associated with floating exchange rates. Membership would also assist in stabilising interest rates that had a tendency to fluctuate.

4. Linked with the above point, membership of the ERM would stabilise sterling and reduce currency speculation. This would eventually lead to lower interest rates and lower inflation.

5. Those countries participating in the ERM were experiencing a greater degree of economic convergence, including a common commitment to fighting inflation.

6. ERM entry would give Britain greater political influence within the Community.

7. Finally, the very existence of the ERM meant that the British government could not just ignore the system. There was a build-up of pressure for British entry within the business sector and the currency markets.

---

line followed by the Treasury (Lawson, 1992: 486). Nigel Lawson had therefore manoeuvred the Treasury into a position whereby it reflected his own viewpoint that entry was beneficial to Britain's interests (see Box 5.4). And it was from this base that he would mount subsequent campaigns for ERM entry. The significance of this was that it reflected the power and influence of the Treasury within government, and demonstrated that the Treasury essentially maintained a 'veto' on all monetary policy decisions (see Chapter 2).

The Foreign Secretary, Sir Geoffrey Howe, who aligned with the Chancellor to pressurise Prime Minister Thatcher to consider the merits of this policy, also shared Lawson's view that ERM entry was favourable for Britain, though Howe's views did not determine the success of this policy. This was despite the fact that the issue of membership was not on the strategic agenda of the Cabinet at that time. That is not to say that it could not, or would not, be discussed at Cabinet meetings, as the Chancellor would have had the opportunity to raise such objections. But Thatcher was fundamentally against the policy and she had also moved herself into a more dominant position within Cabinet,

---

BOX 5.5

Biography of Lady (Margaret) Thatcher (1925–)

Elected Britain's first female Prime Minister in 1979, a post she maintained until 1990. As Prime Minister she advocated the importance of retaining member state influence over the direction of European integration. Yet, at the same time, her acceptance of the single market programme witnessed a whole new tranche of European legislation that applied to Britain. By the end of her period as Prime Minister there was considerable division within her government over the nature of Britain's commitment to European integration, and while she attempted to dominate policy in the manner that she had become accustomed to, this only served to isolate her within Cabinet. The net result was that her position as leader of the party was challenged and she failed to win the November 1990 contest. In the period since her departure from office she has continued to act as an influence on Conservative thinking on European politics.

---

where she tended to lead discussion rather than listen to the viewpoints of her colleagues. This was also representative of her tendency to 'get involved' with policy matters on a direct level, whereby she would regularly engage departmental officials and ministers to find out about recent developments on particular subjects, rather than letting Cabinet Ministers take full responsibility for policy at departmental level.

It was with this in mind that her opposition to entry was again advocated at a meeting concerning the ERM on 13 February 1985. But regardless of her personal opinions, the Prime Minister offered Lawson a second meeting on the question of ERM membership on 30 September 1985. The arrangement of this meeting demonstrated the point that Thatcher could not just ignore the opinions of Lawson and Howe, two of the most senior Cabinet Ministers. During that discussion there was increasing support for membership from the Treasury, Bank of England and Sir Geoffrey Howe, but Thatcher was still not convinced of the merits of membership (Lawson, 1992: 494–6).

The broadening of the support for ERM membership put Thatcher in an ever more isolated position within Cabinet. In an attempt to buttress her own position, she brought more like-minded ministers into the discussions on ERM entry, notably Norman Tebbit (a close ally of Thatcher), though she was also careful to include Willie Whitelaw, who represented the centre ground. Somewhat predictably, the effect of the stage-managed meeting of November 1985 was to emphasise the negative factors surrounding entry (Lawson, 1992: 496).[12] But while Thatcher had essentially rejected membership at this stage, the support of the Treasury and Foreign and Commonwealth Office for membership meant that the issue would not just go away. As Thompson notes, 'Thatcher could keep saying "no", but she would ultimately not be able to end the clamour from within her own government for ERM entry, nor control the economic conditions which would add monetary logic to her ministers' arguments' (Thompson, 1996: 67). Of the two key individuals supporting British entry, Lawson had a far stronger position than Howe within Cabinet. This would soon become virtually unassailable by virtue of the recognition of his role as the architect of the economic growth that was widely responsible for the Conservative Party's victory in the 1987 general election.

In the meantime, however, Margaret Thatcher and her economic adviser, Alan Walters, were opposed to the concept of membership, believing instead that floating exchange rates were the correct option (Walters, 1986). The Prime Minister was politically against the concept, despite the economic merits and Cabinet support for membership and 'ignored the majority feeling that the right time was not far off' and stated that 'if you join the EMS, you will have to do so without me' (Lawson, 1992: 489 and 499). Walters noted that 'there was no question' of joining the ERM in late 1985 due to the turbulence of exchange rates (Walters, 1990: 97). This was because the 'key' issue according to Thatcher was that ERM entry would not reduce the speculative pressure on sterling, while sterling's international role would also be hampered (Thatcher, 1993: 694–8). Furthermore, there was also a belief that it was necessary for Britain's currency reserves to be strengthened before the government could join the system (see Table 5.1, p. 100). Thatcher's position of not wanting to commit to the system was also shared by the Treasury and Civil Service Committee in its October 1985 conclusion on the question of membership:

> While not ruling out eventual British participation in the long term, we consider that the difficulties of securing an appropriate valuation for sterling and the need to keep options open to pursue domestic policies in the national interest lead us to recommend a maintenance of the status quo in the short to medium term (Scott, 1986).[13]

The significance of this statement was that it provided a further bolster to Thatcher's policy of independence. Her economic adviser, Alan Walters, later stated that the Prime Minister's 'intransigence . . . to entering the ERM was a godsend. If we had entered, then raising interest rates to new highs in late 1985 and throughout 1986 would have jeopardised, even ruined, the Conservative Party's prospects in the election of 1987' (Walters, 1990: 101). This suggested that political considerations seem to have been a significant factor in determining the outcome of the government's decision, while the use of advisers such as Walters hinted at a move away from Cabinet responsibility (Major, 1999: 169). Thatcher's very rationale for using Walters was because she wanted to counterbalance the powerful influence of the Treasury (see Chapter 2). In particular, she considered Chancellor Lawson to have a greater knowledge of economic policy than she did. But this decision was also reflective of her desire to control all areas of policy, with a former No. 10 adviser noting that 'she wasn't in the habit of consulting her Cabinet much', while a former member of the Cabinet stated that the growing location of policy within No. 10 was because the Prime Minister was fed up with the number of policy leaks.[14]

In the end, reservations over entry such as the loss of monetary independence,[15] the vulnerability of sterling to oil price movements, the prospect of

---

BOX 5.6

Arguments against ERM membership in 1985

1. One of the primary points raised against British participation in the ERM was the paramount importance of domestic monetary policy. Thus, domestic monetary factors and not exchange rates should determine interest rates.

2. In addition to this point, the benefit of a floating rather than fixed exchange rate was that it reflected the economic conditions particular to the country concerned. In this sense, there was a belief that ERM membership was contrary to the economic reality of the market, namely that it is impossible to buck the market.

3. British non-membership of the ERM would allow an overvalued pound sterling to be devalued, which would help export-led economic growth.

4. British membership of the ERM would remove the government's ability to reduce interest rates, which was considered to be too important an economic lever to give up.

5. Because sterling was a petrocurrency by virtue of North Sea oil, then it was intrinsically different from other ERM currencies. There was also a strong consideration that Britain was subject to a different economic cycle.

6. Some members of the Cabinet were against further European integration and therefore questioned the desirability of closer ties with other member states.

---

speculation in a bipolar system, the exchange control logic of the EMS, the insufficiency of instruments to control competitiveness as well as inflation in the EMS[16] seemed to outweigh the benefits of joining (Artis, 1990: 294–8) (see Box 5.6). This was despite the fact that the use of sterling as a major trading currency had diminished, while concern over its petrocurrency status seemed unjust considering the florin had not suffered through membership, even though similar pressures would have been exerted on it. The case for membership had also been bolstered by the fact that there was a greater proportion of trade with other European countries. This obviously meant that the value of exchange rates against these countries was increasingly important to business competitiveness.[17] Economic conditions for membership were also bolstered by the fact that those countries within the system had experienced a notable improvement in their economic performance. There were in effect fewer currency realignments after 1983, as the system became more stable. Thus, ERM members benefited from being able to trade and cooperate without the hindrance of large currency fluctuations, a factor that was not true for Britain. Indeed, the predominant opinion of senior Bank of England officials at that time was that it was not possible to maintain a sound monetary policy without accepting the discipline of the ERM.

Within a few years such reservations over entry were increasingly being challenged, especially from the business sector. It favoured entry to ensure exchange rate stability, while the Bank of England believed that entry was essential to stop the government from adjusting economic conditions to match its political desires, rather than the nation's economic fortunes. A desire to join was influenced by the growing stabilisation of the ERM; after the eleventh realignment in January 1987 (only nine months after the previous general realignment of April 1986) there was a general agreement among the monetary authorities of the participating countries that future realignments should be increasingly infrequent as well as being small. This was principally because of the converging nature of members' economies, especially with regard to inflation rates. Furthermore, the President of the Bundesbank Karl-Otto Pöhl was favourable to British entry at this time. The then Governor of the Bank of England, Robin Leigh-Pemberton, was convinced that Pöhl would have helped Britain to negotiate a favourable entry rate. Yet Thatcher was still against the concept of membership and stated that she would not be prepared to discuss ERM membership in the same style of meetings as she had in 1985, when she had found herself outnumbered.

The pressure to join

The outcome of these differences of opinion was that by 1987 the previous cracks in the Cabinet had developed into an open split. In particular, the Chancellor of the Exchequer, Nigel Lawson, continued to exercise his belief that ERM membership was vital. In this context, he led the Treasury in a policy of 'shadowing' the Deutschmark within a DM3 ceiling between early 1987 and spring 1988 as part of an effort to demonstrate the case for Britain's participation in the system (Thompson, 1996: 86–95). Somewhat inevitably, this policy of 'shadowing' created tension within Cabinet, as the decision to 'shadow' was one that Lawson had taken without the full consultation of his colleagues. Such a strategy also demonstrated the power and influence of the Treasury as a strategic actor in Whitehall. John Major would later comment that 'it was clear to all that Nigel was no longer working in harness with Margaret; by shadowing the exchange rate of the Deutschmark and pressing, repeatedly, for our entry to the ERM, he was setting out his own economic stall in competition with his prime minister' (Major, 1999: 132). There was moreover no formal consultation between the Bank of England and the Treasury over the policy, while the reality of shadowing meant that government reserves were used to maintain sterling at the desired level. Some $1.8 billion of intervention took place on 2 and 3 March 1988 to hold sterling within the desired level, with an obvious knock-on effect on currency reserves. The Prime Minister was rightly concerned about this level of intervention and made her feelings known to Lawson, though the strength of his position within Cabinet meant that there was little that Thatcher could do to reprimand her Chancellor. The outcome

Table 5.1   UK official reserves, 1980–1990[a]

Date	$ million
1980	27,476
1981	23,347
1982	16,997
1983	17,817
1984	15,694
1985	15,543
1986	21,923
1987	44,326
1988	51,685
1989	38,645
1990	38,464

[a] Reserves at the end of period.

Source: *Economic Trends*, Annual Supplement, 1995 edition, Section 5.1, p. 223.

of this state of affairs was for Lawson to be permitted by Thatcher to operate a limited policy of intervention, which in effect meant that sterling was 'uncapped' due to intense market pressure (Lawson, 1992: 783–804). So while the policy of shadowing had come to an end, Lawson had demonstrated that Thatcher was not able to dominate policy completely. By adopting an economic policy that was at odds with the Prime Minister, the Chancellor had won a key battle in the Prime Minister–Chancellor relationship; Thatcher considered that she could not sack Lawson as his position was unassailable (Thatcher, 1993: 703).

As noted earlier, one of the factors that influenced Thatcher's thinking against membership was the weakness of Britain's reserves. But by the late 1980s this negotiating position within Cabinet was increasingly less tenable as there had been a considerable strengthening of the nation's official reserves (Table 5.1). The fact that the levels of reserves were crucial to British membership was because those nations within the ERM were required to support their own currencies as well as weaker currencies. In this context a strong currency's central bank would be required to purchase the weak currency on the foreign exchange market, while the weak currency's central bank sold the strong currency.

Just as the question of the level of the government's reserves removed a potential barrier to membership, there had also been a sea change in the opinion of key interest groups. While the CBI had not been convinced of the merits of membership in 1985, it was by 1989 favouring British entry 'at the earliest opportunity, simply because the volatility of the pound against European currencies places our industry in particular at a competitive disadvantage'.[18] There were various factors that influenced this change of position. Most importantly, the EMS had undergone a significant strengthening since the mid-1980s (Cobham, 1989). The currencies participating in the system had stabilised and there had

Table 5.2   Bilateral nominal exchange rates against ERM currencies[a]

Country	1979–83	1984–86	1987–89
Benelux	1.1	0.5	0.3
Denmark	0.9	0.5	0.4
Germany	0.9	0.5	0.4
Greece	2.4	2.5	0.6
Spain	2.0	0.9	1.2
France	1.0	0.7	0.4
Ireland	0.8	1.3	0.4
Italy	1.0	0.8	0.6
Netherlands	0.7	0.4	0.3
Portugal	2.1	0.9	0.6
UK	2.4	2.2	1.7
AV1	0.9	0.6	0.4
AV2	1.2	0.8	0.6
AV3	2.3	1.8	1.4

[a] Variability as weighted sum of standard deviation of monthly percentage changes.

Note:

AV1 = weighted average of ERM currencies, ECU weights.
AV2 = weighted average of EC currencies, ECU weights.
AV3 = weighted average of EC non-ERM currencies, ECU weights.
The selected ERM currencies do not include the Spanish peseta or the pound sterling.

Source: Emerson et al. (1992, p. 72, Table 3.6).

been a marked reduction in the number of realignments. This situation was principally influenced by the September 1987 Basle–Nyborg Agreement which had been specifically designed to reinforce the EMS by ensuring greater co-ordination between central banks in the event of tensions (Padoa-Schioppa, 1987: 83; Dyson and Featherstone, 1999: 162–6).

This strengthening in the system was demonstrated by the success of the ERM in promoting exchange rate stability among the member currencies, as realignments became less frequent, as shown in Table 5.2. It demonstrates the differentiation between the stability experienced by ERM members in comparison to the greater degree of fluctuation that sterling suffered. Indeed, the lira's adoption of the narrow band on 8 January 1990, resulting in a −3.7% realignment, was the twelfth realignment of the ERM, but only the sixth since 1983, with the previous realignment taking place on 12 January 1987.[19] The ERM was therefore providing increasing stability in the latter half of the 1980s, while at the same time the majority of participating countries were encountering low-inflationary economic growth, as demonstrated in Table 5.3 (Mcdonald and Zis, 1989).[20]

One effect of this desire by member states to reduce inflation was that Germany became the centre of the system, leading to the suggestion that the ERM was essentially a greater Deutschmark zone. This was because high-inflation

Table 5.3   Consumer price inflation

Countries	1981–85[a]	1986–89[a]	1990[b]
Germany[c]	3.9	1.0	2.8
France	9.6	3.0	3.4
Italy	13.9	5.6	6.4
Ireland	12.3	3.3	2.7
Netherlands	4.2	0.3	2.6
Belgium	7.0	1.8	3.5
Denmark	7.9	4.3	1.9
United Kingdom	7.2	5.1	9.3

[a] Annual averages.
[b] Annual percentage change based on end-of-period figures.
[c] All figures are for West Germany only.

Source: Bank for International Settlements, *62nd Annual Report*, Basle, June 1992, p. 13, and *63rd Annual Report*, Basle, June 1993, p. 29.

countries followed Germany's anti-inflationary example instead of devaluing against the Deutschmark – or leaving the ERM completely. Thus participants were often forced to bring their macroeconomic indicators into line with those in Germany and, therefore, follow the Bundesbank's monetary course. This trend of low inflation and clear monetary policy contrasted with Britain's unsuccessful experiment with monetary targeting. This policy had actually resulted in monetary growth accelerating to nearly 25% per annum in the wake of the Lawson boom, while consumer price inflation increased from 4.9% in 1988 to 9.3% by 1990 as monetary policy was tightened. Such economic difficulties had been partly influenced by the policy of shadowing, which had put a strain on sterling and the exchange rates. Thus the desire to reduce inflation, combined with greater exchange rate stability, were significant factors influencing the decision to join the ERM. Nigel Lawson emphasised these points by stating that the advantages of membership were that it would 'reduce [exchange rate] fluctuations and we would be able to use it to assist us in our anti-inflationary monetary policy'.[21]

Trouble in the ranks

Despite the reality that ERM membership had brought economic benefits to the participating nations, the issue of British involvement was still to be resolved by early 1989. That Britain did join the ERM in 1990 was influenced by the consideration of officials and ministers that the nation was being isolated from the wider debates on Economic and Monetary Union (EMU). As emphasised in Chapter 6, Community member states had taken the decision in

---

BOX 5.7
_____

Arguments in favour of ERM membership in 1989–1990

1. The same arguments that applied in 1985 were equally applicable in 1989/90. There was in addition a strong belief that ERM membership would establish an anti-inflationary discipline in a period of inflationary growth.

2. By the latter years of the 1980s the benefits of ERM membership had been well documented and it was recognised to be a stable and secure system.

3. There was greater support for ERM entry in the City and amongst interest groups such as the Confederation of British Industry. In this context, there was significant concern among business groups that British non-participation in the ERM would have a major impact on the economic well-being of the nation.

4. By 1989/90 ERM membership was intrinsically linked to Economic and Monetary Union. EMU had been put firmly on the agenda by the Delors Report and there was a strong feeling among ministers and business groups that British entry to the ERM would provide the government with greater influence over the direction that EMU was to take. Entry would therefore provide the government with various options, such as undermining or stalling moves to EMU, or allowing Britain to play a constructive and active role in moving towards an EMU that would be of benefit to Britain.

5. The concept of a loss of sovereignty that had previously been so well deployed against membership was seen to be increasingly questionable. To be sure, entry would remove an impression of economic sovereignty, but there was considerable doubt as to the validity of this as domestic economic indicators demonstrated that sterling was affected by currency speculation and therefore the government was not in control.

1988 to appoint a study group to examine the prospects of achieving a single currency. (The group was chaired by the then President of the Commission, Jacques Delors.) The publication in April 1989 of that report brought further attention to sterling's absence from the ERM. The net effect of this was for those Cabinet Ministers who favoured ERM entry, principally Howe and Lawson, to further champion the cause of membership in Cabinet meetings and in individual talks with other officials and ministers, including the Prime Minister (see Box 5.7). To this end they arranged an Anglo-Dutch 'summit' at Chequers (the Prime Minister's country residence) between Thatcher and the Dutch Prime Minister, Ruud Lubbers, on 29 April. But despite the general warmth in relations between the two leaders, the meeting failed to alter Thatcher's stance. If anything it actually stiffened it, because when Lawson met her a few days later on 3 May she told him that 'I do not want you to raise the subject ever again' as 'I must prevail' (Lawson, 1992: 917–18; Dyson and Featherstone, 1999: 549).

We can therefore see that Prime Minister Thatcher's position on joining the ERM was being actively challenged within government. Moreover, at the national level, the stock of the Conservative Party appeared to be in decline. This was exemplified through heavy defeats in the June 1989 European Parliament elections.[22] Tension within Cabinet was equally hostile at this time, with Howe and Lawson having threatened Thatcher with resignation unless Britain gave a commitment to the ERM prior to the June 1989 Madrid European Council, the primary purpose of which was to discuss the implications of the Delors Report (Howe, 1994: 580; Lawson, 1992: 932). It was with this in mind that they sent a draft minute to Thatcher on 14 June 1989, headed 'EC Issues at Madrid' (Lawson, 1992: 929; Dyson and Featherstone, 1999: 550).[23] The premise of this document was that the government would have to take seriously the desire of other member states to proceed to EMU, and that British entry to the ERM could act as an interim measure to demonstrate a commitment to the process (Major, 1999: 156). As the first stage of the Delors Report necessitated ERM entry, Britain could quite rightly say that it was not isolated in this debate. Thus the overall intention was to ensure that Britain was still locked into the discussion on monetary union. Of course, one problem was that other member states were aware that any such commitments did not necessarily come from the heart, but were instead grudgingly given.

It was predictable that Prime Minister Thatcher would not welcome the Howe–Lawson axis. But as John Major noted, 'despite carping at Nigel for wanting to join the ERM, Margaret had no alternative policy of her own to put in place' (Major, 1999: 134). She had, in any case, become increasingly independent of the Chancellor and Foreign Secretary in sourcing information on economic and foreign policy matters. Advisers such as Charles Powell and Alan Walters became the mainstay of her policy-making, a development that would prove to be to her cost in the 1990 leadership election (Thatcher, 1993: 709). For example, Thatcher held a meeting of her No. 10 advisers on 19 June 1989 (including Alan Walters and Brian Griffiths) to discuss the Delors Report, but excluded all her ministerial colleagues. This was because she considered Lawson and Howe had 'mounted an ambush' on 14 June by sending a joint proposal that argued for a constructive British position (Thatcher, 1993: 710; Howe, 1994: 579; Lawson, 1992: 928–35). That is not to say that the Howe–Lawson position was one that favoured immediate British entry to the ERM. Rather, they merely wanted to map a path to entry by 1992. Nevertheless, Thatcher was opposed to their thinking and resisted any conditions for sterling's entry to the system during a meeting with Howe and Lawson on 20 June. Geoffrey Howe remarked that she 'was uncompromising and resistant to our thinking', while Lawson stated that '(S)he was totally opposed to any commitment to join the ERM' (Howe, 1994: 579; Lawson, 1992: 931). As befitted the manner of the Prime Minister, she was not prepared to be dictated to by her colleagues, though she was aware that the stonewalling of their objectives would not resolve the situation. On 21 June Thatcher therefore put forward her conditions for sterling's entry to the ERM so as to demonstrate that it was she who was in control

---

BOX 5.8

Arguments against ERM membership in 1989–1990

1. The same arguments that were applicable in 1985 were also applicable at this time. Some of these points had been reinforced, including a stronger belief that the government could not 'buck the market'.

2. Those who were against ERM membership considered that the government should attempt to establish a firm domestic control over inflation rates rather than having economic policy dominated by the ERM.

3. The experience of shadowing the Deutschmark in 1987 and 1988 had proved unpalatable to many ministers, especially Thatcher. It had also proved costly, as the government had to intervene in the currency markets.

4. By 1989 Germany definitely had the key currency in the ERM and the issue of a loss of sovereignty was a key point in many sceptical minds.

5. The dramatic unravelling of the European continent in 1989 and 1990 through the collapse of the Soviet Union and the removal of its grip on Eastern Europe suggested that this was a period of instability. This point was further emphasised by the unification of Germany and the consideration that there was a divergence between Britain's economic cycle and that of Germany. The time was therefore considered not to be right for British entry.

6. Linked to the previous point, there was a lack of economic convergence within the Community at this time, with countries experiencing different inflation rates.

7. The establishment of a path towards EMU by the Delors Report meant that the ERM had become politicised. A direct effect of this was that the ERM was less flexible because countries considered it was imperative for the system to remain stable for there to be a progression towards EMU.

8. Many government ministers were against the move towards the establishment of a single currency. In this sense, they considered it improper for Britain to join the ERM and at the same time adopt an anti-EMU position.

(see Box 5.8). But these conditions were very demanding and virtually ruled out sterling's participation. Inevitably, Howe and Lawson demanded a further meeting, at which they threatened resignation unless Thatcher agreed to their conditions (Lawson, 1992: 931–2, 932–3; Thatcher, 1993: 712; Howe, 1994: 580). The net effect of these events was for Thatcher and Howe to travel to the Madrid European Council with the issue of membership unresolved. Lawson, for instance, commented that 'Margaret had expressed the view that it would be more sensible to play the summit by ear than to agree terms in advance' (Lawson, 1992: 938). In line with the unpredictable nature of these events, Thatcher established at the Madrid meeting the conditions that would make membership possible[24] – though without setting a date for membership (an objective held by Howe and Lawson). Bernard Ingham (Prime Minister Thatcher's press secretary) commented that 'I have never known a worse atmosphere within the British party than at the European Council in Madrid in June 1989' (Ingham, 1991: 385).

Having changed tack on ERM entry because of pressure from Howe and Lawson, Margaret Thatcher returned to Downing Street to present the Madrid conditions to Cabinet and the Commons on 29 June.[25] This resulted in 'no resignations' as a result of the government not having set a definite date for sterling's entry to the ERM, which meant that Howe and Lawson had acknowledged her 'victory' (Thatcher, 1993: 713; Howe, 1994: 583). In the wake of that meeting she reshuffled the Cabinet with its very scope resembling Harold Macmillan's 1962 'Night of the Long Knives'. At the centre of the July reshuffle, the most dramatic of Thatcher's period in office, was the departure of Sir Geoffrey Howe from the Foreign and Commonwealth Office. Howe had been informed on the 24th that he would have to move from the Foreign Office although he would be offered another post in the government. He was nevertheless 'stunned, almost disbelieving at what had happened' (Major, 1999: 115). Thatcher clearly felt that the growing gulf between herself and Howe merited a change in office, resulting in his appointment as Leader of the House of Commons and Deputy Prime Minister. Thatcher had, however, kept that title as 'a final sweetener' and had been advised by the Chief Whip, David Waddington, to keep Sir Geoffrey in the Cabinet to ensure that he could not vent his anger from the backbenches (Thatcher, 1993: 757). But despite his new title, Howe's change of office 'was a blatant demotion' (Major, 1999: 177). To this end, Thatcher made it clear that the formal authority associated with Howe's position was, in fact, meaningless.

The reality of the reshuffle was that Thatcher had silenced one of the staunchest pro-European members of the Cabinet and demonstrated her long-standing intention of having in her Cabinet 'only the people who want to go in the direction in which every instinct tells me we have to go' (Gilmour, 1992: 4). Howe's ability to influence policy had been reduced to speaking at fringe meetings; he was given no opportunity of addressing the Conservative Party Conference in 1989 and 1990, and from then on 'harboured a deep resentment' against Thatcher (Parkinson, 1992). The reshuffle brought a new wave of MPs into the Cabinet, such as Chris Patten, who was promoted to Environment Secretary, while John Major was elevated from Chief Secretary to the Treasury to Foreign Secretary, despite a poor knowledge of foreign affairs. Major would later comment that this was the one job in government 'for which I was least prepared' (Major, 1999: 111).

John Major's position as Foreign Secretary lasted for only three months before he moved to No. 11 Downing Street, with Douglas Hurd being appointed his successor at the Foreign Office. While Major had not been out of his depth at the Foreign Office he was clearly happy to move to more familiar surroundings, commenting that it was 'the job I most coveted' (Major, 1999: 134). The change of office had been caused by the resignation of Nigel Lawson as Chancellor of the Exchequer on 26 October 1989. Lawson had different views from Thatcher over economic policy and had been irritated by the influence that Thatcher's economic adviser, Alan Walters, had on economic policy (Seldon, 1997: 98). Walters' influence reflected Thatcher's growing use of advisers such as Charles Powell, her private secretary for foreign affairs, in the formation of policy instead of the Cabinet. Ironically, Alan Walters resigned in the wake of Nigel Lawson's resignation, which meant that Thatcher lost her economic adviser at a time when it was evident that she was increasingly isolated in Cabinet (her isolation had in fact begun with the departure of William Whitelaw in 1987).

Such dramatic changes in high Cabinet office marked the lack of consensus that existed within government at this time. In Major, Thatcher hoped to have appointed a minister who would not cause her difficulty in the manner that Howe and Lawson had. But Major was himself not antagonistic to European integration *per se* (Major, 1999: 114, 124–5 and 133). In this context the Prime Minister's continuing hostility in 1990 towards the European process did not result in open wounds being healed. If anything, the strains within government became worse.[26] Big hitters, such as Nigel Lawson, were now free from the shackles of Cabinet responsibility and were therefore able to voice their views in an independent manner.

Into the ERM

Strains within the government were particularly apparent over the issue of ERM membership throughout 1990. As noted earlier, Britain's position since the mid-1980s had been to 'join when the time was right', while conditions had been set at Madrid. Yet Thatcher continued to rebuff any moves towards ERM entry, which were now being championed by Hurd and Major and were reflective of their growing influence within government at the expense of Thatcher's dominance. This was particularly noticeable in July 1990 when the new Chancellor, John Major, considered that the time was right for entry; there had in fact been a high degree of speculation in May and June of that year as to the possibility of membership. The resulting effect of this was for sterling to surge in value as speculators backed the pound through expectations of gaining high yields from a stable currency (Thatcher, 1993: 723).[27] London's financial markets (FTSE 100 share index) surged on 17 May by 63.3 points to 2,284.4, equating to a 2.8% advance that was the biggest daily gain since November 1987.[28] Such increases were further fuelled by the Prime Minister's comments at the Scottish Conservative Party Conference on 12 May, when she noted that Britain's ability to join the ERM had improved as the differentiation between the domestic inflation rate and the European average decreased.[29] This position seemed to suggest that Thatcher was not as vehemently opposed to joining as she had been when Lawson was Chancellor, and similarly suggested that the timing of entry was in the hands of the Chancellor of the Exchequer, John Major.[30] This meant that Thatcher had *de facto* accepted Britain's participation and therefore the primary obstacle to entry had been removed. This statement was further accentuated by a speech made by Major on the same day at the Confederation of British Industry (CBI) annual dinner, in which he noted that entry would take place: 'I am sure we will benefit from joining the ERM, and join it we most certainly will when our conditions are met. But it is an added discipline, which will reinforce domestic monetary restraint, not replace it.'[31]

Moreover, Major suggested to Thatcher in a paper at the end of June 1990 that a two-tier Europe could develop, with Britain isolated (Thatcher, 1993: 724). Thatcher's view was that Major was 'going wobbly' as he clearly favoured entry to the ERM and realised the need for a more compromising stance on monetary union, and she accordingly resisted his desire to enter the ERM in July 1990 (Thatcher, 1993: 723–6).

In the end, Thatcher remained opposed to entry until 5 October, when she accepted the overwhelming pressure for entry from ministers,[32] academics and business people.[33] The validity of this policy was emphasised by an increase in the financial markets.[34] The very policy of entry had been regarded by Hurd, Major and the City as an essential means of regaining influence in the debate over monetary policy as well as a means of strengthening the government's position in the forthcoming monetary union negotiations (Seldon, 1997: 112).[35] As Dyson and Featherstone note, 'The Government was to stumble into the ERM. Political factors determined the principle, the timing and the method' (Dyson and Featherstone, 1999: 553). Sterling's absence from the ERM meant that the government could be detached from the forthcoming intergovernmental conference negotiations, as had previously happened at the Strasbourg summit at the end of December 1989.[36]

Despite the practical requirements of Britain needing to have a greater input in EC decisions, it was notable that the very decision to join came after the announcement that there would be a 1% reduction in interest rates.[37] For Thatcher, the interest rate cut was a means of justifying the policy, while also demonstrating that she had not been defeated and was still in command (Thatcher, 1993: 724; Major, 1999: 158–60 and 164). This could not have been further from the truth, and this public gesture did not mask the depths of division that beset the Conservative Party. For some months, if not over a year, the government had been rudderless. The very decision to join had not been subject to Cabinet discussion, while the Governor of the Bank of England was not consulted and opposed the interest rate reduction, as did the Treasury.[38] The reason given for this lack of divulgence of information was that the policy was too market-sensitive, though such a cloak and dagger approach only added fuel to the poor relations between the Bank of England and the Prime Minister.

Entry was welcomed by other member states, with Karl-Otto Pöhl considering it to be 'an important contribution in the framework of European economic and monetary union', a position that was equally shared by Pierre Bérégovoy, the French Finance Minister, who considered that it was 'a progression along the road of European economic and monetary union'.[39] John Major highlighted that while entry to the ERM was part of Britain's commitment to Stage 1 of EMU, it did not commit the government to the Delors approach for Stages 2 or 3.[40] That reflected Major's position of hostility to the imposition of a common currency, with his view (as argued throughout 1990 and 1991) being that market (and public) opinion would in the end decide whether Britain would take part in a single currency (Major, 1999: 271–3). The government's position was that it had entered the ERM so as to participate in an important EC institution, as well as gaining the functional benefit of keeping inflation at a low level, as later outlined by Major's successor as Chancellor, Norman Lamont, who noted that 'we did not join the ERM as a stepping-stone to monetary union. We joined it for its immediate, practical benefits in getting inflation down'.[41] As Major himself would comment, bringing down inflation 'was the primary reason for our entry into the ERM' (Major, 1999: 138). This meant that ERM obligations were 'the over-riding factor' in setting interest rates (Lamont, 1999: 36).[42]

Upon reflection it is nevertheless evident that there were similarities between the arguments used in favour of ERM entry in 1990 and those used to support Britain's entry to the Community in 1973. In both cases it was evident that British industry, the financial markets (City of London) and academics were able to recognise that there were important developments taking place on the continent and that non-participation would marginalise Britain from future debates on monetary union. Such a negotiating stance therefore demonstrated a traditional British unwillingness to fully commit to Europe. It also evidenced a reactive style of governance that had a greater concern for the effects of non-participation than the benefits of further cooperation.

Conclusion

Despite this demonstration of commitment to the EC, there remained a clear division between the government and other member states over monetary policy and EC affairs in general.[43] There additionally existed a division of views at the domestic level within Cabinet, and in particular between Margaret Thatcher and Geoffrey Howe, John Major and Douglas Hurd. A powerful alliance between the Foreign Office and the Treasury had thus emerged to challenge the decision-making capacity of the Prime Minister. The impending discussions on EMU added a further dimension to domestic and Community negotiating tactics. According to Major 'Europe was a ticking time-bomb' (Major, 1999: 138), and he considered his success in getting Thatcher to accept the case for ERM entry to be a key achievement of his period as Chancellor.[44] Crucially, however, both Hurd and Major were in a stronger position to influence Thatcher's opinions than had been the case for Howe and Lawson. This was both because of a watering-down in Thatcher's own opposition to the ERM, as evidenced by the Madrid conditions, and because Howe and Lawson had expended much of their domestic negotiating influence after a series of difficult confrontations with the Prime Minister. By contrast, being newly appointed to their respective posts at the Foreign Office and Treasury, Hurd and Major commanded a greater degree of authority than their predecessors because Thatcher could not risk losing either (or both) of them, as this would have made her own position untenable.[45] In this way, the Cabinet reshuffle did not bolster the Prime Minister's power, but instead weakened it in the face of increasingly dominant Cabinet ministers.

But despite Britain having committed itself to the ERM, there had not been a noticeable shift in its negotiating influence within the Community. The Prime Minister continued to adopt a hostile stance, stating that she was 'totally against a federal Europe'.[46] Major himself commented that 'her [Thatcher's] deepest hostility was to a single currency and the political implications of surrendering monetary authority' (Major, 1999: 154). The effect of this state of affairs was for Sir Geoffrey Howe to resign from the Cabinet on 1 November 1990.[47] He had, in fact, 'been driven to it' (Major, 1999: 179). A decision to resign had been determined by the gulf that separated him from the Prime Minister on European policy, especially monetary affairs.[48] It was somewhat ironic that it would be Howe's resignation that would have the most immediate impact on Thatcher's grip on office, as he had been one of the quieter members of the Cabinet. His resignation speech of 13 November emphasised the 'growing difference' between himself and Thatcher over the ERM, and he criticised the government for offering little that was constructive with regard to the implementation of a single currency. In specific terms, he stated:

> How on earth are the Chancellor and the Governor of the Bank of England, commending the Hard ECU as they strive to, to be taken as serious participants in the debate against that kind of background noise? . . . It is rather like sending your opening batsmen to the crease only for them to find, the moment the first balls are bowled, that their bats have been broken before the game by the team captain.[49]

His resignation letter spoke of the 'growing difference which has emerged between us on the increasingly important issue of Britain's role in Europe' (Howe, 1994: 648–50). Thatcher had emphasised that she was not prepared to be flexible or constructive in the EC as 'we are determined to retain our fundamental ability to govern ourselves through Parliament'.[50] He stated the need to be at the 'centre of the European partnership' and scathingly criticised Thatcher's stance at the Rome European Council, noting that 'the mood you have struck . . . will make it more difficult for Britain to hold and retain a position of influence' (Howe, 1994: 648–50). And while there was a general awareness within and outwith government of this state of affairs, the emergence of such direct criticism from a senior minister was a severe blow to Thatcher's authority. This isolation abroad, combined with a lack of agreement over her policies at home, represented the beginning of the end of her reign as Prime Minister: 'For it was the Prime Minister herself who was breaking ranks with her own government, with a clear view that Britain would never participate in any EMU arrangements' (Howe, 1994: 643).

That position of hostility towards a single currency did not drastically change when Major became Prime Minister on 28 November. The government had, however, become increasingly serious about engaging in monetary discussions at the European level. This will become evident in Chapter 7, which reviews Britain's position in the 1990–91 intergovernmental conference negotiations on economic and monetary union. But prior to that discussion, the next chapter will illustrate the manner in which the monetary policy negotiations were shaped by France and Germany and the extent to which Britain was once again isolated from this debate.

Key points

- Between 1985 and 1990 there was significant disagreement within government over Britain's policy towards the ERM, with Prime Minister Thatcher being against British participation. By contrast, Nigel Lawson, Geoffrey Howe and John Major favoured entry.

- Prime Minister Thatcher vetoed any concept of Britain's entry to the ERM in the mid-1980s, both on economic grounds (the conditions were not right) and because of more deep-lying political factors which included her reluctance to commit Britain to further European integration.

- By the end of the 1980s the case for British membership was stronger, with support both inside and outside government, for example from industry. The position of Thatcher was weakening at this time and she found it difficult to veto the pressure for membership.

- Britain eventually joined the ERM in 1990, but did so at a time of increasing instability in European currency markets. Whilst policy-makers stressed that Britain had joined to gain the benefits of lower inflation, membership was also seen as a means of demonstrating the government's commitment to Europe. This was an important point, not least because of negotiations which were scheduled to take place in 1991 on EMU and political union. In this sense, the wider debate of EMU partly played a role in determining British policy on the ERM.

Questions

1. For what reasons did Nigel Lawson favour Britain's entry to the ERM?

2. Why did the British government prefer a policy of floating rather than tied exchange rates throughout the 1980s?

3. For what reasons did Nigel Lawson put in place a policy of sterling shadowing the Deutschmark?

4. Why did Britain not join the Exchange Rate Mechanism until 1990?

5. What were the factors that influenced Britain's entry to the ERM in 1990?

6. 'When Britain joined the ERM in 1990 it did so at the wrong rate and the wrong time.' Discuss.

7. How much do the debates on ERM entry in the 1980s tell us about the manner by which Margaret Thatcher took decisions within government?

8. Examine the role that European issues had in bringing about Margaret Thatcher's downfall from office.

9. What factors contributed to John Major's election as leader of the Conservative Party?

10. 'Reactive rather than proactive policy-making': to what extent is this statement reflective of British policy towards the ERM?

Further reading

Blair, Alasdair (1999) *Dealing with Europe: Britain and the Negotiation of the Maastricht Treaty*, Aldershot: Ashgate, Chapter 7.

Dyson, Kenneth (1994) *Elusive Union: The Process of Economic and Monetary Union in Europe*, Harlow: Longman.

Dyson, Kenneth and Featherstone, Kevin (1999) *The Road to Maastricht: Negotiating Economic and Monetary Union*, Oxford: Oxford University Press, Chapter 13.

Gros, Daniel and Thygesen, Niels (1998) *European Monetary Integration*, 2nd edn, Harlow: Longman, Chapter 4.

Howe, Geoffrey (1994) *Conflict of Loyalty*, London: Macmillan, Chapters 30, 35, 38, 40, 43.

Lawson, Nigel (1992) *The View From No. 11*, London: Bantam Press, Chapters 33, 39–40, 52–3, 63–4, 67, 69, 73–7, 80.

Levitt, Malcolm and Lord, Christopher (2000) *The Political Economy of Monetary Union*, Basingstoke: Macmillan, Chapter 3.

Stephens, Philip (1996) *Politics and the Pound*, London: Macmillan, Chapters 2–8.

Thatcher, Margaret (1993) *The Downing Street Years*, London: HarperCollins, Chapters 18, 24.

Thompson, Helen (1993) 'The UK and the Exchange Rate Mechanism 1978–90', in Brian Brivati and Harriet Jones (eds.), *From Reconstruction to Integration: Britain and Europe since 1945*, London: Leicester University Press, pp. 227–40.

Thompson, Helen (1996) *The British Conservative Government and the European Exchange Rate Mechanism, 1979–1994*, London: Pinter.

Notes

[1] Such figures are the average of daily telegraphic transfer rates in London. *Economic Trends*, London: HMSO, Annual Supplement, 1995, Section 5.1, p. 223, and *Economic Trends*, London: HMSO, December 1985, No. 386, p. 50 for 1985 figure.

[2] *Financial Times*, 6–7 October 1990, p. 9.

[3] Resolution of the European Council of 5 December 1978 on the establishment of the European Monetary System (EMS) and related matters. Published as Cm. 7419.

[4] See Chapter 3 for details.

[5] United Kingdom Government, *The European Monetary System*, Green Paper, London: HMSO, 1978. Reprinted in *Financial Times*, 25 November 1978.

[6] Private information.

[7] Nigel Lawson's preference for membership did not mean that he was not aware that the system could result in a reduction in 'flexibility', and that membership could involve the 'vigorous' use of interest rates due to the system becoming bipolar with sterling's participation, whereas it had predominantly been a Deutschmark zone. House of Commons, *Fifth Report from the Treasury and Civil Service Committee*, HC181 (1984–85) paras. 55–60, pp. 12–13.

[8] House of Lords Select Committee on the European Communities, *European Monetary System*, HL39 (1983–84), para. 85, points iv and v respectively, p. xxiv.

[9] UK official reserves declined from $27,476 million at the end of 1980 to $17,817 at the end of 1983. They stood at $15,694 million at the end of the fourth quarter in 1984 and declined to $13,528 million at the end of the first quarter of 1985, while the reserves were subsequently bolstered to $18,750 million at the end of the first quarter of 1986. *Economic Trends*, London: HMSO, Annual Supplement, 1995 edition, Section 5.1, p. 226, and *Economic Trends*, London: HMSO, December 1985, No. 386, p. 50.

[10] House of Commons, *Fifth Report from the Treasury and Civil Service Committee*, HC181 (1984–85), memorandum submitted by Mr Christopher Johnson, 'Full EMS Membership and the Sterling Crisis'.

[11] House of Lords Select Committee on the European Communities, *European Monetary System*, HL39 (1983–84), memorandum submitted by the Confederation of British Industry (CBI).

[12] At the meeting were Thatcher, Howe, Lawson, Whitelaw (Deputy Prime Minister), Tebbit (party chairman), John Biffen (Leader of the House of Commons), John Wakeham (Chief Whip), Brian Griffiths (head of the Prime Minister's policy unit), Peter Middleton (Treasury), Terence Burns (Treasury), Robin Leigh-Pemberton (Governor of

the Bank of England) and Eddie George (Bank of England). The Prime Minister's private secretary attended to take notes.

[13] *Treasury and Civil Service Select Committee*, HC (1984–85) 57-IV, para. 84.

[14] Private information.

[15] A wish to maintain monetary independence was further influenced by the government having responsibility for setting interest rates rather than this task being entrusted to the Bank of England.

[16] House of Lords Select Committee on the European Communities, *European Monetary System*, HL39 (1983–84), paras. 79–81, p. xxiii.

[17] Nigel Lawson, *What Sort of Financial Area?*, speech at the Royal Institute for International Affairs on 25 January 1989, London: HM Treasury, p. 12.

[18] House of Lords Select Committee on the European Communities, *The Delors Committee Report*, HL3 (1989–90), para. 180, p. 46.

[19] *Bull. EC*, Vol. 23, 1/2-1990, point 1.1.3.

[20] *Treasury and Civil Service Committee, Fourth Report, 'The Delors Report'*, HC341 (1988–89) Q. 57 and Q. 116 respectively.

[21] Nigel Lawson, cited in ibid., Q. 120. Also the Bank of England, annual lecture of the Institute of Economic Affairs, 26 July 1989. Reproduced in *Bank of England Quarterly Bulletin*, August 1989, Vol. 29, No. 3, pp. 372–4.

[22] Throughout 1989 the Conservative Party was running behind Labour in the opinion polls as demonstrated by the Labour Party winning the previous Conservative seat in the Vale of Glamorgan by-election on 4 May.

[23] The Lawson–Howe draft had been produced in the Treasury and was then jointly refined by Tim Lankester (senior Treasury official) and John Kerr (senior Foreign and Commonwealth official). Lawson and Howe discussed the final draft after dinner on 13 June 1989 and sent it to Thatcher on 14 June, requesting a discussion with her of its 12 pages of contents.

[24] The conditions included a reduction in the inflation rate, abolition of all restrictions on capital movements, complete liberalisation of financial services, completion of the internal market and a stronger Community competition policy. This stance had been influenced by the fact that the government had managed to keep the Social Charter off the agenda, which meant that the government felt that it had already been victorious, although its absence allowed EMU to dominate the agenda. At the Madrid European Council meeting of 26–27 June 1989 it was agreed that Phase 1 of the Report would begin on 1 July 1990, while the timetable for Phases 2 and 3 were delayed.

[25] *House of Commons Official Report*, Vol. 155, No. 132, cols. 1107–9.

[26] *The Economist*, 21 April 1990, p. 41.

[27] *Financial Times*, 12 June 1990, p. 1; *The Times*, 13 June 1990, p. 28; *The Independent*, 13 June 1990, pp. 1 and 22; and *The Guardian*, 13 June 1990, p. 11.

[28] *Financial Times*, 18 May 1990, p. 1.

[29] *The Economist*, 19 May 1990, p. 29.

[30] *Financial Times*, 14 May 1990, p. 1, and *Financial Times*, 24–25 February 1990, p. 1.

[31] *Financial Times*, 18 May 1990, p. 1.

[32] *Financial Times*, 6–7 October 1990, p. 9.

[33] House of Lords Select Committee on the European Communities, *The Delors Committee Report*, HL3 (1989–90), para. 180, p. 46. Also *Financial Times*, 19 March 1990, p. 12 and *Financial Times*, 6 April 1990, p. 12.

[34] *Financial Times*, 6–7 October 1990, p. 1, and *Financial Times*, 6–7 October 1990, p. 1.

[35] *The Guardian*, 6 October 1990, p. 11, and *Financial Times*, 14 May 1990, p. 1.

[36] At Strasbourg the government had expressed reservations about the Delors Report's prescription for Stages 2 and 3 of EMU. But despite these views, a majority of the member states agreed to the convening of an intergovernmental conference by the end of 1990 to consider further the progress that would be necessary to achieve EMU.

[37] *International Herald Tribune*, 13 June 1990, pp. 15 and 18. It was decided on the date of entry that interest rates would be reduced to 14% from 15% – the highest they had been for nearly eight years. The cut was the first time base rates had been reduced in two and a half years, during which time monetary policy had gradually been tightened with interest rates reaching 13% by November 1988, 14% by May 1989 and 15% by September 1989.

[38] Private information.

[39] *Financial Times*, 6–7 October 1990, p. 7.

[40] *House of Commons Official Report*, 23 October 1990, col. 202, and *The Guardian*, 13 June 1990.

[41] Norman Lamont, 'Britain and the Exchange Rate Mechanism' – speech to the European Policy Forum, 10 July 1992.

[42] *Financial Statement and Budget Report 1991–92*, HC (1990–91) 300, para. 2.02. Also *Bank of England Quarterly Bulletin*, Vol. 30, No. 4, November 1990, pp. 482–4.

[43] *Europe Documents*, No. 1657, 25 October 1990, and *Agence Europe* (n.s.), No. 5355, 22–23 October 1990, p. 7.

[44] *Financial Times*, 27/28 October 1990, p. 6.

[45] *Financial Times*, 18 June 1990, p. 20.

[46] *House of Commons Official Report*, 30 October 1990, col. 889.

[47] *Financial Times*, 2 November 1990, p. 8, and *The Economist*, 3 November 1990, p. 38.

[48] *House of Commons Official Report*, 30 October 1990, col. 870.

[49] *Ibid.*, col. 464.

[50] *Ibid.*, col. 871.

CHAPTER 6

The prospects for monetary union: 1988–1991

Objectives

- Outline British position on monetary union.
- Demonstrate the initial lack of appreciation among government ministers and officials as to the implications of monetary union.
- Examine the role of the Delors Committee in advancing the cause of monetary union.
- Highlight the extent to which Britain was isolated and adrift from debates on monetary union.

Introduction

Just as Chapter 5 noted the difficulty that the British government had in establishing a coherent position on the Exchange Rate Mechanism, this chapter highlights the problems that surrounded the government's position on Economic and Monetary Union. Particular attention is given to the lack of understanding among ministers as to the substance of EMU and the fact that it was more than just a sideshow to other developments at the European level. A lack of appreciation of the impetus behind monetary policy meant that Britain was slow to advance proposals on this topic,[1] the effect of which was to relegate the government from the core debate on monetary union. This state of affairs was principally because of Prime Minister Thatcher's reluctance to countenance monetary union, though the Treasury and especially the Foreign Office encouraged dialogue. And when any proposals did come forward for discussion within Cabinet, most discussion concerned what British ministers thought of the policy. The impact of this was that there was not enough thought as to how other European leaders would respond. In the meantime, while this debate took place in Whitehall, France and Germany were making great progress in the direction of EMU. The net effect of this was for Britain to be left behind in these discussions, and when the government did eventually advance a proposal on monetary union, it was a case of too little, too late. This was because the British proposal (hard ECU) did not offer the benefits of a single currency that other nations wanted, and consequently did not mirror the broader objectives held by the majority of EU member states.[2] That is not to say that the proposal did not have certain merits. It did. Indeed, if it had been advanced at an earlier stage then there may have been a real chance that Britain would have had a greater input to this policy area.

Changing course

Among recent decades, the 1980s stands as one of the most important in the progress of the European polity. It was in this period that the Community finally emerged from the poor economic performance of the 1970s and more importantly resolved long-running disputes that had clogged the policy-making process. Chief among these was the argument over Britain's budgetary contri-butions, a problem that was finally concluded at the Fontainebleau summit of 1984 (Howe, 1994: 397–410). In subsequent years the Community established many significant policies, of which the 1985 negotiations that produced the Single European Act (SEA) were especially crucial.[3] Not only did this document establish the objective of a single market by 1992 and extend the provision of qualified majority voting for Community decision-making, but it also men-tioned EMU in two paragraphs of the Preamble and Article 20 of the text.[4] This may not seem important, but it is worth remembering that the issue of mon-etary policy was not expressly included in the mandate granted by the June 1985 Milan European Council that set the parameters of the SEA negotiations. The net effect of its inclusion was that EMU was now back on the Community agenda.

Not all member states were keen for this development, Britain in particular (Lawson, 1992: 893). But France, and to a lesser extent Germany, supported this policy, with the primary driving force being the French Finance Minister, Edouard Balladur (Gros and Thygesen, 1998: 396; Dyson and Featherstone, 1999: 163–6). An interest in EMU for France was not wholly because it regarded the project as being beneficial to all participants. Rather, more Machiavellian reasons lay at the heart of French policy, as the nation was aware of the power of the German Bundesbank in European financial affairs. A move towards a single currency would consequently provide France with greater input into European financial planning, and therefore help to dilute the dominance of Germany in European monetary policy. As Dyson and Feather-stone note, 'EMU offered France the opportunity to re-establish influence over monetary policy by Europeanising it' (Dyson and Featherstone, 1999: 97). Of the other member states that came forward with proposals, Germany advanced proposals for a European Central Bank in February 1988. This was so as to ensure that any future single currency would be embedded with the same principles of stability that shaped German policy-making on monetary matters. A concern over the operational capabilities of EMU would be a theme that subsequently dominated policy in this area.

Just as Britain was reluctant to take part in the ERM (see Chapter 5), it did not warm to EMU objectives. At that time the government believed that EMU would not lead to anything serious and dismissed the policy as an unnecessary distraction from other important negotiating topics. Of these, it had had its eyes firmly focused on the single market objectives that were established by the Single European Act.[5] But while Britain did not envisage any further policy developments at this time, there was nevertheless a real feeling that monetary union was firmly part of the Community's agenda. As Ben Rosamond notes, 'for the single market's potential to be realised, pure economic logic would contend that EMU is a necessity to maximise economic efficiency' (Rosamond, 2000: 100). To this end, the single market process created a series of 'spillover' effects by which other areas of Community policy-making were given impetus to develop, and demonstrated that the path to further European integration was not completely bound up by state influence (Tranholm-Mikkelsen, 1991).

Such a neo-functionalist approach to integration therefore stressed that greater political integration at the European level was determined by further economic integration (see Chapters 3 and 11). The spillover effect thus referred to the scenario where integration in one area of policy-making produced motivations for further integration in other areas. This approach contrasted with the desire of the British government to have further European integration determined by states (intergovernmentalism). To this end the government, particularly Prime Minister Thatcher, considered that it would be possible to ring-fence certain developments, such as the SEA, with the effect of limiting the potential for spillover.

Such a stance obviously sheds light on the manner in which British policy-makers and decision-takers viewed European events as a sideshow from the real theatre of Whitehall. Somewhat worryingly this had been a consistent, and unwise, continuum of British policy in the post-1945 period. The outcome of this state of affairs was that Britain did not engage in the EMU debate during the first half of 1988. And just as there was an absence of discussion between London and Brussels on this matter, it was conspicuous that the Governor of the Bank of England had no real discussions on this subject with the Prime Minister or the Treasury during the same period.[6] This was reflective of the fact that Britain's response to monetary union was a government, and not Bank of England, matter. To that extent, the Governor of the Bank of England was 'informed' of government policy-making, and therefore was not consulted on the context of that policy.[7] Such a strategy was reflective of the fact that at that time monetary policy was firmly controlled by government.

BOX 6.1

Hanover European Council of 27–28 June 1988

The Hanover European Council agreed to a proposal put forward by Jacques Delors for a new study on EMU. France and Germany stressed the importance of the emergence of a single European currency as an essential complement to the freeing of the internal market. They argued that the EMS needed to be strengthened through the creation of a European Central Bank along with steps to establish the ECU as the common currency of the Community.

The negativity surrounding the British position was evident when Prime Minister Thatcher rejected the creation of a European Central Bank in a statement to the House of Commons the week before the June 1988 Hanover European Council (Dyson and Featherstone, 1999: 604–6; Thompson, 1996: 119–24). Her stance had been influenced not by Cabinet, but by her use of special advisers such as Charles Powell, and she did not even seek the advice of the Chancellor of the Exchequer, Nigel Lawson (Lawson, 1992: 902). But despite this domestic position, there was a growing momentum towards monetary union at the Community level, with France and Germany stressing at the Hanover meeting that a single currency was a necessary linkage to the establishment of an internal market, thus further demonstrating the functional spillover approach to European integration. They argued that the European Monetary System needed to be strengthened by the creation of a European Central Bank and the establishment of a common currency. The eventual outcome of this was that member states took the decision at Hanover to create a committee to examine the means by which monetary union could be established (see Box 6.1).[8] The resulting proposals were to be examined at the June 1989 Madrid European Council.

The idea for the committee (known as the Delors Committee after the chairman Jacques Delors) emanated from the German Finance Minister, Hans-Dietrich Genscher, who considered that it should be composed of independent experts. That proposal was slightly amended by Thatcher who suggested that the committee should be composed of member states' central bank governors. The reason for this point of view was a consideration that she would at least be able to count on the support of the Governor of the Bank of England, Robin Leigh-Pemberton.[9] Such a viewpoint was based on the nature of the relationship between government and the Bank of England, whereby it was the government's responsibility (and not the Bank's) to set interest rates (see Chapter 2). The effect of this was that the Prime Minister was used to the Bank carrying out government instructions rather than offering a distinct series of policy objectives. But Thatcher also thought central bankers would take a more level-headed approach to EMU.[10] Thus, for Britain, the creation of the committee was a means of 'pushing the proposal for EMU into the long grass',[11] with the

---

BOX 6.2

Biography of Jacques Delors (1925–)

President of the European Commission between 1985 and 1995. He was a major force in the further development of the Community, particularly the progression towards the single market, commitment towards a single currency (Delors Report) and the enlargement of the Community from 10 to 15 members. His desire to foster closer European integration was often at odds with Prime Minister Margaret Thatcher, who considered that European policies were encroaching on areas of policy that were the responsibility of member states.

---

view that 'the whole implication at the beginning was that this was not a serious runner'.[12]

In retrospect we can see that this negotiating position was indeed a naive one, with the Prime Minister (and her advisers) being unable to look to the long-term implications of EMU. This was further emphasised by her belief that the removal of any reference to a European Central Bank from the final text agreed at Hanover was a negotiating success. But as the British Chancellor, Nigel Lawson, later noted, the other leaders 'must have been amazed at her innocence' (Lawson, 1992: 903). This was because the Hanover European Council of 27–28 June 1988 emphasised 'the objective of progressive realisation of economic and monetary union'.[13] It was therefore inevitable that the Delors Committee's terms of reference would, in fact, recommend the setting-up of a European Central Bank. Delors consequently informed Thatcher that '[T]here is no way that a committee with those terms of reference can possibly do anything else than recommend the setting up of a European Central Bank' (Lawson, 1992: 903). Differences of opinion as to the reality of the EMU project were therefore rife within government, with Lawson's view that the Delors Committee was a means of advancing towards monetary union not being shared by Thatcher (Lawson, 1992: 903–4).

Committee men

Despite the fact that the government had been somewhat surprised by the developments towards EMU, with one senior official noting that 'we should have had our eyes wider open',[14] there continued to be a lack of policy co-ordination among central government actors. In this context, the first the Governor of the Bank of England knew of the effects of the Hanover meeting was when he was told that he was on the Delors Committee.[15] This development was symptomatic of the way in which decisions were taken. All too often policy (particularly on European matters) was made on a short-term basis with little consideration of the longer-term strategic objectives. As noted in Chapter 5, the decision on ERM entry was very much a reaction to events, and when decisions were taken, they were invariably in the wake of short-term compromises. Thatcher had, for instance, been unwilling to let Major enter the ERM in the summer of 1990, but three months later she acquiesced to this request. Moreover, it is likely that the amount of energy and resources that were spent on ERM discussions impacted on the lack of consideration given to talks concerning EMU.

In this context government ministers displayed little enthusiasm towards the Delors Committee. That did not mean, however, that the government took no further notice of the project. Rather, the tactic it deployed was, if not to oppose the committee, then to emphasise the difficulties of its objectives. The agreed position was that the government's negotiating stance should be alongside the President of the Bundesbank, Karl-Otto Pöhl. Thatcher considered it inconceivable that Pöhl would be in favour of the abolition of the Bundesbank because this would obviously dilute his own power (and that of the Bundesbank). The perceived wisdom within Downing Street was that an Anglo-German alliance would thus halt any progress towards EMU (Lawson, 1992: 902).[16] In many senses, the government was correct to consider that the Bundesbank would be unwilling to relinquish its power over economic policy to a European body (a European Central Bank). Yet the consideration that an Anglo-German alliance would materialise was somewhat fanciful. Britain was, after all, displaying an increasing contempt for Community integration, while Thatcher and Kohl had never been close allies. Moreover, the government seemed to consider that the Bundesbank might take a position independent of the German government, which had displayed support for EMU. This was somewhat ironic, as Thatcher was, of course, insistent that the Bank of England should follow government policy and should not take it upon itself to have an independent position.

The end product of these events was that the committee did not slow down the progression to EMU as Thatcher had expected. If anything, it accelerated matters (Lawson, 1992: 904; Dyson and Featherstone, 1999: 606–10). One of the reasons for this was that the axis between Pöhl and Leigh-Pemberton never materialised, primarily because Pöhl was not interested in the negotiations and felt that it would be difficult to argue strongly for or against policy proposals (Lamont, 1999: 117). He also took the viewpoint that EMU was not going to happen during his tenure as President of the Bundesbank.[17] But despite Pöhl's own scepticism, Thatcher failed to understand that Pöhl was likely to reflect the views of the German government, which favoured EMU.[18] There was in fact a lack of balance to her thinking that, while Pöhl would be a free agent, Leigh-Pemberton would reflect London's point of view.

A further factor that hindered the government's cause during the period when the Delors Committee[19] met was that there was a lack of consensus between the Bank of England and the Prime Minister as to Britain's negotiating position. Prime Minister Thatcher and her senior advisers were disgruntled that Leigh-Pemberton did not fully reflect the views of the British government in the committee's

---

BOX 6.3

Delors Report of 12 April 1989

The Report of the Delors Committee proposed a three-stage process for monetary union, namely linking the currencies together, integration between states, and the creation of a European Central Bank. The Chancellor of the Exchequer, Nigel Lawson, immediately rejected these proposals and stated that Britain would be publishing its own proposals. The Delors Report proposed a three-stage transition to monetary union:

1. Completion of the single market.
2. 'Soft' monetary union. The European System of Central Banks (ESCB) would co-ordinate national monetary policies.
3. 'Hard' monetary union – irrevocable locking of exchange rates and the transfer of monetary authority to the European Central Bank (ECB).

---

negotiations, based on the assumption that the Bank should carry through the government's viewpoints. The government was therefore annoyed with the actions of the Governor, who considered himself to be 'a personal representative and at liberty to take whatever view he thought best'.[20] The Governor himself believed that the remit of the Delors Committee was not to 'answer whether, but rather the question of how' EMU could be achieved.[21] Not surprisingly, Prime Minister Thatcher was 'disillusioned' with him, stating that he had gone 'native' by adopting a position that was entirely out of sympathy with the government's line (Thompson, 1996: 128–30).[22]

When published in April 1989, the Delors Report[23] detailed three stages for currency union: linking the currencies together through strengthening existing procedures, integration between states through a new treaty and, lastly, the creation of a European Central Bank which would ensure that monetary policy was transferred from national authorities, while at the same time currencies would be irrevocably locked (see Box 6.3). The document therefore firmly set down a path to monetary union and consequently contradicted the view held by Thatcher, which was that national governments should retain control over monetary policy. Thus the issue for the government was not so much the move to Stage 1 of the Delors Report but the subsequent transition to Stages 2 and 3, which would involve a loss of national control over monetary policy.[24]

Full speed ahead

Irrespective of British opposition momentum continued, with agreement being reached on the Delors Report's path towards EMU at the Madrid Summit of 26–27 June 1989, the first stage of which was to commence on 1 July 1990 (see

---

BOX 6.4

Madrid European Council of 26–27 June 1989

At the Madrid European Council Margaret Thatcher adopted a more conciliatory tone and made significant progress on the question of British membership of the ERM by stating the conditions that would be necessary for membership. Her previous stance had been that Britain would join when the time was right. Prime Minister Thatcher accepted the implementation of the first stage of the Delors Report. However, at the meeting she still registered her disapproval of plans that would lead to a monetary union as well as the social policy side of the 1992 programme.

Box 6.4). The setting of this deadline signalled acknowledgement among member states of the need for a treaty that highlighted the importance accorded to EMU. By this stage, the disputes that had been raging within Whitehall as to what Britain's position was vis-à-vis the ERM and EMU had led to a degree of policy change. As Chapter 5 mentioned, at Madrid Britain finally set out the conditions that would make membership of the ERM possible.[25] This tactical move won some plaudits from other European governments, particularly Germany, and had a direct effect in blocking (for the time being) France's desire to set a date when the negotiations on monetary union would commence (Grant, 1994: 125–6).

In addition to this setting of the parameters of ERM entry, Prime Minister Thatcher also announced at Madrid that Britain would be advancing its own proposals on monetary union as an alternative to the prescriptions contained in the Delors Report. Yet she had not consulted her Chancellor, Nigel Lawson, about this matter and Thatcher herself did not have 'the faintest idea of what the British alternative might be' (Lawson, 1992: 939). This was a staggering development and demonstrated the breakdown in communication between the Prime Minister and her Chancellor as well as the lack of detailed plans that Britain had to offer in this subject area. The very lack of prior consultation by Thatcher, and the absence of any British proposals on this topic, were markedly demonstrated by the Permanent Secretary at the Treasury, Sir Peter Middleton, who learned about this development by means of a news report. So shocked was he that he nearly crashed his car on hearing the account of the Madrid meeting (Lawson, 1992: 939).

This proved to be only a temporary and brief respite, because France took over from Spain the running of the six-month Community presidency[26] in the wake of the Madrid meeting. For British hopes of a slow path to EMU, this was the knockout punch.[27] With its hands firmly on the levers of Community agenda-setting and policy-making, France accelerated and transformed the progress towards monetary union. Britain was once again to be cast adrift, having obtained no negotiating objectives. The fact of the matter was that the EMU project was being driven at pace by France and Germany, especially Mitterrand and Kohl, with the resulting effect that the Strasbourg European Council reached agreement on the establishment of an intergovernmental conference on monetary union. The path to EMU was therefore firmly set (see Chapter 3).

Apart from this pressure from within the Community, external factors had a significant impact on the process and speed of reform. Of these, the dramatic collapse of Communism in Eastern Europe and the reunification of Germany[28] were the most important. The outcome of this was that all member states, apart from Britain, were united in the objective of achieving EMU.[29] Indeed, at the Dublin European Council of April 1990, which was convened to consider the consequences for the EC of German reunification, agreement was obtained that 'the Community will establish in stages an economic and monetary union'.[30] By October of that year, member states accepted (at the Rome European Council) that the second stage of EMU should commence on 1 January 1994.[31] Somewhat predictably, Britain was against the setting of this timetable for EMU, as it considered that any such decisions were purely the prerogative of the IGC on monetary union when it commenced its work in December 1990.[32]

Alone

The effect of these events was for Britain to remain adrift in the monetary policy debate, with there being no support for the government's preference for pragmatic economic progress[33] that did not involve institutional reform.[34] A fear of being excluded from, or having no impact upon, EMU discussions resulted in ministers and officials considering it necessary for Britain to engage in some form of fruitful discussions with other member states as to the practicalities of establishing a monetary union. A need for Britain to engage resulted in Nigel Lawson attempting to gain throughout 1989 some support from other Finance Ministers for Britain's position towards EMU based on a 'competing currencies' plan (see Box 6.5) (Lawson, 1992: 939–40; Dyson and Featherstone, 1999: 616–18). As its name suggests, this initiative proposed that central banks would 'compete' with each other so that currencies could be used in any member state. In this 'state of nature', the strong currencies would survive and dominate, possibly resulting in the emergence of one single currency. This negotiating position was not, however, mirrored in other member states, especially France, while Lawson was increasingly frustrated at Thatcher's negative negotiating position on EMU and the ERM (see Chapter 5). In the end, disputes between himself and Thatcher, especially over ERM entry, led to his resignation as Chancellor on 26 October 1989. Somewhat ironically, Britain formally advanced Lawson's competing currencies proposal in the wake of his departure, though it made little difference to the negotiating position.[35] In general terms, the new proposal still did not accept the creation of a single currency, or the goal of permanently fixed exchange rates.[36] Rather, it advocated the maintenance of national monetary policies within the context of strengthening the ERM,

---

BOX 6.5

Competing currencies plan

This was a proposal advanced by Britain in 1989, gaining particular support from the Chancellor of the Exchequer, Nigel Lawson, who considered that it was important for the government to get involved in the discussions on monetary union. Up until then the British government had been detached from the EMU negotiations and considered that a single currency would be unlikely to emerge. The competing currencies plan proposed that central banks would 'compete' with each other so that currencies could be used in any member state. In such a scenario, the stronger currencies would emerge as the more dominant, with the possibility of the emergence of a single currency. The proposal was therefore attractive to the British government because it offered the prospect of national control and did not establish a commitment to a single currency. But for this very reason it was unattractive to those countries who wanted to proceed to EMU with a single currency.

---

thereby implying British membership. Thus the government was no further forward in influencing the EMU debate and more importantly its proposals were not perceived by other member states as a workable alternative to Stages 2 and 3 of the Delors Plan.[37] The reality of this situation was not lost on the new Chancellor, John Major, who thought from the outset that the competing currencies plan 'was never going to work' as 'it came too late, and was seen in Europe as a wrecking tactic' (Major, 1999: 139).

The very necessity for a British proposal became even more apparent after the December 1989 Strasbourg European Council's[38] decision to convene an IGC on EMU before the end of 1990.[39] In the classic tradition of Britain's hesitancy to support integrationist policies, engagement was motivated by a desire to slow down the pressure for monetary union by getting central bankers and treasuries involved in the substance of Stage 2 of the path to EMU.[40] Not surprisingly, the recognition of the need to engage in this policy debate did not come from the government (Dyson and Featherstone, 1999: 619–26). Just as the decision to enter the ERM had been influenced by business opinion, so too was the formulation of an EMU policy. It was in this context that the European Committee of the British Invisibles Exports Council (BIEC) originally highlighted the need for engagement in the wake of the Delors Report in May 1989,[41] a view also held by the Bank of England. The BIEC was responsible for policy coordination on monetary union between City institutions, the Bank of England and Whitehall, and had been established on the initiative of the Governor of the Bank of England in 1988.

The BIEC specifically suggested that the existing European Currency Unit (ECU) could be transformed into a hard ECU, whereby member states could obtain the benefit of one currency, while at the same time maintaining control over their own domestic currency (Blair, A., 1999b: 158–62). Such a strategy was reflective of the fear within the City of London and more generally throughout British business that there was a need for the government to offer some form of initiative to gain greater credibility at the European negotiating table. In this context, business interests were notably concerned that government non-engagement would be detrimental to inward investment and the success of the City of London in financial markets by demonstrating a lack of full commitment to the Community. (Some years later a concern over non-participation in the euro was equally viewed as being harmful to inward investment.[42])

Usage of the ECU in this way was particularly attractive to the committee's chairman, Sir Michael Butler, who was himself a former British permanent representative to the Community.[43] The preference of Butler and other senior City figures who participated in the committee was for the hard ECU to be not just an alternative to EMU, but part of an evolutionary approach to a single currency (Richards, 1991).[44] The Treasury and Bank of England 'observers' in the committee also supported that route.[45] Thus, the crux of the matter was that the government should only adopt the hard ECU if it was prepared to accept the generally agreed aim of moving to fixed exchange rates or a single currency. The hard ECU was therefore not to be considered an alternative to a single currency. For them, the primary benefit was that it would 'get the UK back into the centre of the discussion'.[46] In outlining this plan the key consideration was whether Prime Minister Thatcher would accept it. To this end, Butler presented a paper on the hard ECU to Thatcher in March 1990.[47] Thus, at that stage, the plan already had the support of the key officials within Whitehall and, therefore, the primary question was how ministers would respond to it.

It was not unpredictable that Thatcher was reluctant to accept Butler's suggestions, insisting that it could not constitute a route to EMU, though the Chancellor of the Exchequer, John Major, and the Foreign Secretary, Douglas Hurd, considered that it could form such a route (Major, 1999: 155). They repeatedly campaigned for an approach that could advance towards EMU,[48] and there was some belief within government that Thatcher could be pressurised to accept their views. Such thinking had been influenced by her change of position on ERM entry and therefore further concessions might be secured. The necessity for Britain to offer some form of commitment to, and acceptance of, EMU became even greater when it transpired that other member states and the European Commission were seeking to draft the proposed treaty amendments prior to the commencement of the IGC. Readers of this book may think that such developments were reflective of Britain being ambushed. While there is some truth in this, the reality of the matter is that British hesitancy to agree to an EMU negotiating stance, i.e. as a route to EMU or instead of EMU, meant that events would bypass Britain during its period of indecision.

The impending reality of isolation was particularly feared by the City of London, which was concerned that its position as the dominant European financial centre could be threatened if Britain did not act.[49] Active engagement in the discussions on monetary union through workable and sellable proposals was consequently seen as a necessary means of obtaining greater negotiating leverage and an insurance policy for the government to add more clarity to its own proposals.[50] As part of this effort, the government hoped to obtain increased support from other member states for its own proposals. In the end, Thatcher did concede in late June 1990 that the hard ECU plan could form a route to EMU, after the strong recommendation of the majority of her ministers and the Governor of the Bank of England.[51] At the 19 June meeting Thatcher had been persuaded of the imperative of the hard ECU plan by Hurd and Major, although only after there had been a bitter internal wrangle with Nicholas Ridley (Major, 1999: 154–5).[52] Major then transformed the government's acceptance of the plan into a formal British proposal. He suggested, five days before the Dublin European Council of 25 June 1990, that the Community should move beyond Stage 1 by creating a 'hard ECU' which would become a parallel thirteenth currency run by a new institution, the European Monetary Fund.[53] For Major, and other government ministers, the ingenuity of the proposal was that it would allow member states to retain autonomy over their monetary policy, assist in delivering low inflation,[54] ensure economic convergence,[55] and most importantly nobody would be forced to use it (Major, 1999: 151).[56] In effect, the plan signified that the government was prepared to adopt the hard ECU proposal as a means of directing the monetary debate towards a British position.[57]

Acceptance of the proposal demonstrated that Thatcher could no longer resist the pressure of Hurd and Major for British engagement in the monetary debate (and the wider aspect of Community developments), and provided the government with a mechanism for alliance-building, as well as ensuring that the pre-eminence of the City continued. At the same time it provided a mechanism for creating harmony within the Conservative Party because a majority of the parliamentary party could unite behind it, since prior to its announcement no such instrument existed.[58] That was because pro-European MPs could state that the plan was a route to a single currency while the more sceptical MPs could emphasise that it was a means of keeping monetary autonomy, and crucially both would be singing the same tune. As John Major himself noted, the plan 'would ease the divisions opening up in the Conservative Party' (Major, 1999: 151).

The reality that Thatcher had begrudgingly accepted the hard ECU plan, and that the government was not in fact fully united behind this initiative, was demonstrated by a House of Commons statement on 28 June, in which she stressed that the government had yet to agree to Stage 3 of the Delors Report.[59] With his hands tied, Major continued to advocate the proposal to other member states,[60] though all chances of it succeeding had been eliminated by Thatcher' statement. As a former Foreign and Commonwealth Office official noted, 'it would have only been acceptable to other member states if it had been put forward as a sensible second stage of a three stage EMU to which everyone would have been committed, as opposed to being put forward as an alternative plan'.[61] The plan was therefore criticised from within and outwith government.[62] Major would later state that Thatcher's 'comments made people believe that she saw it . . . as a diversion or wrecking tactic. So, as a result of her statement, did our European partners' (Major, 1999: 152).

In many respects Thatcher's viewpoint reflected her inability to consider the need to establish a policy that would unite the Conservative Party. For her, the hard ECU policy was viewed in terms of Britain's relationship with Europe, while for Major it was firstly a means of uniting the party. This distinction between Thatcher and Major is a significant one, and highlighted Major's awareness of his own future vulnerability as Prime Minister. He would later be criticised for taking too much time for establishing Cabinet consensus, but this reflected his need to govern the party. By contrast, Thatcher lost the leadership of the Conservative Party because she had failed to govern it adequately.

The government's growing scepticism towards EMU was despite the fact that there was increasing support for the project within Britain, with the Director-General of the CBI, John Banham, stating that '[W]e believe that a single currency is good for Britain' during a press conference at a CBI Conference in Glasgow on 5 October 1990.[63] The government and the Bank of England, however, continued to advocate the hard ECU proposal based on an evolutionary transition.[64] The reality of the situation was that there existed a clear division between the government and the other member states over monetary policy and EC affairs in general.[65] Britain's belief that EMU did not necessitate a single currency and joint monetary policy contrasted with the broad consensus among the other member states on the fundamental elements of EMU.[66] Such was the extent of the desire of member states to proceed to monetary union, that agreement was reached at the October 1990 Rome European Council[67] on the necessary points that the EMU treaty amendment would cover.[68] The fact that EMU would be more or less a reality irked Thatcher, with her frustration at this development boiling over in a Commons debate on the Rome European Council. Reflective of her independent and increasingly anti-European streak, she announced that the hard ECU plan – whose aim was to tie the Conservative Party together – would be unlikely to be used throughout the Community. The Chancellor, John Major, 'nearly fell off the bench' and reflected that 'with this sentence she wrecked months of work and preparation' (Major, 1999: 176; Dyson and Featherstone, 1999: 632–3). Nevertheless, for some her comments were a welcome development, with Norman Lamont saying that he 'wholly supported her approach' (Lamont, 1999: 111). This was itself reflective of the differences of opinion that would subsequently emerge between himself and Major (Major, 1999: 293; Lamont, 1999: 21).[69]

Conclusion

In retrospect, it is evident that the Rome meeting represented one of the low points of British European foreign policy. Government ministers had certainly been taken by surprise by the speed of developments at the European level.[70] That this took place was not the fault of officials in the Foreign and

Commonwealth Office (the lead government department on European affairs), who had in fact repeatedly informed ministers of the likely developments at the summit meeting.[71] By that stage, British policy resembled something of a farce on European affairs, there being no coherent leadership as to the direction that the ship of state should take. Some may say that the government should not have even bothered to pander to the interests of those who favoured some form of constructive engagement. But the fact of the matter is that to cut the nation off from this important policy discussion would have been a dereliction of responsibility regarding the country's future direction. To just say 'no' could have caused great harm, and we must remember that significant British interests, especially industry and banking, favoured some form of input to the talks by the government. That is not to say that they were smitten with EMU, and in any case a single currency was not likely to happen until the end of the decade.

Therefore, the conclusion of officials, some government ministers and many sectors of the business community was that EMU was going to happen with or without Britain. A cursory glance at our history books tells us that Britain had often been faced with this scenario in the post-1945 era and, on most occasions, such as the Treaty of Rome negotiations, has decided to get involved after the rules of the game had been agreed. Thus a viewpoint that was strongly held at this time was that Britain would in the end have to participate in EMU, and consequently those pressurising for some form of government engagement considered that Britain should have significant input into the design process. This was all the more important as there were many vague details, including the nature of the Delors Report's prescription for Stage 2 of monetary union. It is also important to remember that Britain traditionally displayed an appetite and ability to deal with the nuts and bolts of policy-making, contrasting with the tendency of other European nations such as France to take a broader strategic view. Real input by Britain was still a possibility.

Nevertheless, by the time the delegations arrived at the December 1990 Rome European Council[72] to launch the intergovernmental conferences on monetary union and political union, there were already two main EMU negotiating papers on the table. These were the Committee of Central Bank Governors' draft statute for the European System of Central Banks[73] and the 21 August 1990 Communication of the European Commission.[74] That these documents were adopted obviously inflicted great harm on the British negotiating position.[75] How, for instance, could the government pressurise for the use of the hard ECU when such an approach was no longer on the agenda? And although some governments did warm to the hard ECU proposal, notably Spain, others were not supportive, particularly Germany.

So what were the problems that the proposal suffered from? In the first instance, usage of the hard ECU was not compulsory and it did not bring the benefits of establishing a single currency. Thus, although the proposal envisaged the creation of a common monetary institution, the development of the ECU as a European single currency, and the coordination of exchange rates with regard to third countries, it made no attempt to reduce differences between national monetary instruments.[76] If anything, the presence of a thirteenth currency complicated matters. The Bundesbank was fearful of a competition between the Deutschmark and a harder currency.[77] We can also see that the proposal had not crystallised until quite late in the day, resulting in it not being put on the negotiating table at a time when it might have cultivated wider support.[78] A further factor was that the British government had for some time been negative on a whole range of Community policies. Why then should its views be taken seriously, especially when a British contribution was more likely to be a ploy to influence and stall events rather than reflective of a desire to commit to EMU?[79] As John Major would later reflect, 'We were sidelined. We were not in the ERM. We were not in favour of a single currency. We were out of the debate' (Major, 1999: 150–1). The hard ECU proposal was consequently treated with suspicion,[80] thereby ensuring that the government's alternative to the Delors prescription for EMU had disappeared. Crucially the plan highlighted the government's lack of understanding of the political implications of EMU, which certain member states, such as France, had advocated.[81] This negotiating position on EMU was not even supported by certain strata of the business sector which believed that the development of the Single Market was 'hamstrung' by the imperfections of having different currencies, with the transaction costs involved throughout the Community estimated at £10 billion per annum, while the benefits of exchange rate stability in the ERM could boost UK exports by £3 billion.[82]

John Major's appointment as Prime Minister in November 1990 had therefore not dramatically reversed British negotiating tactics, though it did permit ministers to have greater freedom in selling the hard ECU proposal to their European colleagues (Dyson and Featherstone, 1999: 633–4). He was aware of the need to engage in constructive dialogue with European leaders, having seen at first hand Thatcher's dogmatic negotiating style (see Box 6.6). He had considered that 'The Prime Minister [Thatcher] was flatly opposed to a single currency, and appeared to me to have no idea of how committed our partners were to it. She was confident it wouldn't work, and seemed to believe that if she asserted that it would fail, then it would fail. She did not see the need to confront their determination' (Major, 1999: 151). Thus, Major's leadership victory brought with it the possibility of new alliances with member states that had been previously lukewarm in their friendship when Thatcher was in power. The test for Major was to bring Britain back into the European fold without causing domestic difficulties, and, as Chapter 7 makes clear, this was a difficult balancing act that would dominate the rest of his period as Prime Minister.

BOX 6.6

Thatcher to Major

Elements of continuity included the separation of economic and political integration. The benefits of Community membership were perceived in pragmatic terms of the national interest, including the protection of national sovereignty. The period after the SEA was crucial for Britain as the government faced deeper integration by means of the Delors model of ever closer union. Both the Thatcher and Major governments attempted to create alternatives to the Delors model, based on a British perception of independent nation-states. In this context, Margaret Thatcher wanted to veto further integration and refused to compromise on sovereignty. Her style of diplomatic bargaining became increasingly central to the British position within the Community and was perceived to be hostile. By contrast, Major aimed to negotiate suitable agreements that would protect British interests. But despite such positive tones, his position was quickly undermined by Eurosceptics at home, while the traditional concept of London being 'an awkward partner' meant that other nations did not warm to this vision.

Key points

- France and Germany were the key member states which provided the leadership and momentum behind monetary union in the late 1980s.

- Britain was slow to recognise the desire for monetary union that was held by other member states. Prime Minister Thatcher was sceptical as to whether the study group on monetary union which produced the Delors Report would amount to anything significant.

- Although there was concern within the Bank of England and among industry and business circles (especially in the City of London) that Britain should become engaged in the debate on monetary union, throughout 1988 and 1989 the government was principally concerned with its position towards the ERM.

- When the government realised the importance of getting involved in the monetary union talks, its primary motivation was in slowing down the pressure for EMU within other member states. This strategy was reflected in the advancement of the hard ECU proposal.

- Despite advancing the hard ECU proposal, there was little support for it among other member states who essentially perceived it as a 'wrecking ball' rather than a constructive approach.

- By the end of 1990 the British government was for all intents and purposes isolated from key debates on monetary union. This was a product of an initial lack of appreciation of the seriousness of the proposal as well as part of the wider reluctance of Britain fully to commit to the European project.

Questions

1. Why did the issue of European integration prove increasingly divisive for the Conservative Party after 1984?

2. 'Prime Minister Thatcher was perfectly realistic in thinking that EMU would not result in any developments that would be of a significant nature.' Discuss.

3. Why was Britain opposed to further European integration in the field of monetary policy?

4. 'Doomed from the outset': is this a correct assessment of the Conservative government's strategy towards the Delors Committee?

5. To what extent did the British 'competing currencies plan' have any chance of being accepted as a favourable option by other member states?

6. 'The hard ECU proposal was representative of the extent to which the British government was isolated from key debates on monetary union.' Discuss.

7. What were the main advantages of the hard ECU proposal for the Conservative government?

8. Assess the role of the Delors Committee in advancing the cause of monetary union.

9. Is monetary union the product of the 'spillover' effect of European integration?

10. 'Eyes closed': is this an accurate description of the views of British policy-makers towards monetary union in the late 1980s?

Further reading

Blair, Alasdair (1999) *Dealing with Europe: Britain and the Negotiation of the Maastricht Treaty*, Aldershot: Ashgate, Chapter 7.

Dyson, Kenneth (1994) *Elusive Union: The Process of Economic and Monetary Union in Europe*, Harlow: Longman.

Dyson, Kenneth and Featherstone, Kevin (1999) *The Road to Maastricht: Negotiating Economic and Monetary Union*, Oxford: Oxford University Press, Chapters 2, 4, 14.

Forster, Anthony (1999) *Britain and the Maastricht Negotiations*, Basingstoke: Macmillan, Chapter 2.

Gros, Daniel and Thygesen, Niels (1998) *European Monetary Integration*, 2nd edn, Harlow: Longman, Chapter 10.

Howe, Geoffrey (1994) *Conflict of Loyalty*, London: Macmillan, Chapters 38–9 and 43.

Lawson, Nigel (1992) *The View From No. 11*, London: Bantam Press, Chapters 71–7.

Levitt, Malcolm and Lord, Christopher (2000) *The Political Economy of Monetary Union*, Basingstoke: Macmillan, Chapter 4.

Major, John (1999) *The Autobiography*, London: HarperCollins, Chapters 6–9.

Stephens, Philip (1996) *Politics and the Pound*, London: Macmillan.

Thatcher, Margaret (1993) *The Downing Street Years*, London: HarperCollins, Chapters 24–5.

Notes

[1] John Major would later comment that 'it became clear to me that our European partners were much more set on implementing the Delors Report on Economic and Monetary Union – and moving to a single currency – than I had realised. Whilst we regarded the move as a fanciful long-term ambition faced by enormous problems, they were regarding it as more or less a *fait accompli*': Major, 1999:149.

[2] *Financial Times*, 28 November 1990.

[3] *Bull. EC*, Vol. 18, 11–1985, point 1.1.1.

[4] *Bull. EC*, Supplement 2, 1986.

[5] Private information. The government considered that EMU was a 'damaging diversion' from the single market. Nigel Lawson, *What Sort of Financial Area?*, speech at the Royal Institute for International Affairs, 25 January 1989, London: HM Treasury, p. 17. The Institute of Directors reiterated this point. See memorandum submitted by the Institute of Directors to the *House of Lords Select Committee on the European Communities*, HL3 (1989–90) para. 48, pp. 129–30.

[6] Private information.

[7] Ibid.

[8] *Bull. EC*, Vol. 21, 6–1988, points 1.1.1–1.1.4, and point 3.4.1 (no. 5 – monetary union).

[9] Private information. For an overview of Robin Leigh-Pemberton see *Financial Times*, 25 June 1990, p. 40.

[10] Private information.

[11] Ibid.

[12] Ibid.

[13] *Bull. EC*, Vol. 21, 6–1988, point 3.4.1(5).

[14] Private information.

[15] Ibid.

[16] Ibid.

[17] Ibid.

[18] There has been, over the years, a widespread misunderstanding over the role of the Bundesbank as a separate organ of the state, which can decide policy on its own. This is, in fact, not the case. While the statutes of the Bundesbank require it to work for priorities such as low inflation, such objectives are within the framework of a policy established by the German government. For example, in the course of German monetary union the Bundesbank did not approve of the rate of exchange that the Ostmark was given against the Deutschmark. But once the policy had been decided by the German government the Bundesbank set about ensuring that the decision was implemented in a way that least undermined the value of the Deutschmark.

[19] The Delors Committee met eight times between September 1988 and April 1989 at the Basel offices of the Bank for International Settlements.

[20] Private information. *Financial Times*, 25 June 1990, p. 40.

[21] Private information.

[22] Ibid.

[23] Committee for the Study of Economic and Monetary Union, *Report on Economic and Monetary Union in the European Community* (the Delors Report), Luxembourg, Office for Official Publications of the European Communities, August 1989. The committee consisted of the 12 central bank governors, supplemented by Miguel Boyer, a Spanish banker and former Finance Minister; Frans Andriessen, a European Commissioner; Niels Thygesen, a Danish economist; and Alexandre Lamfalussy, the Belgian general manager of the Bank for International Settlements. Also HM Treasury, 1988–89, pp. xv–xvii, and *Bull. EC*, Vol. 22, 4–1989, Report of the Committee for the Study of Economic and Monetary Union, points 1.1.1–1.1.5.

[24] *Bank of England Quarterly Bulletin*, August 1989, Vol. 29, No. 3, pp. 368–74.

[25] The conditions were a reduction in the inflation rate, abolition of all restrictions on capital movements, complete liberalisation of financial services, completion of the internal market and a stronger Community competition policy by reducing state aids.

[26] The job of the presidency is to guide member states towards a compromise position, having taken into consideration their different points of view and the possible conflicts between them.

[27] *Bull. EC*, Vol. 22, 12–1989.

[28] The April 1990 Dublin European Council noted that German unification was 'a positive factor in the development of Europe as a whole and of the Community in particular'. *Bull. EC*, Vol. 23, 4–1990, point 1.3. On the April 1990 Dublin European Council see speech by Charles Haughey on 16 May to the European Parliament, reproduced in *Bull. EC*, Vol. 23, 5–1990, point 2.3.1.

[29] *Bull. EC*, Vol. 23, 4–1990, point 1.1.1.

[30] Ibid., point 1.7(ii).

[31] Ibid., point 1.5, pp. 8–9, and *Agence Europe*, No. 5353 (n.s.), 19 October 1990, p. 7. Also 'European Council, Conclusions of the Presidency, Rome, 27 and 28 October 1990', *Europe Documents*, No. 1658, 30 October 1990, point I.2, and *The Economist*, 3 November 1990, pp. 57–8.

[32] *House of Commons Official Report*, 30 October 1990, col. 870, and *The Economist*, 3 November 1990.

[33] *Bank of England Quarterly Bulletin*, August 1989, Vol. 29, No. 3, pp. 368–74.

[34] Lawson, *What Sort of Financial Area?*, p. 15. This issue was also emphasised in an explanatory memorandum by HM Treasury to House of Lords Select Committee on the European Communities, *The Delors Committee Report*, HL3 (1989–90) para. 17, p. 55 of Sub-Committee A Evidence.

[35] HM Treasury, 1989. Also John Major, *House of Commons Official Report*, Vol. 159, No. 166, cols. 488–95 and *Survey of Current Affairs*, Vol. 19, No. 11, London: HMSO, November 1989, pp. 408–9. Also *Bank of England Quarterly Bulletin*, February 1990, Vol. 30, No. 1, pp. 62–7.

[36] HM Treasury, 1989, paras 23 and 38 respectively. The inability to accept the irrevocable fixing of exchange rates was because the evolutionary approach would either create a situation whereby one national monetary policy would dominate or where there would continue to exist a number of different policies within the Community. This point was outlined by European Commission vice-president, Henning Christophersen, in a document presented to the IGC reflection group on 21 March 1990. Henning Christophersen, 'Economic and Monetary Union: The Economic Rationale and Design of the System', *Europe Documents*, No. 1604/1605, 23 March 1990, point III.1.

[37] These points were raised in a letter by Sir Michael Butler to the Chancellor of the Exchequer, John Major, on 7 November 1989, paras. 2 and 3 especially.

[38] *Bull. EC*, Vol. 22, 12–1989, Economic and Monetary Union, point 1.1.11; *Agence Europe*, 9 December 1989; and *Survey of Current Affairs*, Vol. 19, No. 12, London: HMSO, December 1989, pp. 457–9.

[39] Some four months prior to Strasbourg, in August 1989, Paul Richards of Samuel Montagu Bank had suggested that the ECU could be transformed into a 'hard ECU' as a means of providing an alternative to monetary union, rather than a route to monetary union. Interview with Sir Michael Butler.

[40] This was highlighted in correspondence between key individuals and ministers involved in the EMU debate in November 1989. Based on private information.

[41] The committee was set up in 1988 as a coordinating mechanism between the government and the City of London to ensure that a consensus emerged on policy issues in the run-up to 1992. The committee brought together senior personnel from the City with senior personnel from Whitehall and the Bank of England. The chairman of the committee was Sir Michael Butler of Hambros Bank, the deputy chairman was Sir Michael Franklin, and the secretary was Nigel Carter from the Bank of England.

[42] *The Guardian*, 1 July 2000, p. 24 and *The Guardian*, 4 August 2000, p. 21.

[43] *Financial Times*, 23 June 1990, p. 6.

[44] Private information.

[45] Ibid.

[46] Paper by the chairman considered at the European Committee of the BIEC on 27 March 1990, *Stage 2 of Economic and Monetary Union*, para. 3.

[47] Ibid. Butler also presented the paper on the usage of the ECU by Paul Richards, *The Next Stage in an Evolutionary Approach to Monetary Union*, 28 March 1990.

[48] Correspondence with Foreign and Commonwealth Office official.

[49] *Financial Times*, 12 June 1990, p. 1, 13 June 1990, p. 2 and 18 July 1990, p. 14.

[50] These points were highlighted in a letter from Sir Michael Butler to Charles Powell on 11 June 1990. The government's desire to slow the pace of the EMU negotiations, and avoid a rapid move to EMU, was emphasised by John Major in a speech in London to the German Chamber of Commerce and Industry. *Financial Times*, 13 June 1990, p. 2.

[51] The accepted formula was that 'a common currency which could become a single currency one day if the Governments and Parliaments so wished'. Private information. Also *Financial Times*, 9 July 1990, p. 8, 12 July 1990, p. 20, 17 July 1990, p. 7, 21 June 1990, p. 12, and 18 June 1990, p. 20.

[52] Nicholas Ridley resigned from the government less than one month later, as a result of his comments on Germany. His resignation suggested that Thatcher's grip on policy

had been loosened, although an equally Eurosceptical MP and Thatcherite supporter, in the form of Peter Lilley, replaced him. For an analysis of the Ridley resignation see *Financial Times*, 16 July 1990, pp. 1 and 6.

[53] John Major, speech to the German Industry Forum, 20 June 1990. Also *Survey of Current Affairs*, Vol. 20, No. 7, London: HMSO, July 1990, pp. 242–3; *Treasury Bulletin*, London: HMSO, Summer 1990, pp. 14–16; *Financial Times*, 21 June 1990, p. 1, and *The Economist*, 23 June 1990, p. 64.

[54] The issue of low inflation was important for Major who had been concerned that a European Central Bank would not necessarily adopt 'rigorous anti-inflationary policies', while the move to a single currency would involve the loss of control over interest rate policy or exchange rate policy. Major also emphasised the need for prior economic convergence before a single currency could be adopted, a stance also echoed by the Governor of the Bank of England.

[55] House of Commons, *Treasury and Civil Service Committee, European Monetary Union*, HC620 (1989–90) paras. 1–2, pp. 7–8. Also *Bank of England Quarterly Bulletin*, Vol. 30, No. 3, August 1990, pp. 374–7.

[56] House of Lords Select Committee on the European Communities, *Economic and Monetary Union and Political Union*, HL88 (1989–90)I, para. 55, pp. 24–5, and press release by Bank of England, 21 June 1990, 'EMU: Beyond Stage 1 – The Hard ECU', in House of Lords Select Committee on the European Communities, *Economic and Monetary Union and Political Union*, HL88 (1989–90)II – Evidence. On Hard ECU, also see *Treasury Bulletin*, Autumn 1990, pp. 1–9.

[57] House of Lords Select Committee on the European Communities, *Economic and Monetary Union and Political Union*, HL88 (1989–90)I, para. 55, pp. 24–5, and press release by Bank of England, 21 June 1990, 'EMU: Beyond Stage 1 – The Hard ECU', in House of Lords Select Committee on the European Communities, *Economic and Monetary Union and Political Union*, HL88 (1989–90)II – Evidence. On hard ECU, also *Treasury Bulletin*, Autumn 1990, pp. 1–9.

[58] Private information.

[59] *House of Commons Official Report*, 28 June 1990, col. 493. Also cols. 489–93 for other comments on hard ECU. Also *Financial Times*, 19 June 1990, p. 12.

[60] For example, John Major presented the hard ECU proposal at the October 1990 Rome European Council meeting. *House of Commons Official Report*, 23 October 1990, col. 203.

[61] Private information.

[62] *Financial Times*, 22 June 1990, p. 1 and 3 July 1990, p. 1.

[63] *Agence Europe*, No. 5364 (n.s.), 5–6 November 1990, p. 15.

[64] *Bank of England Quarterly Bulletin*, Vol. 30, No. 4, November 1990, pp. 500–2, and *Bank of England Quarterly Bulletin*, Vol. 31, No. 1, February 1991, pp. 43–8.

[65] *Financial Times*, 22 June 1990, p. 20. It notes that 'Ever since the Madrid summit of June 1989, the UK Treasury has been searching for the philosopher's stone: a proposal that would turn Mrs Thatcher's opposition to Mr Delors' vision of economic and monetary union into an acceptable alternative to it. The proposals from the Chancellor of the Exchequer represent another failure, but not an irredeemable one.'

[66] 'Economic and Monetary Union: Report by Mr Carli to the European Council', *Europe Documents*, No. 1657, 25 October 1990, and *Agence Europe* (n.s.) No. 5355, 22–23 October 1990, p. 7.

[67] *Bull. EC*, Vol. 10, 1990, point 1.5, pp. 8–9.

[68] *The Guardian*, 26 October 1990; *The European*, 26 October 1990; *House of Commons Official Report*, cols. 870–1 and *Daily Telegraph*, 30 October 1990.

[69] Major noted that 'although Norman had helped me win the leadership contest in 1990, our relationship was a working one which never ripened into personal friendship, affable in manner and engaging company though he was. Perhaps some of the grit that was to cause the ugly split between us after Black Wednesday was already present.'

[70] *Bull. EC*, Vol. 23, 10–1990, point 1.1.9. Thatcher was furious when she returned from Rome because she believed that the EC leaders were debating issues that were not relevant to present economic difficulties that the member states faced, such as the World Trade talks.

[71] Correspondence with Foreign and Commonwealth Office official.

[72] *Bull. EC*, Vol. 23, 12–1990, point 1.10.

[73] 'Draft Statute of the European System of Central Banks and of the European Central Bank', *Europe Documents*, No. 1669/1670, 8 December 1990. Also *Agence Europe* (n.s.), No. 5369, 14 November 1990, p. 10. The governors of the 12 central banks reached an agreement on the basic principles of the future European Central Bank in the context of EMU in Basle on 13 November 1990.

[74] European Commission's 'Draft Treaty Amending the Treaty Establishing the European Economic Community with a View to Achieving Economic and Monetary Union', *Europe Documents*, No. 1675/1676, 20 December 1990. Also the accompanying European Commission document, 'Comments on the Draft Treaty on Economic and Monetary Union', *Europe Documents*, No. 1678/79, 27 December 1990.

[75] *The Guardian*, 14 December 1990, p. 1.

[76] The hard ECU proposal provided for national control over monetary policy without developing multilateral cooperation between central banks. It consequently reflected Britain's vision of an open Europe which other countries could join, with this form of monetary union not involving the erection of new barriers. But the proposals did not lend themselves to a rapid transition to monetary union that was necessary to move from Stages 1 to 3. Such a desire to move quickly to Stage 3 was because the cost/benefit analysis suggested there would be greater benefits from monetary union in comparison to an economic union, particularly through the adoption of a single currency.

[77] Private information.

[78] Ibid.

[79] House of Lords Select Committee on the European Communities, *Economic and Monetary Union and Political Union*, HL88 (1989–90)1, para. 72(v), p. 30. Also statement by Lord Alexander of Weedon, the chairman of National Westminster Bank plc, para. 47, pp. 21–2.

[80] Private information.

[81] Ibid.

[82] David Lees, chairman of GKN and of the CBI European Monetary Union Working Group, cited in House of Lords Select Committee on the European Communities, *Economic and Monetary Union and Political Union*, HL88 (1989–90)1, para. 37, p. 19.

CHAPTER 7

Negotiating monetary union: 1991–1992

Objectives

- Outline the lack of support for Britain's negotiating proposals on monetary union.
- Demonstrate the extent to which John Major was constrained by divisions within the Conservative Party.
- Examine the implication of Britain's negotiation of an opt-out from the single currency.
- Explain the details concerning the mechanics of monetary union.
- Demonstrate the extent to which the Maastricht Treaty reflected British interests on monetary union and highlight the implications of government policy.

Introduction

We have seen in previous chapters the difficulty that surrounded the formation of the government's position as regards entry to the Exchange Rate Mechanism (ERM) and its negotiating stance towards Economic and Monetary Union (EMU). That political factors took precedence in shaping the British negotiating strategy is further demonstrated in this chapter, which examines Britain's involvement in the EMU negotiations that formed part of the Treaty on European Union.

A hard ECU to sell

Just as Britain had been slow to respond to the Delors Committee, it had been largely isolated in the preparatory work that preceded these talks. As with many other areas of Community affairs, the then Conservative government did not want to be forced to adopt policies that clashed with its domestic political objectives. It was therefore inevitable that the majority pressure among other member states for the creation of a single currency would cause difficulties for British negotiators who considered that only Parliament could decide when, or if, the nation would take part in monetary union. The great fear within Whitehall was that Britain should not, and moreover could not, be committed to (or locked into) the objective of a single currency (Lamont, 1999: 116). In essence, the government did not want to change its ability to alter domestic economic activity, for example by decreasing or increasing interest and inflation rates. Most policy-makers were, however, realistic enough to consider that a single currency would be established, though without British participation.

In contrast to this negative outlook, most of the other member states favoured the adoption of a single currency. But the very establishment of a single currency that spanned many different countries raised issues over the design of the system. After all, not all of the countries within the Community shared similar economic fortunes, with, for instance, Greece, Portugal and Spain not mirroring the economic development and wealth of Germany, or for that matter Britain and France. A single currency would have to deal with these economic differences, while the very rules that established the criteria for participation would have to reflect the need for economic stability and take account of the need to include as many members as possible. This question of inclusion and exclusion proved to be a particularly thorny element of the monetary union talks.

Of the states that demanded the setting of tough criteria to determine which countries were best suited to take part in EMU, Germany was the most vociferous. Its insistence on strict convergence criteria was not because it was antagonistic towards those countries that did not share its economic fortunes. Rather, it was based on the hard reality that the Deutschmark was the strongest of all the currencies within the Community and that any replacement of it would have to be as strong and as stable. For Germany, therefore, economic rigour took precedence over political niceties. By contrast, Italy was far more lenient towards a set of tough convergence criteria. This was itself a reflection of Italian national politics, as the establishment of tough conditions impinged on the nation's ability to proceed to EMU as a result of the government's indebtedness. In a different vein, Greece was realistic enough to accept that its economic situation did not lend itself to progressing towards a single currency.

Although the British government had not been successful in obtaining a great deal of support for its hard ECU proposal in the period prior to the negotiations, that did not stop ministers and officials advancing the plan when the talks commenced. The realists within government considered that it had the greatest opportunity for success in influencing the transition from Stages 2 to 3 of EMU, rather than offering an alternative route to a single currency. To that end the government put forward the hard ECU text at the very start of the intergovernmental conference discussions in early January 1991.[1] Somewhat predictably, there was not a great deal of support for the plan, with the Bundesbank

---

BOX 7.1

Hard ECU proposal

The hard ECU proposal did not envisage the creation of a single European currency. Rather, it was a common, or parallel, currency proposal. The idea was to transform the ECU into a currency that could be used in competition with national currencies. The very use of the term 'hard ECU' signified that it could not be devalued. In this sense, if there was an increase in the value of any of the currencies that made up the ECU, then there would be an increase in the weighting of that currency in the basket that constituted the ECU. Thus, the value of the ECU would not change. The idea was supposed to be attractive to business, whilst it also offered the government an evolutionary path to monetary union. There would therefore be time for the government to revise its proposals and get more involved in the monetary union discussions. But the very feature that made the proposal attractive to Britain was also its downfall. For instance, the proposal only envisaged the creation of a parallel currency and therefore there would still remain national currencies. But for other member states, the whole idea behind the monetary union project was the creation of a single currency, and whilst the hard ECU offered some movement in this direction through an evolutionary approach, it crucially did not resolve the problem of there being other currencies in circulation.

---

providing the fiercest opposition. This was not surprising, as the hard ECU proposal ran counter to the Bundesbank's negotiating objectives, as it created the possibility of a two-tier Europe by weakening pressure for economic cohesion among the existing 12 member states.[2] This was because the hard ECU only represented a thirteenth currency that would operate in parallel with national currencies, with governments therefore not having to adhere to stringent economic conditions (see Box 7.1). That opposition to the hard ECU plan was obvious from the start of the talks highlighted the degree of difficulty the government faced in attempting to influence the negotiations.

The lukewarm response that the hard ECU proposal received from officials was duplicated at ministerial discussions, with member states not being prepared to challenge the objectives set at Rome in October 1990 (when Britain had been isolated).[3] And while some elements of the hard ECU plan were reflected in French[4] and Spanish[5] texts, this did not constitute wholehearted support on any deviation from the goal of a single currency. The effect of this was for the hard ECU plan to vanish to the margins of the negotiations from February 1991 onwards. This state of affairs was influenced by the agreement in Brussels on 28 January that the European Commission Working Paper would act as the basis for discussions on EMU.[6] The fact of the matter was that the majority of member states had not responded well to the proposal, and although the Spanish submission involved some elements of the plan, they did not resemble it. This situation was acknowledged by Treasury mandarins who were aware that 'from spring 1991 onwards there was not the political willingness on the part of the other member states to accept the hard ECU'.[7]

Crucially, Germany[8] and the Netherlands did not support the plan and the only potential allies were the southern European members of the Community, such as Portugal and Spain. Therefore, the problem that the government faced was that it could not obtain enough member states to support it, while those that might have given allegiance did not carry enough negotiating influence for such an alliance to win. This meant that there was little, if any, likelihood of the plan being successful. The reality of this situation did not stop the government from continuing to advocate the merits of the hard ECU in the monetary union discussions. Of the reasons that influenced this course of action, the government was consciously aware that if it tore up its only negotiating proposal at such an early juncture, then it would have had even less of an input in the monetary union talks. A further reason, which is also reflective of the domestic political constraints imposed upon the government at this time, was that the hard ECU plan provided the linchpin that kept the Conservative Party together. Its removal from the negotiating table could thus have been conceived as defeat by those MPs who favoured a Eurosceptic approach. A by-product of this would have been to stir up concern over other areas of the negotiations. The flawed hard ECU plan nevertheless managed to inject some form of unity into a rebellious Conservative Party, and acted as a damage limitation exercise for a government that had little of a constructive nature to offer in these discussions. Thus the government was from the very beginning of the negotiations hamstrung by not being able to drop policies, such as the hard ECU, which had not gained widespread acceptance, because such a course of action would be viewed as a defeat. At the same time, the government could not adopt a more flexible approach due to the divisions within and outwith the Cabinet, especially from those segments of the parliamentary party that were becoming increasingly sceptical (and vocal) about the reality of a single currency.

As noted earlier, government negotiators also considered that the hard ECU could have some influence on the wider aspects of EMU, especially the institutional design of Stage 2 and the convergence requirements for movement to Stage 3. This was influenced by the fact that a whole range of questions still needed to be answered, including the nature of the transition and the institutional balance. Thus, by maintaining the proposal in public – though privately accepting that it was without influence – the government hoped to affect the EMU debate. Any adherence to the plan did, nevertheless, reflect the fact that the government had little else to offer in this area of the negotiations. Both European and domestic negotiators were aware that British influence in this area of the treaty talks was far less significant than that of Germany. Thus, whereas the government could expect to have its views taken into consideration on such policy discussions as common foreign and security policy (where the military presence of Britain was an important consideration to any European policy), the reverse was true for discussions on EMU (Blair, A., 1998a; 1998b). Maintenance of the hard ECU plan right up to June 1991 therefore became an illusionary objective in the course of the negotiations.[9]

Negotiating an opt-out

Despite publicly adhering to the hard ECU until the summer of 1991, with Douglas Hurd noting 'that some form of hardened ECU will form an important element in Stage 2',[10] the government's priorities had shifted by late February from selling the proposal to that of ensuring that a single currency would not be imposed on Britain.[11] In favouring this course of action, the government advocated a general provision whereby member states would have to seek national ratification before they proceeded to Stage 3 of EMU. While Britain accepted the objective of a single currency, it crucially did not want member states to be locked into a path to EMU. Individual national choice therefore offered maximum flexibility, and contrasted with the situation whereby Britain would have been specifically highlighted in the treaty text as not wanting to proceed to EMU. This strategy was not without its problems, as the government's pursuit of an acceptable opt-out meant that it was less concerned with other aspects of the negotiations, including the timetable for EMU (Grant, 1994: 182).

That Britain did not want to be tied into an imposed future single currency became a central feature of these talks (see Box 7.2).[12] To that extent, at a Finance Ministers' meeting on 12 May 1991, Jacques Delors launched the concept of a 'unilateral declaration' for Britain, which would ensure that Britain would be able to sign the treaty, though any acceptance of a single currency would require a positive vote in the House of Commons.[13] The importance of this strategy was that it would not hinder the other member states' progress towards a single currency, while the very resolution of the question of British participation would permit more time to be spent on other important issues. These included the nature of the transition from Stage 2 to Stage 3 of EMU.[14] But the merits of this plan were far from evident when it was reviewed in Whitehall. The Chancellor of the Exchequer, Norman Lamont, regarded it as premature to discuss this proposal, which had the knock-on effect of marginalising Britain in the discussions on monetary union.[15] There was, nevertheless, some domestic support for the Delors proposal, especially within the European Reform Group, which with 70 MPs was the largest Eurosceptic grouping within

---

BOX 7.2

UK opt-out

Along with Denmark, the Maastricht Treaty made provision for both countries not to be obliged to move to the third stage of monetary union at any time. The ability of the British government to decide whether it wants to proceed to EMU is set out in a protocol attached to the Maastricht Treaty, stating that Britain will not be obliged to move to the third stage of EMU without the approval of government and Parliament. The further condition of a popular vote in a referendum has since been added to these conditions.

the Conservative Party.[16] At the European level, there was greater support for the Delors approach by June, with agreement being reached at a Finance Ministers' meeting that no member state would be obliged to take part in Stage 3, while at the same time no member state could prevent the rest from proceeding to Stage 3.[17]

The importance that Britain attached to not being committed to take part in a single currency was further evidenced at the Luxembourg European Council of June 1991, when Prime Minister Major was insistent that he would not sign an agreement at Maastricht that included a legally binding obligation for Britain to join a single currency. As a measure of the importance of this issue, the other member states, especially France, Germany, Luxembourg and the Netherlands, agreed to this strategy in a private meeting (Dyson and Featherstone, 1999: 654–6).[18] In this context, while it was possible to conceive of the motivation for monetary union having come from the functional spillover effect of the single market programme (Chapters 3 and 6), the negotiations on the nuts and bolts of monetary union were very much shaped by the member states themselves. Such an intergovernmental account thus played down the role of supranational institutions, such as the European Commission (Moravcsik, 1991; 1993). But while it is possible to examine the monetary union negotiations from a standpoint whereby decision-making was the result of intergovernmental negotiations, the British position was nevertheless confined by the absence of an overall strategic plan in which concrete preferences were formulated.

The June meeting was nevertheless a significant development for Britain as it meant that it could not be tied into Stage 3 and, as Douglas Hurd stated, 'the Government will not recommend to this Parliament acceptance of a commitment to a single currency'.[19] In advancing this opt-out policy, Britain was insistent that it did not want to be singled out as a special case through specific treaty text, as reflected in the Dutch draft text of 28 October 1991.[20] The very presence of British objectives within the Dutch text was regarded as a tactical success in London,[21] though the government was incredibly optimistic to consider that such provisions would be reflected in any final treaty document. This was primarily because the creation of a general exemption provision ran counter to France and Germany's desire to establish a framework whereby countries would be locked into a route to EMU.[22] The leaders of both of these countries, Mitterrand and Kohl, were particularly conscious that any deviation from a fixed path to EMU would create a situation whereby countries other than Britain would not participate in a single currency, at which time the very validity of the monetary union project could be called into question. 'Political leadership for Kohl and Mitterrand acted as the vital animating and organising force behind the EMU negotiations, assisted by Delors in oiling the wheels of the process' (Dyson and Featherstone, 1999: 757). As a member of the Council Secretariat commented, 'the British provision was shot down by Chancellor Kohl because he considered the clause unacceptable as he wanted to ensure that once the Treaty had been ratified that the course for EMU was set, without any further involvement of national parliaments'.[23]

A consequence of this was that yet again a British negotiating position had been undermined, with the government realising by early November 1991 that the general exemption clause would not be accepted by a majority of the other member states.[24] This was a view evidenced in Finance Ministers' discussions, with Jean-Claude Juncker, the Luxembourg Finance Minister, noting that a generalised clause 'would take away all the credibility of the current exercise'.[25] The reality of this state of affairs meant that, for Britain, the primary issue became the need to draft an acceptable exemption clause that was particular to its own needs. As a mark of the awareness in London that a specific opt-out text would be necessary, British negotiators had been working on such a strategy since the summer of 1991 (Major, 1999: 279). At a basic level, the idea was to examine what aspects of the treaty the government did not wish to be subjected to and then to include them in the opt-out text.[26] Such an amendment would consequently provide Britain with the ability to decide whether it would take part in Stage 3 of EMU.[27] The effect of this was for the government to proceed to the December 1991 Maastricht European Council having resolved the opt-out issue. As far as Treasury Ministers were concerned, 'when we went into the final rounds of the negotiations, none of us had any serious doubts that we would have an opt-out, whether it was single or general. That was not an issue that bothered any of us at Maastricht.'[28] For Britain, acceptance of the opt-out text by other member states was a 'non-negotiable' issue and, therefore, the intention was to present it at Maastricht as a *fait accompli*.[29]

The mechanics of EMU

Discussion of the details surrounding the path to EMU was aided by the great amount of dialogue that had taken place on this topic prior to the commencement of the negotiations. Within this policy arena, Germany,[30] the Netherlands and Britain advocated tough convergence criteria. The German government and the Bundesbank[31] were particularly eager to ensure that a future EMU did not include countries with a weak currency, as they rightly perceived that this could lead to instability in the system as a whole (see Box 7.3). Germany therefore advocated the need for economic convergence to precede monetary union,

---

BOX 7.3

Convergence

This term refers to the narrowing of the differences between economic conditions in different countries. In this context, such economic indicators as inflation rates, interest rates and government debt tend to be of a similar level in each country.

and that any EMU text should include such priorities as low inflation (Lamont, 1999: 118).[32]

As noted earlier, not all member states shared the opinion that a treaty with specific details should be created. Of those member states that followed a more flexible approach, Italy was particularly concerned that the imposition of a strict route to EMU would place substantial obstacles in its path to participating in a single currency. Such a concern was also supported by the European Commission Directorate General for Economic and Financial Affairs. An effect of this was that the talks on convergence criteria were subject to pressure from two separate negotiating positions. Of the two, the first was that certain member states, such as Italy, considered that the most important aspect for Stage 2 of EMU was the setting of a date for the establishment of a single currency rather than creating specific conditions that countries had to conform to. This broad approach, which placed emphasis on the goal of EMU, advocated that all member states should proceed to a single currency on an automatic basis unless it was blatantly obvious that the essential conditions had not been met. In contrast to this broad-brush approach, other nations, especially Britain and Germany, regarded the conditions for convergence to be crucial and believed that member states should not proceed to EMU unless they had specifically met these conditions, a point that was emphasised at the Luxembourg European Council of 28–29 June 1991.[33] That there was a huge gulf between these negotiating positions meant that a divergence of views was a constant factor throughout the whole of the talks.[34]

The very creation of EMU also necessitated the establishment of institutional apparatus that was capable of effectively managing a single currency. As to the nature of that organisation, the key debate was between France and Germany, with France wanting the new institution to commence operation on 1 January 1994, while Germany preferred it to be established at the final phase of EMU – a position that was also supported by the Netherlands.[35] But this difference of opinion between France and Germany (who had provided much of the impetus behind European integration in recent years), was not perceived to be as serious a problem as the setting of the convergence criteria. Kohl himself commented that 'I am sure that, as always, we will find a common line and take the decision together.'[36] In any event, the central bank negotiations were somewhat depoliticised, as the key players in these talks were the central bank governors themselves. To that extent they managed to get every aspect of their proposals accepted when they were presented in April 1991.[37] Within the discussions, the Bundesbank played a particularly active role, with the President of the Bundesbank, Karl-Otto Pöhl, stating that the future European Central Bank could only be set up 'if and when it has been decided what countries are prepared and capable of creating a monetary union, of establishing irrevocably fixed exchange rates and enacting the necessary transfer of sovereignty'.[38]

As the negotiations progressed into the second half of the year after a summer recess, the question of the transition from Stage 2 to Stage 3 of EMU received far more attention, especially at official and ministerial discussions on 3 and 9

September.[39] This included confirmation of earlier proposals[40] that Stage 2 would commence on 1 January 1994 and agreement on the creation of a European Monetary Institute (EMI).[41] The establishment of growing consensus among the member states, primarily through time constraints, resulted in a significant breakthrough in the EMU negotiations at an informal Finance Ministers' meeting in Apeldoorn on 20–22 September 1991.[42] This included the decision that Stage 2 would begin on 1 January 1994 and that the Council would report within three years on the number of countries that had met the convergence criteria. Agreement was further reached on the point that a minimum of six countries would be required for a single currency to be established, thereby reflecting the consensus that currencies could be expected to unite at once.[43]

On their return from their European foray, British ministers were treated to severe criticism from those on the Conservative backbenches.[44] But despite this public debate, British negotiators were quietly content with the outcome of the monetary union discussions (Lamont, 1999: 129).[45] The fact of the matter was that the proposed EMI strongly reflected the government's earlier plan to establish a European Monetary Fund (EMF) as part of the hard ECU approach.[46] To be sure, the Apeldoorn meeting had put EMU firmly on the cards. For many months, the government had been struggling to hold the tide of support that had gathered around the single currency. And in making its objections known, there was at least some semblance of policy that represented British interests. The drive to a single currency had been decelerated with the establishment of the EMI, while the fact that national central banks would maintain autonomy throughout Stage 2 at least meant that the move towards a single currency and the creation of a European Central Bank was not as stark a process as it could have been (see Box 7.4).

Discussions concerning economic convergence became a primary negotiating topic in the wake of the Apeldoorn meeting. As mentioned earlier, there

---

BOX 7.4

European Central Bank

The ECB was formally constituted on 1 June 1998, with the formal inauguration on 30 June. It is part of the European System of Central Banks in conjunction with the national central banks of EU member states. The primary objective of the ECB is to maintain price stability (as set out in its statute). The basic tasks of the ECB include conducting foreign exchange operations, holding and managing the official foreign reserves of EU member states, and the definition and implementation of monetary policy for the euro area. The independence of the ECB is provided for in Article 107 of the TEU. Article 105a provides the ECB with the exclusive right to authorise the issue of banknotes within the EU, though the actual process of issuing banknotes is shared with national central banks. Finally, only those notes and coins issued by the ECB or national central banks have legal tender within the EU.

BOX 7.5

European Monetary Institute (EMI)

The EMI, which is based in Frankfurt, was established under the terms of the Maastricht Treaty (Article 109f) to coordinate the monetary policy of the central banks of member states within the ESCB. The EMI specifically assisted the preparation of the third stage of EMU, and when the European single currency was introduced in 1999 the EMI was renamed the ECB. The specific task of the EMI was to: (1) strengthen cooperation between member states' central banks; (2) strengthen the coordination of member states' monetary policies so as to ensure price stability; (3) supervise the operation of the EMS; (4) assume the tasks of the European Monetary Cooperation Fund; (5) ensure the maintenance of the use of the ECU.

---

was a substantial difference of views on this policy, with Britain, Germany[47] and the Netherlands advocating a stricter set of conditions than Greece and Italy.[48] The key question was the establishment of a set of economic criteria that had to be adhered to for participation in a single currency, which was both strict enough to placate Germany and also flexible enough to appease the views of Greece and Italy. Apart from these points, the negotiations had yet to resolve the exact role of the EMI, especially with regard to the proposed president of the Institute, the powers to be delegated to it and the resources it should have (see Box 7.5).[49] Key to these discussions was the role of France and Germany, with the former wanting the Institute to be a true embryo for the Central Bank, while the latter did not want to provide it with any monetary power during Stage 2.[50] That issue was eventually resolved at the Brussels Finance Ministers' meeting of 11–12 November. Agreement was reached that the EMI would be given the task of coordinating monetary policies (although they would remain the responsibility of national authorities). It was also agreed that the EMI would be able to present recommendations that could be adopted by a qualified majority vote. Its duties would additionally include establishing the technical preparation of the final stage of EMU. In terms of personnel, the agreed solution was that offered by Spain and Denmark, which noted that the EMI's president and vice-president should be chosen from its council, and the managing director (who would not have voting rights) should be appointed by an EC summit.[51]

The effect of the negotiating outcomes of the previous 11 months of discussion was that the British position had become even more restricted. From the outset of the negotiations, the hard ECU proposal had been ruled out, with the majority of the member states favouring a swift transition to EMU rather than the prolonged and gradual evolution favoured by Britain. As the talks approached the endgame at the December 1991 Maastricht European Council, British negotiators were effectively left hoping that the outcome of the discussions would be as favourable as possible. This included the preference that monetary responsibility would continue to be a national responsibility in

Stage 2 and that the convergence criteria would be both clear and quantifiable. In these remaining weeks prior to the final negotiations at Maastricht as many as possible of the outstanding issues were resolved. Discussion at ministerial level in early December produced agreement on various points, including there being a 'no opting-out' clause in the treaty, as the British and Danish problems would be solved through separate protocols, and that all member states (except Britain) would commit themselves to an 'irreversible process' that would result in the creation of a single currency. Moreover, any movement towards Stage 3 would be based on objective economic criteria listed in the body of the treaty, and those who did not meet the established economic criteria in 1996 would be unable to prevent the others from moving to Stage 3.[52] The path to EMU was therefore well established, both in terms of the mechanics and the proposed timeframe. British negotiators had had little impact in altering the overall project. For British negotiators, the key issue that remained was the need to resolve the exact nature of the British opt-out text.

Into the abyss

As British negotiators set off for the December 1991 Maastricht European Council, the outcome of the preceding months of discussion within the monetary union intergovernmental conference had resolved many of the questions on the establishment of a single currency (Dyson and Featherstone, 1999: 659–63).[53] In many respects, this was also true of the negotiations on political union. Only those issues of an unresolvable nature were therefore left to the finale. For British negotiators, the Maastricht meeting represented the culmination of a great deal of hard work at the domestic and European levels. Although the foregoing analysis has painted a negative picture of the government's stance in the monetary union talks, this position was to a large degree determined by the Prime Minister having to act as a broker between the influence exerted upon

---

BOX 7.6

Biography of John Major (1943–)

Served as Prime Minister from 1990 to 1997, though never a commanding influence over Cabinet and government. He favoured a consensual style of decision-making, which reflected the weakness of his own position. Throughout the 1992–97 Parliament serious divisions over the issue of Europe within the Conservative Party beset his leadership. Having advocated that Britain should be 'at the heart of Europe' in 1991, his own policies reflected a more sceptical viewpoint towards the end of his period as Prime Minister. This was partly as a means of pandering to the interests of Eurosceptics within the Conservative Party (so as to keep it united).

him from members of the Cabinet and from other parliamentary colleagues. John Major considered that 'politically the position I faced was dire' (Major, 1999: 275). In this final phase of the year-long talks, the parliamentary party had become ever more fractious and Major was especially concerned about the need to keep the party united in the face of an impending general election campaign (Blair, A., 1998a: 178). Domestic political priorities were paramount in the Prime Minister's mind (Lawson, 1992: 1013; Major, 1999: 275–6). As he would later comment: 'In a foretaste of what I was to encounter in 1997, I also wanted to prevent my backbenchers from binding themselves to an anti-European posture that could either blow our election chances apart or, if we won, undermine my future negotiating strategy' (Major, 1999: 293).

In advancing to Maastricht, British objectives included the retention of national control over monetary policy throughout Stage 2 and for economic policy to remain a primary responsibility of member states. The government was also clear that it wanted to retain the right to decide if it wanted to progress towards a single currency.[54] The government also stated that the arrangements should be based upon the principles of free competition and open markets. The fourth, and last, condition was that it retained the right to decide if it wanted to move to a single currency and monetary policy. At Maastricht it was decided that the remaining restrictions on capital flows should be abolished during Stage 1 of EMU (1990–94) and that direct central bank lending to the public sector would be terminated.[55] It was also agreed that Stage 2 would commence on 1 January 1994 when the responsibilities of the Committee of Central Bank Governors of EC central banks would be transferred to the new European Monetary Institute (EMI). And while the responsibility for monetary policy would remain with member states during Stage 2, there would be a strengthening in the co-ordination of national monetary policies. Some of these outcomes therefore reflected British objectives. Others, however, did not.

One of the points that Britain had been opposed to was the setting of a deadline for monetary union. Yet this was the very outcome of the Maastricht meeting which stated that Stage 3 would begin no later than 1 January 1999, although with the possibility of commencing in 1997 if there was sufficient economic convergence and a qualified majority vote was in favour (see Box 7.7).[56] This development took British negotiators somewhat by surprise and evidenced the thinking within government that whilst EMU might happen at some stage in the future, it was unlikely in the short term. That this was the very result highlighted the lack of reality surrounding ministerial opinions. Major commented that 'suddenly, the likelihood of the single currency loomed larger' (Major, 1999: 283). In moving to Stage 3 there would be a permanent locking of exchange rates, while a European Central Bank and European System of Central Banks (ESCB) would assume full powers to formulate and implement a single monetary policy, with the single currency being managed by the ECB (see Box 7.8). Whilst the setting of the 1999 deadline ran counter to German desires, its establishment was necessitated by French pressure. Indeed, this was one of the few points that were crucial to French objectives at Maastricht. As Dyson and

---

BOX 7.7

Maastricht Treaty provisions on EMU

The Treaty on European Union established a three-stage approach to monetary union:

1. Stage 1 commenced on 1 July 1990 with the completion of the Single Market.

2. Stage 2 began on 1 January 1994. The European Monetary Institute (EMI) was established to administer the EMS, coordinate national monetary policy and monitor progress towards convergence. The EMI was established as an independent body with a commitment to price stability. It would be replaced by the ECB in Stage 3.

3. Stage 3 involved the irrevocable locking of exchange rates, the adoption of a single currency, and the ESCB and ECB's responsibility for monetary policy. Stage 3 provided the opportunity for EMU to start on 1 January 1997 if the Council decided (by QMV) that a majority of states had met the 'convergence criteria'. This proved not to be possible. The convergence scheme included a deadline date of commencing EMU on 1 January 1999 for states that did meet the criteria. In order to do so, many states, including Italy and France, established a policy of cuts to public expenditure as a means of reducing deficits. Convergence criteria provide for: (1) a high degree of price stability – an average rate of inflation of not more than 1.5% higher than that of the three best performers; (2) a sustainable financial position – a budget deficit of not more than 3% of GDP and a public debt ratio not exceeding 60% of GDP; (3) currency stability – participation in the narrow bands of the ERM for two years without severe tension or devaluation; (4) interest rate convergence – average nominal long-term interest rate not more than 2% higher than that of the three best performing states.

Featherstone note, 'The President's preoccupation was with the political direction of the EMU negotiations, particularly the putting in place of a timetable that would bind future negotiators to make sustained progress and prevent them slipping back into a conservative and cautious approach that would undermine progress towards the final goal of a single currency' (Dyson and Featherstone, 1999: 97). In terms of the convergence criteria, the outcome reflected both the interests of those who wished for tough conditions and those who advocated a more flexible stance. Thus whereas the convergence criteria set out in the protocol on Article 109j provided a detailed set of conditions relating to budget deficits, public debt, long-term interest rates and ERM membership,[57] the treaty provided for flexibility, as allowance could be made if a country's deficit had 'declined substantially and continuously' or 'is only exceptional and temporary' (Article 104c).

The outcome of the monetary union negotiations reflected certain British interests, including the concern that national economies should have attained greater levels of symmetry prior to the establishment of a single currency. Apart from these points, the government faced the additional challenge of securing its EMU opt-out. As previously mentioned, there had been a great deal of pre-

---

BOX 7.8

European System of Central Banks

The ESCB has been responsible for managing monetary union since the start of the third stage of EMU (1 January 1999). The primary objective of the ESCB is to maintain price stability (Article 105(1) of the TEU), while it shares the right to propose new policies with the European Commission. The basic tasks to be carried out through the ESCB are: (1) to define and implement the EU's monetary policy; (2) to conduct foreign exchange operations; (3) to hold and manage member states' official foreign reserves; (4) to promote the smooth operation of the payments system; and (5) to assist with the regular behaviour of policies linked to the prudential supervision of credit institutions and the stability of the financial system. The body comprises the ECB and national central banks and it is independent of national governments and the institutions of the EU. The governing council of the ECB is composed of members of the executive board and the governors of national central banks, with the executive board consisting of four members plus a president and vice-president, all of whom are appointed for eight years by the European Council. By contrast, national central bank governors have to be appointed for a minimum of five years, with the ability to appeal to the Court of Justice in the event of dismissal.

BOX 7.9

Biography of Norman Lamont (1942–)

Served as Chancellor of the Exchequer from 1990 until 1993. During that time he presided over a difficult economic climate which witnessed Britain's exit from the ERM and a dramatic rise in levels of unemployment. His tenure as Chancellor was often subject to controversy. A committed Eurosceptic, he attacked John Major's government after his departure from office.

---

negotiation over Britain's attainment of an opt-out and it was therefore not a great concern to a majority of the governments at the European Council meeting. The reality of this situation was evidenced by the British Chancellor of the Exchequer's belief that the opt-out text would be presented as a non-negotiable issue at a meeting of Finance Ministers on the second day of the Maastricht talks.[58] Not all governments had discussed the acceptance of the opt-out, with the talks at Luxembourg in June being confined to France, Germany, Luxembourg, the Netherlands and the Commission (Dyson and Featherstone, 1999: 655). Norman Lamont's wish to present the opt-out text as a complete and final document was somewhat influenced by his concern that its contents could have been altered in discussion with the other Finance Ministers. But it was surely inevitable that they would want to examine the text. Their governments would after all have to sign the final treaty. This point was lost on Lamont, who stormed out of the Finance Ministers' meeting with the rest of the British negotiating team when his fellow Finance Ministers subjected the text to scrutiny (Dyson and Featherstone, 1999: 660–3). Lamont would later justify such tactics by saying that he needed to discuss this matter with the Prime Minister (Lamont, 1999: 132). Major was taken aback by this development: 'It was an extraordinary way for Norman to behave. He could simply have asked for a recess. Instead, he just upped and went. Yet the opt-out we were seeking was part of the treaty, and every government would have to pass it in their own domestic legislation. The other finance ministers were quite within their rights to query it, and reacted with irritation to Norman's departure' (Major, 1999: 284). Lamont's view was unsurprisingly different: 'At no stage did John Major express the slightest concern. Far from endangering the negotiations, I am quite sure the walk-out had exactly the desired effect' (Lamont, 1999: 132).

The reality of the situation was that the Chancellor had seriously misjudged the temperament of his fellow Finance Ministers and this negotiating juncture reflected on his own status as having been sidelined in the EMU discussions. It was Major (not Lamont) who had discussed the possibility of an opt-out at the June meeting. Moreover, after Lamont's walk-out from the Finance Ministers' discussion, about which the Prime Minister was seemingly furious, it was Major who resolved the matter in a side meeting with Ruud Lubbers and Helmut Kohl (Major, 1999: 286).[59] Both leaders were central to the text's success; Lubbers had the key position of holding the presidency chair while it was unthinkable to obtain any movement on EMU without German consent. In retrospect it is evident that this piece of history was not central to the conclusion of the Maastricht agreement; member states had been aware of Britain's desire to have an independent opt-out since the summer. Prior to Maastricht, Major considered that 'the divisions over economic and monetary union were not my main worry' (Major, 1999: 279). But the way in which the discussions unfolded mirrored Britain's position within the monetary union talks. Even up to the last minute, the government bizarrely considered that it was able to dictate terms. To be sure, agreement at Maastricht was dependent on common accord by all member states, and therefore the government had some negotiating leverage. And while many of the decisions on EMU broadly reflected its own concerns, the same concerns were also held by other states, such as Germany. A confrontational stance towards the end consequently did not reflect the relative lack of influence that the government could bring to bear in these discussions.

Conclusion

From the British perspective the monetary union negotiations were the one area of the intergovernmental conference talks where successive governments had failed to engage sufficiently. John Major had been aware of Prime Minister Thatcher's lack of enthusiasm towards monetary union and the ERM, although

he did manage to persuade her of the merits of joining the latter, however reluctantly (Major, 1999: 142). Such reluctance during the early stages of the talks
on monetary union, including the Delors Report, did considerable damage to
subsequent attempts to culture a constructive British negotiating position. The
attainment of such a position was perfectly achievable; government officials
had after all warned ministers of the impending likelihood of EMU. But ministers treated this desire for monetary union with disdain and did not consider
it likely that a single currency could be achieved. Such decision-taking was particularly reckless. Did not Britain, and especially the City of London, have much
to be concerned about the creation of a single currency? And what about the
voice of business? Prime Minister Thatcher, however, seemed blind to such
views, and only reluctantly considered the hard ECU a worthy proposal.

Such foot-dragging was of course not kept secret. Other member states were
perfectly aware that there was not a consensus within Cabinet as to the government's position on EMU. So when John Major was appointed Prime Minister
he assumed a negotiating position on monetary union that was unlikely to
succeed. By late 1990 the reality of the matter was not whether a single currency
would be created, but when. However, the government (now led by Major)
proved reluctant to accept the possibility of a single currency. Both the hard
ECU and the competing currency plans were launched to challenge this impending reality. Their very construction reflected British foreign policy at the time,
which included the advance of well-thought-out proposals that were often
technically brilliant, but which fundamentally failed to appreciate the political
reality in other member states. This was, of course, partly determined by the
reactive nature of decision-making, whereby initiatives were often advanced
without Britain being party to the groundwork of the negotiations.

In essence, because Britain refused to accept the goal of a single currency, it
was inevitable that its voice would (and could) not be taken seriously in the
monetary union discussions. As part of its defence, the government continued
to advocate the hard ECU proposal long after the policy received any external
support. From then on its ability to shape and influence the negotiations was
minimal, although it was a key player in the tough but flexible convergence
criteria (Blair, A., 1998a: 175–6). There was a realisation that this policy was not
something that the government would be able to alter, or stop the others from
engaging in.[60] But while the government may have come in for criticism for its
naivety in advancing suitable proposals, or for keeping them on the negotiating table for too long, there was some domestic reason for this. The hard ECU
proposal had helped to inject some glue into a fractious Conservative Party, as
did the subsequent unilateral opt-out proposal. Major in effect 'managed his
party with an adroitness that few of his peers could have matched' (Dyson and
Featherstone, 1999: 646).

The attainment of the opt-out was of prime importance to John Major, and
had been assisted by Chancellor Kohl, with Germany having had the strongest
influence in the overall negotiations (Dyson and Featherstone, 1999: 421–2).
The treaty had been largely written on German terms – monetary rigour taking
precedence over economic integration, with the European Central Bank designed

---

BOX 7.10

Treaty on European Union

The TEU is also commonly referred to as the Maastricht Treaty because its terms were agreed at the Maastricht European Council meeting of December 1991. The treaty was actually signed in February 1992, and it established numerous policy objectives, including monetary union to take place by January 1999 and a European Central Bank to administer a single currency and monetary policy.

---

to be as independent as the Bundesbank. That strength and influence in the negotiations assisted Britain at the June Luxembourg European Council, when Major was not 'ambushed' by the acceleration of the negotiations, as Thatcher had been at Rome the previous October.[61] Support from Kohl[62] was substantiated at a bilateral meeting at Chequers on Sunday 9 June,[63] and that relationship proved to be a recurring factor throughout the negotiations (Major, 1999: 267).

To conclude, Britain was effectively bereft of influence on the EMU talks. This was nevertheless a situation that did not seem to bother the government, partly because of the scepticism that the Chancellor of the Exchequer had towards the whole process of monetary union. That scepticism was based on a consideration that it would be difficult for EMU to be reached by 1999, while at the same time Chancellor Lamont believed that the government would at a later stage take a definite decision not to participate in EMU and, therefore, the 'wait and see' approach that the Prime Minister had advocated and obtained would be transformed into a definite stance against EMU. Distrust and distaste for the whole monetary project by Lamont was thereafter emphasised by his refusal to sign the Treaty on European Union in February 1992 (see Box 7.10). This was because he did not consider the text to be worthy of signing, as it firmly stated that a single currency would be established – a development that he was opposed to (Lamont, 1999: 123–6).[64] As will become apparent in Chapter 8, Lamont's Euroscepticism would be further tested by British participation in the ERM.

Key points

- A great deal of work on EMU had already been conducted prior to the commencement of the intergovernmental conference negotiations. During this period Britain had been hesitant to get engaged in the monetary debate and this resulted in the government being somewhat sidelined from key debates on monetary union.

- Once it became evident that the hard ECU proposal lacked support from other member states, a key objective of the government was to ensure that Britain would not be directly committed to adopting a single currency. At the same time, the government also wanted to ensure that the possibility of joining in the future remained open.

- Britain's preference for an opt-out from the third stage of monetary union (adoption of the single currency) had an impact on its overall ability to influence the EMU discussions. Nevertheless, the government did play an important role in certain aspects of the EMU talks, particularly those on the technical nature of the convergence criteria.

Questions

1. How far did the government of John Major achieve its aims in the Maastricht Treaty negotiations?

2. 'The failure of the hard ECU plan meant that the British government was for all intents and purposes isolated from key discussions on monetary union.' Discuss.

3. What were the key benefits of the hard ECU plan for the British government?

4. 'The prime motivation for the adoption of EMU was, and is, political rather than economic.' Discuss.

5. 'The agreement on monetary union was primarily determined by Germany's concern over economic rigour.' Discuss.

6. Assess French objectives in the establishment of a commitment to create a single currency.

7. Why was the setting of convergence criteria an important aspect of the monetary provisions of the Maastricht Treaty?

8. Assess the main features of the Maastricht provisions on EMU.

9. 'The British negotiating position at the Maastricht European Council was constrained by a divided and Eurosceptic Conservative Party.' Discuss.

10. What were the implications of the British opt-out from the third stage of monetary union (establishment of a single currency) for the nation's influence within the European Union?

Further reading

Blair, Alasdair (1998) 'UK Policy Coordination during the 1990–91 Intergovernmental Conference', *Diplomacy and Statecraft*, Vol. 9, No. 2, pp. 160–83.

Blair, Alasdair (1999) *Dealing with Europe: Britain and the Negotiation of the Maastricht Treaty*, Aldershot: Ashgate, Chapter 8.

Dyson, Kenneth (1994) *Elusive Union: The Process of Economic and Monetary Union in Europe*, London: Longman.

Dyson, Kenneth and Featherstone, Kevin (1999) *The Road to Maastricht: Negotiating Economic and Monetary Union*, Oxford: Oxford University Press, Chapter 15.

Forster, Anthony (1999) *Britain and the Maastricht Negotiations*, Basingstoke: Macmillan, Chapter 2.

Gros, Daniel and Thygesen, Niels (1998) *European Monetary Integration*, 2nd edn, Harlow: Longman, Chapter 10.

Hogg, Sarah and Hill, Jonathan (1995) *Too Close to Call*, London: Little, Brown, Chapters 5 and 9.

Lamont, Norman (1999) *In Office*, London: Little, Brown, Chapter 5.

Levitt, Malcolm and Lord, Christopher (2000) *The Political Economy of Monetary Union*, Basingstoke: Macmillan, Chapter 4.

Major, John (1999) *The Autobiography*, London: HarperCollins, Chapter 12.

Stephens, Philip (1996) *Politics and the Pound*, London: Macmillan, Chapter 9.

Notes

[1] 'Economic and Monetary Union – Beyond Stage I: Possible Treaty Provisions and Statute for a European Monetary Fund', *Europe Documents*, No. 1682, 10 January 1991. Also *Agence Europe*, No. 5405 (n.s.), 9 January 1991, p. 12. On hard ECU, *The Times*, 9 January 1991 and *Daily Telegraph*, 9 January 1991.

[2] *Agence Europe*, No. 5406 (n.s.), 10 January 1991, p. 12.

[3] 'European Council, Conclusions of the Presidency (Rome, 27 and 28 October 1990)', *Europe Documents*, No. 1658, 30 October 1990.

[4] The possibility of France's contribution including some elements of the hard ECU was outlined in *Agence Europe*, No. 5410 (n.s.), 17 January 1991, p. 5.

[5] The core elements of the proposal by Spain's Minister of Finance, Carlos Solchaga, is documented in *Agence Europe*, No. 5419 (n.s.), 28–29 January 1991, p. 11. 'The Ecu and the ECSB during Stage Two', 28 January 1991, *Europe Documents*, No. 1688, 1 February 1991.

[6] *Bull. EC*, Vol. 24, Issue 1/2, 1991, point 1.1.2.

[7] Interview with Treasury official.

[8] The German text of February 1991 ruled out support for the hard ECU plan. 'EMU: An "Overall Proposal" by the FRG for the Intergovernmental Conference', *Europe Documents*, No. 1700, 20 March 1991; *Agence Europe*, No. 5441 (n.s.), 28 February 1991, pp. 7–8; and *The Economist*, 9 March 1991, pp. 43–5.

[9] For example, Norman Lamont noted in a speech to the Royal Institute for International Affairs on 30 May 1991 that 'I am happy to rebut suggestions that we are "abandoning" the hard ECU. On the contrary, the ideas which led us to put forward our proposals are making some headway with our partners.' Quoted in *Financial Times*, 31 May 1991, p. 6. Also *Daily Telegraph*, 31 May 1991; *The Times*, 31 May 1991; *Financial Times*, 31 May 1991. Later, at the Luxembourg European Council, Boris Johnson from the *Daily Telegraph* reported that 'At least one British negotiating ploy – the celebrated "hard ecu", a 13th parallel Euro-currency which would co-exist with the pound and others – has run its course.' *Daily Telegraph*, 28 June 1991.

[10] *House of Commons Official Report*, 26 June 1991, col. 1012.

[11] Interview with Treasury official. 'Non-Paper by the Luxembourg Presidency concerning the draft articles 2 to 4 bis and 102A to 104A of the treaty establishing the EEC, amended with a view to the creation of Economic and Monetary Union', *Europe Documents*, No. 1693, 27 February 1991 and *Agence Europe*, No. 5458 (n.s.), 23 March 1991, p. 9.

[12] Douglas Hurd said that 'the Government will not recommend to this Parliament acceptance of a commitment to a single currency'. *House of Commons Official Report*, 26 June 1991, col. 1012.

[13] *The Guardian*, 13 May 1991, p. 9.

[14] *Agence Europe*, No. 5490 (n.s.), 13–14 May 1991, p. 7.

[15] *The Times*, 14 May 1991.

[16] *Agence Europe*, No. 5507 (n.s.), 7 June 1991, p. 3.

[17] *Bull. EC*, Vol. 24, Issue 6, 1991, point 1.1.2; *Agence Europe*, No. 5510 (n.s.), 12 June 1991, p. 9; and *Financial Times*, 11 June 1991, p. 4.

[18] Interview with former Foreign and Commonwealth Office Minister.

[19] *House of Commons Official Report*, 26 June 1991, col. 1012.

[20] Article 109 G.2 stated that: 'The Council shall not oblige a Member State to participate in the third stage if a Member State has notified the Council that the National Parliament of the Member State does not feel able to approve of the irrevocable fixing of its currency at the provisional date. Such a Member State shall be exempted from the decision as mentioned above, and will in this Treaty be called "Member State with an exemption". The Articles referred to in paragraph 4 do not apply to it.' 'Draft Treaty on Economic and Monetary Union', *Europe Documents*, No. 1740/1741, 1 November 1991, Article 109 G.2.

[21] *Financial Times*, 29 October 1991 and 30 October 1991; *The Guardian*, 29 October 1991; *The Independent*, 29 October 1991, p. 10; *Daily Telegraph*, 29 October 1991.

[22] Interview with Treasury official.

[23] Interview with former Council General Secretariat official.

[24] Interview with Treasury official.

[25] Quoted in *Agence Europe*, No. 5621 (n.s.), 2–3 December 1991, p. 7.

[26] Interview with Treasury official.

[27] 'Draft Treaty on Economic and Monetary Union', *Europe Documents*, No. 1740/1741, 1 November 1991, Article 109F.3. It stated that: 'On the basis of these recommendations of the Council and of the opinion of the European Parliament, the European Council: – shall assess whether it is appropriate for the Community to enter into the third stage of economic and monetary union; – shall formulate a conclusion on the date for the beginning of the third stage.'

[28] Interview with former Treasury Minister.

[29] Interview with former Treasury Minister.

[30] *Financial Times*, 7–8 December 1991, p. 3.

[31] For example, the Bundesbank's vice-president, Hans Tietmeyer, in a speech in Italy on 22 November 1991, warned of the dangers of EMU without convergence, and the absolute

necessity for EMU to include strict rules and sanctions against any member state that failed to keep its budget deficits under control. *Financial Times*, 23 November 1991.

[32] 'EMU: An "Overall Proposal" by the FRG for the Intergovernmental Conference', *Europe Documents*, No. 1700, 20 March 1991; *Agence Europe*, No. 5441 (n.s.), 28 February 1991, pp. 7–8; and *The Economist*, 9 March 1991, pp. 43–5. Also *Agence Europe*, No. 5441 (n.s.), 28 February 1991, p. 7.

[33] The Luxembourg meeting stressed the need for the Community to make progress on economic and monetary convergence, with particular reference to price stability and sound public finance. *Bull. EC*, Vol. 24, Issue 6, 1991, point 1.12.

[34] This was evidenced at the Brussels personal representative meeting on 19 March 1991. *Bull. EC*, Vol. 24, Issue 3, 1991, point 1.1.1 and *Agence Europe*, No. 5456 (n.s.), 21 March 1991, p. 8. Differences in opinion were also evident at the Finance Ministers' meeting on 8 April 1991. *Agence Europe*, No. 5466 (n.s.), 6 April 1991, p. 5, and *Agence Europe*, No. 5467 (n.s.), 7 April 1991, pp. 7–8. That meeting paid attention to draft Article 109C of the presidency 'non-paper' regarding Articles 73 to 73E and Article 109.

[35] The Dutch Finance Minister, Wim Kok, in a letter addressed to the president of De Nederlandsche Bank on 2 April, stated that the second stage should not commence before the member states had reached agreement on the basic characteristics of the final stage and that they had been accepted as treaty provisions. Also, economic and monetary developments should strongly resemble each other and that, in particular, inflation levels must be similar. *Agence Europe*, No. 5463 (n.s.), 3 April 1991, pp. 7–8, and *Agence Europe*, No. 5464 (n.s.), 4 April 1991, pp. 7–8.

[36] *Agence Europe*, No. 5480 (n.s.), 26 April 1991, p. 8.

[37] *Agence Europe*, No. 5468 (n.s.), 10 April 1991, p. 10.

[38] *Agence Europe*, No. 5455 (n.s.), 20 March 1991, p. 13. These points were outlined in a press conference after a meeting with the European Parliament's Committee on Economic and Monetary Affairs in Brussels.

[39] *Agence Europe*, No. 5564 (n.s.), 11 September 1991, p. 5.

[40] In April 1991 the Luxembourg presidency presented a negotiating paper that advocated Stage 2 commencing on 1 January 1994. The non-paper entitled 'Draft Articles 109D and 109E of the Treaty Establishing the EEC with a View to Achieving Economic and Monetary Union' is reproduced in *Agence Europe*, No. 5479 (n.s.), 25 April 1991, pp. 9–10. Also *Agence Europe*, No. 5458 (n.s.), 23 March 1991, p. 9.

[41] The European Monetary Institute (EMI) was designed to act as a coordinating body for the monetary policy of the central banks of the member states within the European System of Central Banks (ESCB). The EMI was specifically involved in the preparation of the third stage of EMU, at which time it was renamed the European Central Bank. 'Role of the EMI', *Bank of England Quarterly Bulletin*, February 1994.

[42] The breakthrough in the EMU negotiations that was provided by Apeldoorn was noted in an editorial, 'EMU – (1) The (Virtuous) Gears are Turning', *Agence Europe*, No. 5574 (n.s.), 25 September 1991, and the *Wall Street Journal*, 23 September 1991, p. 1. Also *International Herald Tribune*, 23 September 1991.

[43] *The Times*, 23 September 1991 and the *Financial Times*, 21 September 1991, p. 2.

[44] *Bull. EC*, Vol. 24, Issue 9, 1991, point 1.1.3. Also *The Guardian*, 23 September 1991, p. 22; *The Independent*, 23 September 1991. The possible softening of the government's

position also resulted in one Conservative MP, Tony Favell, demanding a referendum on the issue of EMU. *The Independent*, 25 September 1991.

[45] *House of Commons Official Report*, 20 November 1991, col. 271.

[46] *International Herald Tribune*, 29 October 1991, and *Financial Times*, 30 October 1991.

[47] *The Times*, 19 September 1991; *Financial Times*, 19 September 1991; *The Guardian*, 19 September 1991.

[48] *Agence Europe*, No. 5584 (n.s.), 9 October 1991, p. 5.

[49] *Financial Times*, 29 October 1991, p. 2.

[50] *Agence Europe*, No. 5604 (n.s.), 7 November 1991, p. 11; *Financial Times*, 14 November 1991; *The Independent*, 15 November 1991. Also *Agence Europe*, No. 5603 (n.s.), 6 November 1991, p. 6, and *Agence Europe*, No. 5604 (n.s.), 7 November 1991, p. 11.

[51] *Agence Europe*, No. 5607 (n.s.), 12–13 November 1991, pp. 7–8, and *The Economist*, 16 November 1991.

[52] *Agence Europe*, No. 5621 (n.s.), 2–3 December 1991, pp. 7–9; *Agence Europe*, No. 5622 (n.s.), 4 December 1991, p. 7; and *Agence Europe*, No. 5625 (n.s.), 6 December 1991, p. 7.

[53] *Survey of Current Affairs*, Vol. 22, No. 1, London: HMSO, January 1992, pp. 3–12.

[54] *House of Commons Official Report*, 20 November 1991, col. 274. Also 'Economic and Monetary Union: the Agreement at Maastricht', *Treasury Bulletin*, HM Treasury, London: HMSO, Vol. 3, Issue 1, 1991–92, pp. 2–3.

[55] *Bull. EC*, Vol. 24, Issue 12, 1991, points 1.1 – 1.19. *Bank of England Quarterly Bulletin*, February 1992, Vol. 32, No. 1, pp. 64–8.

[56] *Agence Europe*, No. 5627 (n.s.), 11 December 1991, p. 6 bis.

[57] The convergence criteria detailed that member states should have a budget deficit not exceeding 3% of GDP; a public debt not exceeding 60% of GDP; consumer price inflation of not more than 1.5% per annum; long-term nominal interest rates no more than 2% above those of the three most stable member states; and a smooth performance within the Exchange Rate Mechanism during the preceding two years.

[58] Interview with former Treasury Minister.

[59] The British opt-out from EMU recognised that 'the United Kingdom shall not be obliged or committed to move to the third stage of economic and monetary union without a separate decision to do so by its government and Parliament'. *Treaty on European Union*, Protocol on Certain Provisions Relating to the United Kingdom of Great Britain and Northern Ireland.

[60] Interview with Treasury official.

[61] Britain's desire not to be ambushed at Luxembourg was conveyed by John Major to Jacques Santer during a working lunch in Downing Street on 5 June. *Financial Times*, 6 June 1991, p. 14.

[62] *Agence Europe*, No. 5510 (n.s.), 12 June 1991, p. 9.

[63] *The Times*, 6 June 1991, and *Financial Times*, 10 June 1991, p. 1.

[64] Interview with former Treasury Minister.

CHAPTER 8

Tied to the ERM: 1992–1993

Objectives

- Examine whether Britain entered the ERM at the correct time (and at the correct rate) in October 1990.
- Highlight the extent to which the ERM was becoming an unstable system at the time of British entry.
- Explain the reasons why Britain left the ERM in September 1992.
- Outline British tactics on monetary policy after leaving the ERM.

Introduction

Upon his return from the Maastricht European Council, John Major could have been forgiven for feeling rather pleased with the outcome of the negotiations. Britain had, after all, secured an opt-out (opt-in) that did not necessitate an immediate commitment to a single currency. At the same time, those member states that were to progress towards a single currency would have to adhere to fairly strict economic convergence criteria. To be sure, the government had not managed to stop EMU, but that was an unlikely objective, and was never really raised as a negotiating point. As for the other areas of the Maastricht talks, Britain had obtained pleasing outcomes in the discussions on common foreign and security policy (which noted the importance of the North Atlantic Treaty Organisation), while it managed to remove any commitment to the Social Chapter. The outcome of this state of affairs was that Major was widely congratulated by Conservative MPs on his return to Westminster. The fact of the matter was that despite the subsequent disputes over Europe, the vast majority of the parliamentary party at that time thought that the government had negotiated a good treaty (Blair, A., 1998b: 210–15; Young, 1998: 433). The Prime Minister reflected that 'in Cabinet all was sweetness and light . . . It was the modern equivalent of a Roman triumph' (Major, 1999: 288). And it was not only on the domestic stage that Major was feted. His stock had increased on the continent, where such leaders as Helmut Kohl and François Mitterrand realised he was a man that they could do business with.

Upon reflection, it is evident that Prime Minister Major's report card of his first year in office was very positive.[1] Here was a man who had managed to heal some of the wounds that had festered in the Conservative Party in recent years and also steered a potentially difficult course through the intergovernmental conference negotiations. Few could then imagine that 1992 would represent a quite different set of achievements. In the course of that year the government managed, against all odds, to win a fourth successive term for the Conservative Party in the April general election.[2] As made clear in previous chapters, the maintenance of party unity with a view to being successful in the election had been a primary objective of John Major. Domestic politics had always taken precedence over European events. And while the government's majority was reduced to 21 in that election, it was nevertheless a significant achievement.

John Major had, in effect, secured many of the objectives that seemed unobtainable under Thatcher. But, despite these achievements, 1992 would be remembered as the year when Britain exited the Exchange Rate Mechanism (ERM) and when 'the Conservative Party began tearing itself apart' (Major, 1999: 310). The Prime Minister was already concerned about the narrowness of the election victory and the likelihood of future difficulties.[3] As noted in Chapter 5, there had been a division of views within the Cabinet and parliamentary party as to the validity of ERM entry. In the end, the decision to join had been influenced by the consideration that Britain should play a more constructive role in the Community and that entry would provide a more stable environment for business growth (Young, 1998: 419). But, as mentioned earlier, in entering the ERM the government was once again late in joining a Community policy, and when it did so, it was at a time of dramatic change on the European continent. The collapse of the Berlin Wall and the reunification of Germany evidenced this. Such turbulence placed extra strain on the ERM. This chapter reviews Britain's position within the ERM from 1990 until 1992 and highlights the difficulty that the government had in maintaining membership during a period of great instability.

The right time of entry?

With the government not being able to exert pressure in the discussion over monetary union, entry to the ERM was viewed as an essential means of regaining influence in the monetary debate (see Chapters 5 and 6). That is not to say that the government did not consider that entry would assist in reducing inflation.

BOX 8.1

Capital controls

The free movement of capital was principally established in the Single European Act, though measures permitting partial liberalisation were established in 1960 and 1962. The importance of the SEA was that it placed the free movement of capital in the same framework as that of goods and services. This resulted in the adoption of a directive in June 1988 which had the purpose of liberalising capital movement with effect from 1 July 1990. This applied to transactions between member states and with third countries, although Greece, Ireland, Portugal and Spain were permitted a transitional arrangement that allowed them to maintain restrictions until 31 December 1992, and Greece and Portugal were granted an extension of a further three years. In terms of the movement towards monetary union, the liberalisation of capital controls is part of the first stage of the process (as set out in the conclusions of the June 1989 Madrid European Council). Article 73b of the Maastricht Treaty abolished all restrictions on the movement of capital and payments between member states and member states and third countries with effect from 1 January 1994.

It did. However, the more immediate reason was the need to demonstrate a commitment to Stages 2 and 3 of EMU. A combination of Cabinet pressure, business influence and economic and political necessity had urged Prime Minister Thatcher in the direction of joining, while demonstrating that she no longer dominated Cabinet discussions. As already noted, British participation was welcomed on the continent, while domestic supporters considered entry would provide a more stable platform for economic growth. The latter point was influenced by the ERM having become a stable system of exchange rates, influenced by the growing convergence of European economies and the momentum behind monetary union.

Despite this perception of Britain joining a stable system, the ERM was increasingly unstable at this time. One of the reasons for this was that the removal of exchange controls in July 1990 (as part of the Single European Market initiative) meant restrictions, such as those forbidding the direct export of foreign capital, no longer existed (see Box 8.1).[4] Britain had, in fact, been in the vanguard of those countries which supported the abolition of capital controls, as it was a policy that the government had advocated as part of the 'Madrid conditions' for ERM entry (see Chapters 5 and 6).[5] But their removal offered the opportunity for currency speculators to sell weak currencies that were expected to be devalued, thereby adding further pressure to them, at which time the speculators were able to buy them back at a lower price. The difference in value between the selling and buying of the currency therefore represented the profit margins. Thus, prior to their abolition, capital controls had offered a short-term (but not long-term) protection to weaker currencies by limiting the total amount of currency that could be sold (Gros and Thygesen, 1998: 128–37). Somewhat predictably, upon their abolition, currency speculators were aware of the opportunities that existed to make profits by selling the weaker currencies, although by doing so they added a further element of uncertainty to the stability of the ERM. And with the entry of Spain (June 1989) and Britain (October 1990) to the ERM, the scope for disruptive capital movements increased.

The result of these developments was that from the second half of 1990 onwards there was a greater volume of money flowing in and out of countries. In particular, money flowed into high-inflation countries due to an anticipation of higher rates of interest, resulting in a strengthening of the lira in the narrow band of the ERM and the peseta in the wider band of the ERM. In contrast, the French franc and the Deutschmark weakened. But whereas in previous years such movement would have resulted in a realignment of those currencies, there was a growing reluctance on the part of governments to make any adjustments to the ERM at this time. We have to remind ourselves that just as Britain's entry to the ERM was motivated by a desire to curry greater favour in the monetary union discussions (Major, 1999: 156), the very stability of the ERM had a great deal of impact on the path to EMU. Governments wanted to demonstrate that the stability of European currencies, evidenced by an absence of ERM realignments, meant that progress towards monetary union was the natural step forward. But an unwillingness to realign ensured that excess pressure was kept within the system and therefore not released, as had happened with previous realignments. Additionally, sterling's value began to rise throughout 1990 due to the prospect of a 'floor' to the currency as markets began to expect British membership, as highlighted in Table 8.1 (Major, 1999: 157). During the period April to June 1990, sterling increased by 4.3% against the Deutschmark and 6% against the US dollar.[6] The effect of this was for sterling to enter the ERM at a rate (DM2.95) that was higher than the normal ratio, and one that would eventually prove unsustainable. As Hugo Young commented, 'In the matter of timing, the decision was calamitous' (Young, 1998: 365).

At the same time that the value of sterling was increasing (thereby causing concern that when it entered the ERM it would do so at an 'unnatural rate'),

Table 8.1   Sterling/Deutschmark exchange rates, 1989–1990[a]

Date	£/DM
29 December 1989	2.7275
22 February 1990	2.8641
30 March	2.7870
29 June	2.9067
18 July	2.9892
29 August	3.0298
28 September	2.9286

[a] Close of business rates in London.

Source: *Bank of England Quarterly Bulletin*, Vol. 30, No. 1, Feb. 1990, p. 34; No. 2, May 1990, p. 189; No. 3, August 1990, p. 332; No. 4, Nov. 1990, p. 470.

European governments faced the additional task of having to respond to the effects of German unification (Marsh, 1993: 202). While being a momentous event for Germany, it placed extra financial burdens on the German government, which faced the challenge of the reunification of the two Germanies. And as the German Deutschmark was the benchmark currency within Europe, the German government's need to spend large sums of money in assisting the former East Germany affected the Deutschmark's value (Major, 1999: 313). Within Whitehall there was an awareness of these factors, with the Treasury's chief economic adviser, Sir Terence Burns, stating:

> Clearly, at the moment, there are some different pressures in Germany than in some of the other countries but it is not clear that they need necessarily last for very long. I would have every hope that the system would be able to live with that.[7]

We can therefore see that the ERM was becoming increasingly unstable at a time when sterling was looking for security. The irony for Britain was that having spent five years resisting ERM membership, the government joined at one of the most difficult times, when European economies were unstable due to the effects of recession – the very time when financial discipline is difficult to maintain and when calls for lower interest rates dominate (Major, 1999: 315). For this reason, Britain's rate of GDP growth had begun to fall from 1988 onwards, while the level of GDP fell from the second quarter of 1990 to the second quarter of 1992 (except the fourth quarter of 1991 when the level of output slightly increased). Added to this was that Britain's economic performance was worse than that of other European countries (Table 8.2), reflected in a rising unemployment rate. Thus, as Britain's entry to the ERM coincided with a downturn in the economic performance of the majority of European member states, there was some concern that the time was in fact not right for membership.[8] And although it is possible to state this point in hindsight, the fact of the matter is that the decision to join had been determined on political and not economic grounds.

The benefits of participating in the system were immediately noticeable, with inflation rates decreasing during the first year of membership (Table 8.3). As Chancellor Lamont stated, 'we did not join the ERM as a stepping-stone to monetary union. We joined it for its immediate, practical benefits in getting inflation down.'[9] Other benefits of membership were equally apparent, including a reduction in interest rates by 4.5% to 10.5% during the first 12 months of membership. At the same time that sterling was evidently a more stable currency, there was also a decrease in the variability of the sterling–Deutschmark exchange rate, all of which assisted business growth. Such developments were, nevertheless, dependent on a weak Deutschmark, and consequently, when the Deutschmark began to appreciate by the end of 1991 due to a tougher German monetary policy, it was evident that cuts in British interest rates were less likely. One can therefore say that ERM membership had effectively tied British monetary policy to that of Germany. This was demonstrated by the December

Table 8.2   Developments in real GNP/GDP (percentage changes)

Countries and Periods	GNP/GDP[a]
Germany	
1989	3.9
1990	4.7
1991	3.2
1991 Q IV[b]	0.9
France	
1989	4.1
1990	2.2
1991	1.1
1991 Q IV[b]	1.8
Italy	
1989	3.0
1990	2.2
1991	1.4
1991 Q IV[b]	1.5
Britain	
1989	2.3
1990	1.1
1991	−2.3
1991 Q IV[b]	−1.5

[a] GNP for Germany, GDP for the other countries.
[b] Change over four quarters.

Source: Bank for International Settlements, *62nd Annual Report*, Basle, June 1992, pp. 20–1.

Table 8.3   Consumer price inflation

Countries	1990	1991	1992[a]
Germany	2.8[b]	6.1	3.6
France	3.4	3.1	1.9
Italy	6.4	6.0	4.6
Ireland	2.7	3.6	2.3
Netherlands	2.6	3.7	2.3
Belgium	3.5	2.8	2.4
Denmark	1.9	2.3	1.5
Britain	9.3	4.5	2.6

[a] Annual percentage change, based on end-of-period figures.
[b] West Germany only.

Source: Bank for International Settlements, *63rd Annual Report*, Basle, June 1993, p. 29, and *64th Annual Report*, Basle, June 1994, p. 14.

1991 rise in official German rates pushing British short-term interest rates above 11%, while at the same time weakening sterling's value within the system, with it falling below DM2.84 in November.[10]

Tensions: 1992–1993

The foregoing analysis has demonstrated that while ERM entry brought benefits to Britain in the form of lower inflation and interest rates, the very decision to join coincided with the system becoming more turbulent, while countries outside the ERM, such as Finland and Sweden, also experienced exchange rate difficulties.[11] As has been made clear, there was a direct linkage between the continuing stability of the ERM and the successful negotiation of a Treaty on European Union that set a path to EMU. In essence, EMU was dependent on a smooth-running ERM. The appetite that many officials and ministers had for this project was, however, not shared by all nations, most notably Britain. But others, including Denmark, had expressed reservations over the monetary union project, and Denmark had also negotiated a similar opt-out (opt-in) to Britain. The uncertainty that was prevalent at this time was not lost on the various currency speculators who operated in the numerous financial markets. For them, the absence of capital controls had provided an opportunity for making large profits by speculating against national currencies. Thus, when the Community Foreign and Finance Ministers formally signed the Treaty on European Union at Maastricht on 7 February 1992, they set their member states on a process of ratifying the necessary changes to the EC Treaty in their parliaments. And just as speculators had been able to destabilise weak currencies in the ERM, the setting of ratification dates provided a focus for market expectations. If, for instance, a government received a no vote for the adoption of the treaty, then speculators would be able to take advantage of the uncertainty. For Britain, the very ability of the ERM to cope with tension in the exchange markets was viewed as the rationale for participation,[12] with Chancellor Lamont noting that:

> the Government's policy is that we intend to stick within our ERM bands. We believe that the benefits of the discipline of the ERM, the benefits of sticking to the existing parity, are paramount. We have no intention whatsoever of altering the parity.[13]

During the course of 1992, the first significant focus for market expectations was the Danish referendum of 2 June. Despite the fact that the Danish Folketing approved the treaty by 130 votes to 25 on 12 May, a referendum was necessary because of a constitution stipulation. The outcome of that vote was to strike fear about the process of ratification in other member states, with 50.7% of the population voting 'no' versus 49.3% voting 'yes', a margin of only 46,269 votes (Worre, 1995).[14] As a mark of his own scepticism, Lamont recollected that 'I leapt into the air, punching it with my fist. It was an incautious reaction of sheer delight' (Lamont, 1999: 198). Inevitably, the Danish 'no' increased scepticism within the Community concerning the very progress towards monetary union, with sterling weakening by around 1.5 pfennigs against the Deutschmark to DM2.9149 by 5 June, while by 30 June it had moved further down to 2.8992.[15] And although Ireland achieved a comfortable 'yes' vote of 68.7% to 31.3% in favour of the treaty on 19 June, there was no let-up in the pressure that the ERM was under. As part of a predictable strategy, currency speculators targeted the weaker currencies first, especially the lira, throughout June and July, with the government attempting to counter this pressure by means of intervention (buying the currency on the foreign exchange markets) and interest rate rises. Such turbulence was despite there being strong support for ratification in other member states. The Luxembourg Chamber of Deputies ratified the treaty on 6 July by 51 votes to 6, the Belgian Chamber of Deputies approved it 11 days later by 143 votes to 33, while the Greek parliament (the Vouli) ratified the treaty on 31 July by 286 votes to 8. But irrespective of these comprehensive votes in favour of the treaty, the ERM continued to experience relentless pressure.

Tension within the system was particularly concentrated on the weaker economies, which meant that the Italian lira and sterling were clear targets, although Chancellor Lamont maintained Britain would stay within the ERM.[16] Such pressures were exacerbated by the Bundesbank's decision to raise the discount rate (its key interest rate) on 16 July from 8% to 8.75%. This decision had been influenced by the desire to control inflation (4.7% in the first half of 1992), which had increased as a result of German economic and monetary union. This had the knock-on effect of decreasing the likelihood of other European economies emerging from recession (although not necessarily suffering from inflation), as their interest rates tended to follow Germany's, which meant that their currencies were artificially high and consequently exposed to speculators. This vulnerability was highlighted when the lira came under speculative attack in the latter half of August and early September, with the Italian authorities allowing it to reach its lower limit for the first time since it had entered the narrow band of the ERM. This fall in the lira nevertheless did not alter the degree of speculation that it was subjected to, irrespective of the authorities' continuing use of interest rates and market interventions. At the same time the peseta and sterling, which were both in the wide band, underwent speculative attack.

Regardless of such pressure, and the glaring reality that market forces were outwith the control of central government, member states continued to adhere to the system.[17] Britain reiterated its commitment not to devalue from its ERM parity of DM2.95, with Chancellor Lamont announcing on 3 September that the government would borrow 10 billion ECUs so as to shore up sterling's value.[18] Italy, too, demonstrated its willingness to maintain the lira within the ERM, with discount rates being increased by 1.75% to 15% on 4 September (the highest level since 1985). That these measures were taken was reflective of the value that member states attached to ERM membership. Somewhat ironically,

---

BOX 8.2

Bath Ecofin meeting of 5 September 1992

1. Prospect of a general realignment of currencies within the ERM was dismissed at the informal Finance Ministers' meeting in Bath.

2. The decision not to realign had been taken because it was deemed not appropriate at the time, while there was a perception that realignment would have further fuelled the amount of speculation surrounding the forthcoming French referendum on 20 September.

3. At that meeting the Bundesbank had resisted pressure to lower its interest rates – from the UK in particular, which wanted to pursue a looser monetary policy to tackle the severe recession. The decision not to realign pushed speculation towards the currencies that were considered overvalued.

---

they also demonstrated the need for realignment within the system (which governments were reluctant to adhere to) and therefore provided added impetus for speculators to target these troubled currencies.

Although it is apparent that realignment could have benefited the system, Finance Ministers dismissed this very possibility at a meeting in Bath on 5 September 1992[19] (see Box 8.2) (Lamont, 1999: 235). Such a decision was based on the assumption that any realignment would have further fuelled the amount of speculation surrounding the forthcoming French referendum.[20] At the meeting, Britain (which was aware of the constraints that membership placed on sterling) pressurised the German government to lower its interest rates so that the British government could pursue a looser monetary policy in order to tackle the severe recession that was now gripping the country. The need for a change in German policy had already been set out by John Major in a July letter to Helmut Kohl, for which Major 'received no immediate reply' (Major, 1999: 315–16). Both the government in Bonn and the Bundesbank were unsympathetic to the British case and 'were not going to give way' on British pleas for an interest rate cut (Major, 1999: 323). Much of the lobbying for that cut had been done by Lamont, whose somewhat aggressive chairmanship of the Bath Finance Ministers' meeting led to some speculation that this had directly influenced Germany's reluctance to alter interest rates (Lamont, 1999: 259–60). Such linkage is in fact unlikely as 'it was clear that the Germans were not prepared to give way on interest rates *without a realignment, and the French were not interested in that*' (Major, 1999: 324, italics in the original). But despite the technicalities of these details, the fact of the matter was that the events at Bath did not bode well for future German support in defending sterling's value. To this end, Sarah Hogg, the head of John Major's policy unit, seemingly noted that 'I don't think we can rely on the Germans' (Major, 1999: 323). Nevertheless, it was the lira, and not sterling, which was subject to the greatest pressure, primarily because there was concern that the forthcoming French referendum would produce a 'no' vote.[21]

The desperation of the lira's plight was emphasised by the Italian government selling its shares in such companies as Credito Italiano and Nuovo Pignone as a means of raising capital to support the lira.[22] This action did not go unnoticed, with speculators continuing to place pressure on the lira, with it twice falling through its DM floor of L765.4 on 11 September. The effect of this was for the government to seek a 7% devaluation of the lira on 13 September so as to relieve the pressure that it was under.[23] Later that day the Bundesbank announced that it would reduce its Lombard rate and discount rate by 0.25% and 0.5% respectively on the following day, though 'as the first reduction for five years, it was distressingly small' (Major, 1999: 327; Lamont, 1999: 241). Although Italy had devalued, the concept of a general realignment had not taken place. This was despite the fact that a statement by the Bundesbank on 30 September noted that it had requested a general realignment on 11 September,[24] a point reiterated by the chairman of the Bank of Italy.[25] The Bundesbank's request had been prompted by unsustainable interventions to support the lira, which had resulted in a massive inflow of foreign exchange that inflated the money supply and bank liquidity. Yet the option of a general realignment was not conveyed to Britain, with the Chancellor noting that 'we received no request during the weekend from the German authorities that the pound should realign with the lira, or an indication that if we had, the cuts in German interest rates would have been higher'.[26] Furthermore, the Bank of England was also unaware of the request for a more general realignment,[27] and this lack of understanding had been partly because there was no meeting of the Monetary Committee on the weekend of the Italian devaluation.

This attempt to reduce tension within the ERM did not result in a change of British policy, with the government continuing to dismiss any suggestion of a realignment or devaluation,[28] and Lamont stated that it would 'take whatever action is necessary' to defend the central parity of sterling against the Deutschmark.[29] This was despite the fact that the depreciation pressures, which continued to haunt the lira, had spread to sterling with it hovering above its DM2.778 floor on the foreign exchange markets. Indeed, exchange markets were increasingly focused on sterling, as the second most vulnerable currency in the system after the lira, which was itself still subject to speculation as it was still considered to be overvalued.[30] Britain's slow economic growth and rising unemployment had influenced sterling's troubles.[31] Major acknowledged the government's economic difficulties by cancelling a trip to Seville, but such an unusual procedure only managed to fuel the existing pressure on sterling. This was displayed by sterling falling to a new low of DM2.78 on 15 September – the lowest level since Britain entered the ERM, and only one-fifth of a pfennig above the DM2.778 floor.[32]

The mounting pressure on sterling resulted in the Bank of England intervening on 16 September to ensure that it did not fall below the lower margin of the Deutschmark band (Major, 1999: 329–34). To counter sterling's fall,

Table 8.4 Britain's official reserves 1990–1992[a]

Date		$ million
1990	Q1	39,295
	Q2	39,014
	Q3	39,060
	Q4	38,464
1991	Q1	42,258
	Q2	44,264
	Q3	44,593
	Q4	44,126
1992	Q1	45,027
	Q2	45,700
	Q3	42,677
	Q4	41,654

[a] Reserves at the end of period.

Source: *Economic Trends*, Annual Supplement, 1995 edition, Section 5.1, p. 226.

base rates were raised from 10% to 12% at 11 a.m., with a subsequent increase to 15% later in the afternoon. This was the first time that the Bank of England had raised interest rates twice in one day. But such measures did little to alleviate the pressure on sterling, despite the fact that between £1.8 billion and £3 billion had been used,[33] while the underlying fall in the reserves was some $7.7 billion (see Table 8.4).[34] At that stage Lamont 'knew the game was up' (Lamont, 1999: 249). It was estimated that some £10 billion of capital flowed out of Britain on 16 September (commonly referred to as Black Wednesday) as corporate treasurers and fund managers tried to reduce their exposure to sterling (see Box 8.3).[35] Therefore, on the evening of Black Wednesday (the 15% rise was to be effective from the following morning) it was announced

---

BOX 8.3

Black Wednesday

This is the term commonly used to describe Britain's exit from the Exchange Rate Mechanism on 16 September 1992. On that day sterling came under a great deal of pressure from currency speculators who considered that it was too weak to stay in the ERM. The ERM had, in fact, been unstable for much of the summer after Denmark rejected the Maastricht Treaty in a June referendum. On the fateful 16 September the government desperately tried to support sterling by increasing interest rates from 10% to 12% and then subsequently to 15%. The Bank of England also used nearly £3 billion of official reserves to support the currency. This had little effect, with the result that Britain withdrew from the ERM.

that sterling would be 'suspended' from the ERM along with the lira, while the peseta was devalued by 5%.[36] This meant that sterling was left to float in the clutches of the markets and, therefore, rapidly depreciated.[37] In his statement of 16 September, Lamont said that:

> Today has been an extremely difficult and turbulent day. Massive financial flows have continued to disrupt the functioning of the ERM . . . The government has concluded that Britain's best interests are served by suspending our membership of the exchange rate mechanism.

The exit of the lira and sterling from the ERM did not alleviate all of the pressure that the system had been subjected to, as there was still a great deal of uncertainty as to the outcome of the 20 September French referendum.[38] At that time there was a clear perception that the treaty hinged on the French vote, with the British government stating that the narrowest of rejections would result in the ratification process being stopped.[39] Therefore, the narrow margin in favour of the treaty, 51.04% of valid votes cast to 48.95% (a difference of only 539,410), did not immediately remove the pressure that the ERM had been under. Nevertheless, the franc was able to remain within the system, primarily because the French economy was stronger than, for example, that of Britain. At the same time, the centrality of France to the monetary union project meant that it benefited from German support, which was less clear when it came to defending sterling. With the German authorities believing in the French parity, all the central banks were, therefore, lined up against the speculators. Thus, as the Governor of the Bank of England stated, the French franc 'was very much stronger than in our case'.[40] But despite these developments, the narrowness of the French 'petit oui' sent serious shocks to other member states, such as Britain, which expected ratification difficulties. Thus, for the first time since Delors took office, the very nature of the destiny of an ever more integrated Europe was being questioned, and not just by the archetypal sceptical partners.

Postscript on entry

Although the British government was aware from the announcement of the French referendum that the events leading up to 16 September would be 'very difficult ones in the foreign exchange market', it had continued to adhere to the ERM discipline, while strengthening government reserves.[41] The economic difficulties had been predicted by City analysts,[42] as sterling's ERM divergence indicator had fallen below its maximum divergence spread in August. This position was also pointed out by the president of the Bundesbank in his statement of 30 September,[43] and, according to the Bundesbank, sterling had overstepped 'the warning mark'. Nevertheless, the Chancellor did not act on this advice by raising interest rates from June onwards because it would have been a 'very desperate thing to have done' and 'would have undermined rather than strengthened our position'.[44]

Ironically, when the government was eventually forced to increase interest rates, Norman Lamont was not 'enormously optimistic' about the success of the policy and felt that 'frankly, the game was up'.[45] An interest rate rise had been part of a futile attempt to keep sterling in the ERM, while the course of action was necessary due to the rules governing the system.[46] But the underlying weakness of the British economy meant that any rise in interest rates would have had a negative effect on any potential economic recovery. As the Governor of the Bank of England pointed out, 'it was very difficult for us to establish credibility through an increase in interest rates'.[47] For the rise to be effective then it would have been necessary for it to be sustained long enough to stem speculation, by which time any increase would most definitely have percolated through to the wider economy and, therefore, have had an impact on Britain's economic performance.[48]

The government's viewpoint was that the strains in the ERM were due to 'two unique events', the first of which was the French referendum which provided foreign exchange markets with a fixed date against which they could speculate. The second and more 'fundamental' reason was German reunification and the differential that existed between Germany's needs and those of other countries, especially Britain.[49] However, this viewpoint seems somewhat shortsighted, as it is clear that the ERM crisis was caused by something more fundamental, i.e. the lack of realignments. Clearly, the ERM 'stiffened' in the latter part of the 1980s and this seems to have been the product of a political desire for a stable Exchange Rate Mechanism rather than the economic necessity to realign. Indeed, realignments would have ensured that the external value of currencies, i.e. exchange rates, would have been brought into line with their internal value. The lack of realignments meant that pressure built up in the system and, therefore, far from being stable the system was ready to explode. It should, however, be noted that realignments would also have suggested that the system was not stable. Stability was necessary because of the desire to achieve EMU. This process was a further source of tension as it created a dichotomy between the political desire to pursue an ever more integrated Europe and the economic reality that European economies were not ready for such a move due to economic recession. Therefore, a combination of factors resulted in the system being subject to tension, while the abolition of capital controls ensured that speculators had greater freedom to hedge against particular currencies.

Analysis of Britain's exit from the ERM suggests a lack of realism on the part of government. This is because it believed that while the system had been subject to turbulence, the very fact that there had not been any major realignment (until 16 September) for some five years suggested that the system was fundamentally stable.[50] The Governor of the Bank of England admitted that while possible strains such as German unification were recognised, 'we did not foresee the degree to which they would develop when the decision was taken to enter the ERM two years ago'.[51] But this perception demonstrates the traditional inability of the British government to evaluate future developments, while the ERM had in reality been under severe stress since the Danish referendum, and the system's stability had been in question since 1990. There was a lack of awareness among member states for the need for a realignment in the wake of German unification, as pointed out by Helmut Schlesinger's deputy, Hans Tietmeyer (Marsh, 1993: 255, fn 73). Furthermore, the government was aware of the weakness of the British economy which, combined with the fact that sterling had been regarded as overvalued since it entered the system in September 1990, suggests a lack of 'realism' and 'flexibility' on its part. Karl Otto Pöhl commented that Britain joined the ERM with the wrong rate at the wrong time (Marsh, 1993: 255, fn 71).

Once in the ERM the decision to continue to adhere to the system, despite the reality that the foundations supporting sterling were crumbling, was taken because ERM participation was central to the British government's domestic policy of reducing inflation. It also provided a method of demonstrating Britain's commitment to the Community. Thus, if Britain withdrew, then a key aspect of the government's policy would have disappeared, ensuring that the very legitimacy of the Chancellor and the Prime Minister would have been questioned. In this context, Britain's exit damaged Lamont and Major's credibility, while at the same time denting the government's confidence.[52] This meant that there was a need to establish a line of policy that brought renewed confidence and a return to growth, and the Chancellor said that this was 'more essential than ever'.[53]

BOX 8.4

The ERM crisis of 1992–1993

The ERM crises of September 1992 and July–August 1993 were among the most testing periods that the EU had faced. Before the turbulence experienced on the foreign exchange markets during 1992 and 1993, the ERM of the EMS represented the cornerstone of monetary arrangements within Europe. It was viewed as providing the operational framework that would eventually lead to complete monetary union among EC member states. Why then did the system suffer such a significant change of fortunes? The first point is that it was evident that the ERM had been under strain for some time. The last major adjustment of exchange rates had occurred in 1987 and it is clear that the decision not to revalue the Deutschmark following German unification in 1989 had an impact on monetary instability in later years. Second, the exchange market crisis was somewhat triggered by the uncertainty surrounding the referenda on the Treaty on European Union. Denmark rejected the TEU in early June 1992, and the resulting strengthening of the Deutschmark put considerable pressure on sterling and the lira. The lira was not helped by concern over Italy's high level of public debt and excessive budget deficit, while sterling was not helped by the recession in the UK and the weak current account position, which meant that market perceptions suggested that it might be devalued within the ERM.

Opponents of monetary union view Britain's exit from the ERM as justification for their policy stance. For them, the chaos of September 1992 demonstrated that the construction of a single currency was an unworkable objective. Such an opinion does not, however, take into account the fact that there is a distinction between the mere cooperation between national central banks that characterised the ERM, and the integrated nature of EMU. In this context, monetary union involves a pooling of monetary policy rather than just cooperation. And, crucially, such pooling of monetary policy means that EMU could not be witness to the same type of currency speculation that did so much damage to the ERM. The crisis of 1992–93 therefore created a hurdle to monetary union and added fuel to those sceptics who were against a single currency, but it did not take away the motivation for monetary union. Indeed, if anything it added to the need for monetary union, though significantly it left a strengthened hostility in the Conservative government for future European cooperation.

Life after death

The government's position after the ERM crisis was that it would 'resume membership of the ERM as soon as conditions allow', as outlined in a speech by Lamont to the International Monetary Fund only four days after Black Wednesday.[54] This desire (or need) to re-enter the ERM was particularly advocated by Michael Heseltine and Kenneth Clarke. Reflective of their belief that Britain should play a full part in the Community, they warned the Prime Minister in late 1992 that the country could not expect to survive outside the ERM discipline (Balen, 1994: 250). But despite this pressure to re-enter the system, there was awareness within government of the need to deal with the problems that had arisen because of the crisis.[55] In the emergency debate in the House of Commons on 24 September, Chancellor Lamont noted that:

> First, there can be no question of resuming our membership until the current tensions within the foreign exchange markets have subsided. Secondly, I have made it clear to our European partners that we need to have a proper review of the whole way in which the ERM works, the intervention rules, the co-operation procedures and the obligations that it places upon those currencies at the top and the bottom of the exchange rate mechanism bands. Thirdly, and most fundamentally . . . the root cause of the current turbulence has been the unique event of German reunification . . . I do not believe that it would be right for me to recommend that sterling should reenter the ERM unless and until the German economy and ours is more in step.[56]

Chancellor Lamont reiterated the latter point by stating that 'it is not practical to return to the ERM until there is greater symmetry between the policy of this country and Germany'.[57] He later added a further condition that we could not rejoin the ERM until 'we are firmly out of recession'.[58] By late 1992 there was therefore a realisation that sterling's absence from the ERM was not going to be as temporary as Kenneth Clarke and Michael Heseltine had initially thought.

With sterling outside the ERM the government stated that it would pursue the monetary strategy set out in the Medium-Term Financial Strategy, which was published in the Financial Statement and Budget Report. The central objective of the government's policy was to keep the underlying inflation rate within the range of 1–4% per annum, and to bring it down to the lower part of the range by the end of the Parliament. Thus, the irony was that while Lamont had described the ERM as 'our main vehicle for getting inflation down',[59] he noted that the decision to leave the mechanism was a 'watershed',[60] with the government's priority being a reduction in inflation combined with economic growth – the very policies that membership was originally expected to provide.[61] As Helen Thompson notes, 'the core of the post-Black-Wednesday policy was to allow sterling to float downwards and to cut interest rates aggressively to achieve a recovery as soon as possible' (Thompson, 1996: 199). The government's very ability to control inflation benefited from the fact that it had greater flexibility to reduce interest rates as a result of the floating pound. A relaxation of monetary policy was possible because interest rates were no longer needed to support sterling. This meant that base rates were reduced on 22 September and 16 October, while the average £/DM rate in October was DM2.45, which was 13% below its August level and 13% below the average throughout 1991.[62] The dramatic reduction in sterling's exchange rate after 16 September, and continuance of the sterling/DM rate at around 2.40 as illustrated in Tables 8.5 and 8.6, highlighted the degree that sterling had been overvalued.

Conclusion

In analysing Britain's position within the ERM, it is apparent that entry was caught up with the debate on EMU, with membership being in the first instance dictated by a desire to exert some form of influence on the monetary union negotiations. The benefit of a stable exchange rate regime and a low inflation rate seem to have been of secondary importance. The government in effect used ERM membership as a fallback option to convince its European partners of its commitment to European integration. From the outset the government was aware that its views on EMU were different from the majority of the other member states and must have been aware of the likelihood that it could not accept the majority position on EMU. This meant that the government 'blindly' adhered to the ERM discipline irrespective of the tensions within the system, as it had to convince other European governments of its commitment. This assurance was particularly necessary in the wake of the negotiation of the EMU opt-out at the December 1991 Maastricht European Council.

With Britain outside the ERM, the policies that had been central to the 1992 election of the Conservative Party evaporated. John Major had viewed Britain

Table 8.5   Sterling/Deutschmark exchange rates, 1992–1993[a]

Date	DM/£
1 July	2.8970
3 July	2.8955
13 July	2.8532
13 August	2.8199
24 August	2.8001
26 August	2.7970
4 September	2.8017
14 September	2.8131
16 September	2.7784
18 September	2.6100
30 September	2.5095
1 October	2.4840
5 October	2.3930
13 October	2.5281
28 October	2.4317
2 November	2.4063
9 November	2.4255
12 November	2.4126
27 November	2.4186
8 December	2.4942
31 December	2.4520
4 January	2.4571
26 January	2.4267
5 February	2.3961
12 February	2.3555
25 February	2.3387
12 March	2.3887
16 March	2.3985
31 March	2.4254

[a] Close of business rates in London.

Source: 1 July–30 September, *Bank of England Quarterly Bulletin*, Vol. 32, No. 4, November 1992, p. 390; 1 October–31 December, *Bank of England Quarterly Bulletin*, Vol. 33, No. 1, February 1993, p. 63; 4 January–31 March, *Bank of England Quarterly Bulletin*, Vol. 33, No. 2, May 1993, p. 206.

Table 8.6   The sterling exchange rate, 1992–1993[a]

	30 June	15 Sept.	31 Dec.	5 Feb.	7 May
US$	1.90	1.89	1.52	1.45	1.58
DM	2.90	2.78	2.45	2.40	2.49
ECU	1.41	1.38	1.26	1.30	1.27

[a] Close of business rates.

Source: *Bank of England Quarterly Bulletin*, Vol. 33, No. 1, February 1993, p. 17 and No. 2, May 1993, p. 161 for figures for 7 May.

BOX 8.5

Developments in the EMS, 1979–1993

1. Between 1979 and 1983 the ERM was the 'crawling peg' of stable but adjustable exchange rates. There were eight realignments as currencies found a settled parity.

2. The period from 1983 until 1987 is often referred to as the 'old EMS'. This was the most successful period of the system, as states viewed the ERM as the instrument of domestic monetary discipline. Weaker states gained anti-inflationary credibility by tying monetary policies to those of the Bundesbank. The Deutschmark therefore became an anchor currency. This resulted in a minimisation of exchange rate fluctuations and lower inflation rates, while there were only four realignments throughout this period.

3. After 1987 the ERM became increasing inflexible. The 1987 Basle–Nyborg agreement on closer coordination of monetary policy set an informal rule that realignments were to be avoided. This represented a political desire to move towards EMU. The ERM therefore became a quasi-fixed exchange rate system. But the result of this was that the ERM lost its flexibility, causing asymmetry. The removal of exchange rate controls meant that it was harder to resist currency speculation. Turbulence in the ERM was also caused by German unification, which caused high interest rates across the EC during a recession. But there was no broad realignment of the ERM, with the UK refusing to devalue. The Bundesbank became concerned about ERM rigidity and focused on the domestic economy. In September 1992 the lira and sterling were forced out of the ERM as speculators attacked currencies. In addition, the peseta, escudo and punt were devalued in 1992/93.

4. Pressure on the French franc led to the August 1993 decision to widen the ERM bands by 15% for all but the DM and guilder. There was a retreat to hard floating, but by 1994 many states were informally operating in narrow bands. Bands of 15% were accepted as 'normal' for EMU purposes. There was a pre-EMU division into strong and weak currencies – the lira was readmitted in 1996, while the peseta and escudo were devalued in 1995.

as 'at the heart of Europe,'[63] with him being part of the European troika – a partner with Helmut Kohl and François Mitterrand in helping to determine the future direction of Europe. A strong pound had remained at the heart of Britain's monetary policy and Major had stated as recently as 10 September that to devalue would be 'a betrayal of Britain's future'. After Black Wednesday the Prime Minister was 'not sure whether Norman and I could reconstruct economic policy' (Major, 1999: 334). The ERM withdrawal caused cracks in the leadership of the Conservative Party, with Major's instinct being to resign, as he had taken Britain into the ERM as Chancellor in 1990. He would later comment that 'my own instinct was clear: I should resign' (Major, 1999: 334). That he subsequently took Britain out of the system (at the same time that Britain held the presidency of the Community[64]), was a setback for the policies that he had advocated. As he himself later reflected, 'we entered the ERM to general applause, and left it to general abuse' (Major, 1999: 340). The ERM exit increased the tone of scepticism within the Conservative Party concerning the ratification of the Treaty on European Union. As Dyson and Featherstone point out, 'the September 1992 crisis in the ERM emboldened the Eurosceptics, cast a shadow over claims that Britain was at the "heart of Europe", necessitated a redirection of government economic policy and seriously damaged its electoral fortunes' (Dyson and Featherstone, 1999: 73–4). A further overriding concern for Major was that the political effectiveness of the Chancellor of the Exchequer, Norman Lamont, was increasingly in doubt due to his role in the inept attempt at defending the pound.

In many respects the government became a hostage to its own fortunes. Having won the 1992 general election, it suffered the humiliation of having to leave the ERM. As interest rates were reduced, the economy slowly emerged from recession. Economic recovery was nevertheless not translated into a political recovery for the Conservative Party. It continued to be hammered in the opinion polls, not least because the government continued to advocate many unpalatable policies. Chief among these was the coalmine closure programme and a subsequent increase in indirect taxation. More fundamentally, the government increasingly appeared to be incapable of governing. As Chapter 9 points out, the Prime Minister became unable to steer the ship of state in a clear direction. His premiership was dogged by Cabinet splits, an unhealthy dose of ministerial 'sleaze' and an inability to construct a united policy on European affairs. And even when there appeared to be a semblance of agreement on European policy, ministers continued to leak policy documents to the press and counter the government line. In such a situation, the Prime Minister appeared ineffectual and unable to impose any form of control on his party. As the 1992 Parliament neared its end, Major attempted to confront these demons by holding a leadership election in 1995. But although he won that victory, the government was still unable to establish any form of coherent policy, particularly on European affairs.

Key points

- Britain entered the ERM in 1990 at a time when the system was becoming increasingly unstable. This instability was influenced by the lack of realignments among ERM members in recent years, whilst the removal of capital controls in July 1990 meant that there was greater freedom for currency speculators.

- The stability of the ERM was directly linked to the success of EMU. In the course of 1992 a number of referendums took place on the Treaty on European Union, the first of which took place in Denmark on 2 June and resulted in a vote against the treaty. The immediate impact of this took the form of a weakening in the Danish currency.

- Throughout 1992 currency speculators considered that the ERM was unstable, whilst at the same time member governments refused to countenance a realignment of currencies as this might have been perceived as a recognition of a weakness in the system.

- Currency speculators considered that the value of the British pound should fall through a realignment and were therefore prepared to sell the weaker British pound in anticipation of such a decision. At the same time the government refused to consider a realignment or devaluation and attempted to support the value of sterling through intervention by the Bank of England in the foreign exchange markets.

- In attempting to support the value of sterling the government raised interest rates to 15%, but this proved ineffective and the government was forced to leave the ERM in September 1992 (Black Wednesday).

- The ERM continued to remain unstable throughout 1993 and this was influenced by the general uncertainty over Europe's competitiveness and the likely success of EMU.

- Britain had entered the ERM at a time when the system was showing signs of greater volatility and in hindsight some commentators consider that entry should have taken place earlier, in the mid-1980s.

Questions

1. 'Britain entered the ERM at the wrong time and for the wrong reasons.' Discuss.

2. What factors influenced the instability within the ERM in the early 1990s?

3. What were the implications of the lifting of capital controls in July 1990?

4. 'Britain's exit from the ERM demonstrated the fallacy of the argument that national governments have sovereign control over their currency.' Discuss.

5. To what extent did Britain's exit from the ERM highlight the unrealistic nature of monetary union?

6. 'Instead of pacifying the Conservative Party, the Maastricht Treaty tore it apart.' Discuss.

7. To what extent was Britain's entry to the ERM determined by the need to engage in the EMU negotiations rather than as a means of promoting economic stability?

8. Why, and with what results, did Britain leave the ERM in September 1992?

9. 'In retrospect, Britain's exit from the ERM signalled the end of John Major's ability to act as an effective leader of the Conservative government.' Discuss.

10. To what extent did Britain remain at the 'heart of Europe' after Britain's exit from the ERM?

Further reading

Gros, Daniel and Thygesen, Niels (1998) *European Monetary Integration*, 2nd edn, Harlow: Longman, Chapter 5.

Lamont, Norman (1999) *In Office*, London: Little, Brown, Chapters 9–10.

Major, John (1999) *The Autobiography*, London: HarperCollins, Chapter 14.

Stephens, Philip (1996) *Politics and the Pound*, London: Macmillan, Chapter 10.

Thompson, Helen (1996) *The British Conservative Government and the European Exchange Rate Mechanism, 1979–1994*, London: Pinter.

Notes

[1] *The Economist*, 20 July 1991, p. 33.

[2] *Survey of Current Affairs*, Vol. 22, No. 4, London: HMSO, April 1992.

[3] Major noted that 'Whatever my own forebodings, Tory MPs could not conceal unfeigned delight that their party had managed to win a fourth term in office' (Major, 1999: 310).

[4] The Governor of the Bank of England highlighted the possibility that the abolishing of capital controls could result in large speculative movements in a speech at the 1988 Forex Conference of the Forex Club, Luxembourg, 15 November 1988. *Bank of England Quarterly Bulletin*, February 1989, Vol. 29, No. 1, pp. 59–63.

[5] The Madrid conditions for ERM entry included a reduction in the inflation rate, abolition of all restrictions on capital movements, complete liberalisation of financial services, completion of the internal market and a stronger Community competition policy (Howe, 1994: 583; Lawson, 1992: 934).

[6] Sterling reached its highest level against the dollar for eight and a half years on 23 August when its value hit $1.9590, while it touched DM3.0335 on 29 August, the highest level it had been since October 1989. *Bank of England Quarterly Bulletin*, Vol. 30, No. 3, August 1990, p. 334 and No. 4, November 1990, p. 470.

[7] Sir Terence Burns, *First Report from the Treasury and Civil Service Committee*, HC41 (1990–91), p. 20.

[8] This was a view held by Patrick Minford and Sir Alan Walters. *Economic Outlook*, February 1992, pp. 31–4.

[9] Norman Lamont, 'Britain and the Exchange Rate Mechanism' – speech to the European Policy Forum, 10 July 1992. Also *Survey of Current Affairs*, Vol. 22, No. 8, London: HMSO, August 1992, pp. 332–5, and *Treasury Bulletin*, Vol. 3, No. 2, London: HMSO, summer 1992. Similar views are noted in Lamont, 1999: 217. Also *Financial Statement and Budget Report 1991–92*, HC (1990–91), Q. 300, para. 2.02, and *Bank of England Quarterly Bulletin*, Vol. 30, No. 4, November 1990, pp. 482–4.

[10] *Bank of England Quarterly Bulletin*, Vol. 32, No. 1, February 1992, pp. 30–1. Also *The Guardian*, 29 November 1991, p. 14.

[11] Finland experienced a major exchange rate crisis in November 1991 when large capital outflows meant that by 14 November its foreign exchange reserves were virtually depleted, resulting in the government having to abandon its pegged link to the ECU. At the same time, the Swedish krona was subjected to pressure in late 1991, with the Riksbank raising interest rates on 5 December by 6% to 17.5%. Such events provided clear warning signals to the members of the ERM that the exchange markets were unstable.

[12] *Bank of England Quarterly Bulletin*, Vol. 32, No. 2, May 1992, pp. 205–9.

[13] Norman Lamont, *First Report from the Treasury and Civil Service Committee*, HC58 (1991–92), Q. 330.

[14] *Survey of Current Affairs*, Vol. 22, No. 6, London: HMSO, June 1992, pp. 166–80.

[15] *Bank of England Quarterly Bulletin*, Vol. 32, No. 3, August 1992, pp. 274–5.

[16] Norman Lamont, 'Britain and the Exchange Rate Mechanism' – speech to the European Policy Forum, 10 July 1992. Helen Thompson reflected: 'But for all Major's and Lamont's bravura in the face of the foreign exchange markets, the systemic crisis could not disguise the fact that sterling and the lira confronted unique difficulties in the ERM credibility stakes' (Thompson, 1996: 191).

[17] EC Finance Ministers issued a statement on 28 August insisting that 'a change in the present structure of central rates would not be the appropriate response to the current tensions in the EMS'. Quoted in Bank for International Settlements, *63rd Annual Report*, Basle, June 1993, p. 185.

[18] *Financial Times*, 4 September 1992, p. 1.

[19] Treasury press notice, 5 September 1992.

[20] Robin Leigh-Pemberton, *Treasury and Civil Service Committee, The Future Conduct of Economic Policy*, HC (1992–93) 201–ii (minutes of evidence 28 October 1992), Q. 166.

[21] *Financial Times*, 1 September 1992, p. 1; 8 September 1992, p. 2; 16 September 1992, p. 2.

[22] *Financial Times*, 10 September 1992, p. 1.

[23] *Financial Times*, 14 September 1992, pp. 1 and 18. Also *EC Bulletin*, Issue 9, 1992, point 1.2.1.

[24] Published in the *Financial Times* on 1 October 1992. See *Financial Times*, 16 September 1992, p. 1.

[25] Interview with the *Financial Times*, 12 October 1992.

[26] Norman Lamont, *Treasury and Civil Service Committee, The Future Conduct of Economic Policy*, HC201-ii (1992–93) (minutes of evidence 28 October 1992), Q. 7.

[27] Robin Leigh-Pemberton, ibid., QQ. 151–5 and 161–4.

[28] John Major, 'The British Economy', speech to the Scottish CBI, 10 September 1992.

[29] Treasury press notice, 13 September 1992. Also see *Financial Times*, 11 September 1992, p. 1.

[30] *Financial Times*, 16 September 1992, p. 3 and 17 September 1992, p. 2.

[31] *Financial Times*, 14 September 1992, p. 2.

[32] *Financial Times*, 16 September 1992, p. 1.

[33] *The Sunday Times*, 13 December 1992 and *Financial Times*, 30 November 1992, p. 14.

[34] Norman Lamont, *Treasury and Civil Service Committee, The Future Conduct of Economic Policy*, HC201-i (1992–93) (minutes of evidence 12 October 1992), Q. 3.

[35] *Financial Times*, 17 September 1992, p. 6.

[36] *Financial Times*, 17 September 1992, p. 2. Also *Bull. EC*, Issue 9, 1992, point 1.2.2.

[37] For a review of the suspension of ERM membership see *Survey of Current Affairs*, Vol. 22, No. 10, London: HMSO, October 1992, pp. 430–3.

[38] *Financial Times*, 3 September 1992, p. 2 and 16 September 1992, p. 2.

[39] *Financial Times*, 3 September 1992, p. 1 and 14 September 1992, p. 1.

[40] Robin Leigh-Pemberton, *Treasury and Civil Service Committee, The Future Conduct of Economic Policy*, HC201-ii (1992–93) (minutes of evidence 28 October 1992), Q. 168.

[41] Norman Lamont, *Treasury and Civil Service Committee, The Future Conduct of Economic Policy*, HC201-i (1992–93) (minutes of evidence 12 October 1992), Q. 5.

[42] *Goldman Sachs UK Weekly Comment*, 28 August 1992.

[43] Statement by the Bundesbank, published in the *Financial Times*, 1 October 1992, p. 2.

[44] Norman Lamont, *Treasury and Civil Service Committee, The Future Conduct of Economic Policy*, HC201-i (1992–93) (minutes of evidence 12 October 1992), Q. 10.

[45] Ibid.

[46] Robin Leigh-Pemberton and Eddie George, *Treasury and Civil Service Committee, The Future Conduct of Economic Policy*, HC201-ii (1992–93) (minutes of evidence 28 October 1992), QQ. 158 and 160 respectively.

[47] Ibid., Q. 160.

[48] See Robin Leigh-Pemberton, ibid., Q. 160.

[49] Norman Lamont, *House of Commons Official Report*, 24 September 1992, C. 101. With regard to monetary tension between Germany and the UK see Norman Lamont, *Treasury and Civil Service Committee, The Future Conduct of Economic Policy*, HC201-i (1992–93) (minutes of evidence 12 October 1992), Q. 50.

[50] Norman Lamont, *Treasury and Civil Service Committee, The Future Conduct of Economic Policy*, HC201-i (1992–93) (minutes of evidence 12 October 1992), Q. 52.

[51] Governor of the Bank of England, speech to the CBI Eastern Region, 8 October 1992.

[52] Philip Stephens, 'Major Faces the Most Serious Test of his Career', *Financial Times*, 17 September 1992, p. 4, and Norman Lamont, *Treasury and Civil Service Committee, The 1992 Autumn Statement*, HC201-iii (1992–93) (minutes of evidence 16 November 1992), Q. 179.

[53] Norman Lamont, *House of Commons Official Report*, 12 November 1992, col. 991. The need to pursue a more balanced domestic policy was noted by the Governor of the Bank of England in a 'speech at the Lord Mayor's dinner for the bankers and merchants of the City of London', 29 October 1992, reproduced in the *Bank of England Quarterly Bulletin*, November 1992, Vol. 31, No. 4, pp. 458–60.

[54] Norman Lamont, speech to the Interim Committee of the IMF/World Bank Annual Meetings, 20 September 1992. Also *Financial Times*, 21 September 1992.

[55] *House of Commons Official Report*, 24 September 1992, col. 3.

[56] *House of Commons Official Report*, 24 September 1992, col. 104. These points were also emphasised by John Major, *House of Commons Official Report*, 24 September 1992, col. 3. Also *Financial Times*, 25 October 1992.

[57] Norman Lamont, *Treasury and Civil Service Committee, The Future Conduct of Economic Policy*, HC201-I (1992–93) (minutes of evidence 12 October 1992), Q. 78.

[58] Norman Lamont, *Treasury and Civil Service Committee, The 1992 Autumn Statement*, HC201-iii (1992–93) (minutes of evidence 16 November 1992), Q. 205.

[59] Norman Lamont, *Treasury and Civil Service Committee, The Future Conduct of Economic Policy*, HC201-I (1992–93) (minutes of evidence 12 October 1992), Q. 39.

[60] Norman Lamont, Mansion House speech, 29 October 1992.

[61] See Norman Lamont, *Treasury and Civil Service Committee, The 1992 Autumn Statement*, HC201-iii (1992–93) (minutes of evidence 16 November 1992), Q. 178 and Robin Leigh-Pemberton, *Treasury and Civil Service Committee, The Future Conduct of Economic Policy*, HC201-ii (1992–93) (minutes of evidence 28 October 1992), Q. 92.

[62] *Bank of England Quarterly Bulletin*, Vol. 32, No. 4, November 1992, p. 380.

[63] John Major, *The Evolution of Europe*, Speech to the Konrad Adenauer Foundation, London: Conservative Political Centre, 11 March 1991. Also *The Economist*, 9 March 1991, pp. 27–8.

[64] See *Survey of Current Affairs*, Vol. 22, No. 1, London: HMSO, February 1992, pp. 31–3.

CHAPTER 9

Into the darkness: 1993–1997

Objectives

- Demonstrate the extent to which divisions within the Conservative Party hampered the ability of John Major to govern in an effective manner.
- Examine whether the Conservative government had a clear strategy on European policy and the extent to which initiatives were determined by Eurosceptic views.
- Highlight that the 1995 Conservative Party leadership contest did not resolve divisions within the Conservative Party.

Introduction

The evidence presented so far has demonstrated the difficulties encountered by successive British governments in responding to policy developments at the European level, especially those of a monetary nature. Conservative Party managers had increasingly found it difficult to establish a set of policy guidelines that could bind the party together, including those MPs of a Europhile and Eurosceptic persuasion. Moreover, just when it appeared that a common ground had been brokered, this proved more often than not to be a temporary achievement. This state of affairs was certainly accentuated by Britain's humiliating exit from the Exchange Rate Mechanism in the autumn of 1992, which accentuated divisions over European policy (Major, 1999: 312–41; Lamont, 1999: 246–66).[1] Many MPs became supporters of the Eurosceptic cause, despite having defended the agreement brokered by John Major at the Maastricht European Council in December 1991.

From within and outwith Parliament it was plainly evident that John Major's government not only suffered criticism from the opposition Labour Party, but from Conservative MPs too. Of the factors that influenced this state of affairs, the most obvious was the slim majority of 21 that the government had obtained in the April 1992 general election. A carefully marshalled group of disloyal Conservative MPs thus had the potential to cause serious damage to government policy-making. A second and very much related factor was that many of the new intake of Conservative MPs from the 1992 general election were of a Eurosceptical nature (Major, 1999: 358). They were somewhat brasher, and for them the party did not always come first. Personal promotion was a significant factor that influenced their beliefs. From the summer of 1992 onwards, the fashionable cause was to attack the European Union, especially the Maastricht Treaty and the progression towards EMU.

Losing control

Throughout his period in office, John Major constantly had to grapple with the difficult task of maintaining unity within the Conservative Party. In many respects this was a factor that completely dominated all areas of policy-making and affected the strategic direction of government. As the 1992–97 Parliament progressed, it became ever more evident that policy-making was more often than not of a reactive nature, responding to problems and crises as they emerged rather than being part of an overall plan. As Philip Stephens notes, 'mesmerised by internal divisions, the government lost a sense of purpose – policy-making was abandoned in favour of crisis management' (Stephens, 1996: 307). This state of affairs was primarily dictated by a desire to maintain party unity, influenced by Major's own preference for consensus in decision-making. From the moment he was elected Prime Minister, he was aware that he was *primes inter pares* rather than someone who dominated policy. As Prime Minister he therefore acknowledged his dependence on fellow Cabinet colleagues and the wider parliamentary party. More fundamentally, he was also aware that the lack of discussion under Thatcher (especially in the latter years of her premiership) had played a significant part in her own downfall as Prime Minister. It was consequently not surprising that there was a great deal more discussion of policy matters during Major's time as Prime Minister (see Chapter 2). Reflecting on this difference in policy styles, Major commented that 'Margaret had often introduced subjects in Cabinet by setting out her favoured solution: shameless, but effective. I, by contrast, preferred to let my views be known in private, see potential disasters ahead of the meeting, encourage discussion, and sum up after it' (Major, 1999: 209). Though this is a rather simple contrast, Major was nonetheless capable of being ruthless and devious when handling some policy issues. Discussion does, however, not necessarily make for better decision-taking, while it also makes it more difficult to establish core issues that determine the direction of policy-making. This was something that became more evident as the 1992–97 Parliament progressed, the effect of which was for the Prime Minister to become a weather vein for Conservative Party policies.

The difficulty of maintaining a balancing act between the differing interests within the Conservative Party was a particularly complex problem throughout the 1992–97 Parliament because the government had only obtained a working majority of 21 in the 1992 general election. From the outset it was evident that the government, and especially John Major, had a limited degree of scope for dominating policy. The absence of a comfortable parliamentary majority consequently meant that the government could not afford to ostracise many Conservative MPs, a situation that was accentuated by the charged emotion that surrounded European policies. This balancing act became more difficult during the course of the 1992–97 Parliament through the defection of some MPs, including Alan Howarth to Labour and Emma Nicholson to the Liberal Democrats. The main reason, however, for a reduction in the government's majority (and ergo its ability to govern) was the steady run of by-election defeats,[2] as highlighted in Table 9.1. And, as Table 9.2 demonstrates, some of

Table 9.1   By-election results for 1992–1997 Parliament

Constituency	Result
Newbury	Conservative to Liberal Democrat
Christchurch	Conservative to Liberal Democrat
Rotherham	Labour to Liberal Democrat
Barking	Conservative to Labour
Eastleigh	Conservative to Liberal Democrat
Newham North East	Conservative to Labour
Bradford South	Conservative to Labour
Dagenham	Conservative to Labour
Monklands East	Labour to SNP
Dudley West	Conservative to Labour
Perth and Kinross	Conservative to SNP
Islwyn	Labour to Plaid Cymru
Littleborough and Saddleworth	Conservative to Liberal Democrat
Hemsworth	Labour hold
Staffordshire South East	Conservative to Labour

Table 9.2   Biggest swings to Labour (%)[3]

By-election	Year	Swing
Liverpool Wavertree	1935	30 to Labour
Fulham East	1933	29 to Labour
Dudley West	1994	29 to Labour
Staffordshire South East	1996	22 to Labour
Mid Staffordshire	1990	21 to Labour

the most significant changes of voting behaviour in the twentieth century took place during this period.

The by-election defeats inflicted on the Conservative Party dealt a savage blow to the ability of the government to shape policy and took away all hope of winning the forthcoming general election. Major considered the first of these defeats, that at Newbury on 6 May 1993, to be 'calamitous', while his Chancellor, Norman Lamont, thought it 'disastrous' (Major, 1999: 377; Lamont, 1999: 364). The 28% swing against the Conservative candidate represented the worst by-election defeat since 1979. The election had provided the electorate with an opportunity to inflict damage on the government, the scale of which had the effect of ministers appearing to be almost punch drunk. It was clear to Major that this result necessitated immediate action and the most obvious target was the replacement of Norman Lamont as Chancellor. His position had been in doubt since the ERM debacle of September 1992 (Lamont, 1999: 362), while he had in the meantime done little to instil confidence in himself or the government's economic policy. It became clear to the Prime Minister that his Chancellor was a liability. As Stephens notes, 'Lamont had lost the confidence of a broad swathe of the party at Westminster, and his credibility in the City had never been lower' (Stephens, 1996: 284; Lamont, 1999: 375). On 27 May 1993 Major asked Lamont to leave the Treasury with the option of becoming Environment Secretary, which although a serious offer, was nonetheless a demotion (Lamont, 1999: 371–5). For his part, Lamont refused the post at Environment and then embarked on a rather terse series of exchanges with the Prime Minister in which he offered no future support to the government. The extent of the breakdown in the relationship between Lamont and Major was demonstrated by the former's resignation speech on 9 June 1993. Lamont stated that 'there is too much short-termism, too much reacting to events, and not enough shaping of events. We give the impression of being in office but not in power' (Lamont, 1999: 524, 518–24; 281–4). In his memoirs the Prime Minister commented that Lamont's soundbite 'was, sadly, rather better than any he coined in office' (Major, 1999: 681).

Major's decision to remove Lamont from the Treasury had been determined by three main factors (Seldon, 1997: 375–9). In the first instance, it had become evident that the Chancellor did not have the support of the electorate, the City or the Conservative Party. As Major himself commented: 'gradually he [Lamont] lost the confidence of industry, the City, the media and a large part, though not all, of the Cabinet and the parliamentary party' (Major, 1999: 679). Secondly, while Lamont had put in place a series of economic reforms to stimulate growth in the economy, he had been conspicuously absent in promoting the nation's economic fortunes and thereby campaigning for the Conservative Party. Finally, Major was aware that the vulnerability of his Chancellor reflected a weakness in his own leadership and if he did not act to remedy this state of affairs then his own position as Prime Minister was under threat.

In making such changes, it was evident that Lamont was seen from within government as a scapegoat for the wider ills that beset the Conservative Party.

To be sure, his position had become more difficult (even untenable) since Britain's exit from the ERM. But Major could not credibly replace Lamont in the immediate aftermath of the ERM exit because the Prime Minister had been a strong supporter of the ERM policy, which had also been the collective Cabinet policy (Lamont, 1999: 269). Thus, the removal of Lamont at that time would have further weakened and exposed Major's own position within government. But eight months later, in May 1993, Lamont's status had worsened, primarily as a result of a ferocious media campaign against the Chancellor, to which 'Norman fitted the bill as if born to the role' (Major, 1999: 678). Such stories as Lamont's house being let to a 'sex therapist' and his credit card payments being in arrears did little to instil public confidence in him (Lamont, 1999: 93–5 and 314). More importantly, silly quotes such as 'singing in the bath' after sterling left the ERM and *'Je ne regrette rien'* at the Newbury by-election presented the image of a carefree Chancellor (Major, 1999: 678–9). The cumulative effect of these factors therefore made Lamont's position untenable (Lamont, 1999: 315–16).

In response to these developments, Major decided that Kenneth Clarke was best suited to the vacant post at the Treasury (see Box 9.1). Although Clarke was by no means an economist, he had been one of the staunchest defenders of government policy in the wake of sterling's exit from the ERM. Clarke also provided Major with a heavyweight politician in a key government post. More importantly, he also offered the Prime Minister a loyal ally and confidant, something which Major had lost since the departure of Chris Patten to the governorship of Hong Kong after the 1992 general election.[4] A change in office did not, however, produce a change in the government's fortunes. Although the economy

---

BOX 9.1

Biography of Kenneth Clarke (1940–)

Served as Chancellor of the Exchequer from 1993 to 1997, having had previous Cabinet posts at the Home Office, Education, Health, Trade and Industry, and Employment. He replaced Norman Lamont as Chancellor and advocated a more pro-European strategy. His views on Europe often put him at odds with many Conservative MPs and he appeared to be isolated in Cabinet discussions as the Conservative government leaned towards a more Eurosceptical outlook. Other significant advocates of a pro-European strategy within Cabinet included Michael Heseltine. However, as Chancellor Clarke was particularly concerned that the government should not box itself in by adopting too strong a Eurosceptical position, this inevitably resulted in serious divisions within Cabinet. In the wake of the Conservative defeat in the 1997 general election and John Major's decision to stand down as leader, Clarke unsuccessfully stood for the leadership of the party. But despite being one of the most influential Conservative politicians and certainly one of the most popular among the electorate, his pro-European views meant that he was not included in the Conservative shadow Cabinet from 1997 to 2001.

continued to show signs of recovery, the government's luck in successive by-elections fared no better. By the time the Conservative Party lost the Stafford-shire South East by-election in April 1996, the government had been reduced to an overall majority of only one.[5] Under normal working conditions the Conservative Party in government would have benefited from the support of the Ulster Unionist MPs, but the difficult state of the Northern Ireland peace process at this time meant that such support could not be relied upon. And just as support for the Conservative Party ebbed away at the national level, the same was true at the local level, when heavy defeats were recorded in the local elections. In this context, the Conservative Party lost control of 18 councils in the 1994 local elections,[6] while some 2000 Conservative councillors lost their seats in the 1995 local elections – a result Major regarded as 'appalling' (Major, 1999: 607). Conservative fortunes did not fare much better in the local elections of May 1996.[7]

The maintenance of party unity was hence of prime importance to Major. But whereas the strategy of governing prior to the 1992 general election had been determined by the Prime Minister's own belief in consensus decision-taking, after the 1992 election it was predominantly dictated by the need to stay in government. Any defections, by-election defeats or maverick MPs who voted against the government made the possibility of ejection from office ever more likely. For Prime Minister Major, this also meant that he could be faced by MPs who suddenly found that their negotiating leverage had dramatically increased. It was in this context that eight Eurosceptic MPs lost the Conservative whip at the end of November 1994 (Major, 1999: 602–3). Although this development had been sparked off by a refusal to vote for the imposition of VAT on fuel (a measure agreed to at the 1992 Edinburgh European Council to increase the EU's resources[8]), the reality of the matter was that this band of sceptics were looking for a reason for trouble.[9]

The effect of this was that the removal of the discipline of the Conservative Party provided the rebel MPs with even greater room to cause embarrassment than before and for a period of time they essentially became a separate party (Lamont, 1999: 419–23). Major was all too aware of the damage that this group of individuals was doing to the government, not least in terms of the further reduction in the government's parliamentary majority. A more funda-mental factor was that this was a clear challenge to his leadership and it publicly demonstrated his inability to impose authority on the Conservative Party and offered further incentives for other MPs to engage in similar tactics. The reality of this situation meant that the government finally backed down and restored the whip to the rebel MPs in April 1995, though without imposing any restric-tions upon them – something which Major later realised he should have done (Major, 1999: 607). The rebel MPs were therefore back in the fold of the Conservative Party and were able to continue their policies as before; Major was truly humbled. For his part, Richard Body only agreed to take the whip again in January 1996.[10]

To make matters worse, criticism of government policy did not just come from backbenchers who could be regarded as maverick MPs. Former senior ministers too berated government policy. After his resignation as Chief Secretary to the Treasury in 1995, Jonathan Aitken was particularly critical of government policy. In a similar vein, Norman Lamont, the former Chancellor of the Exchequer and Major's campaign manager during the 1990 Conservative Party leadership contest, undertook a fault-finding mission. At a fringe meeting of the 1994 Conservative Party Conference he mooted the possibility of a British withdrawal from the EU, though the peripheral nature of this encounter highlighted the isolation that the former Chancellor now found himself in (Lamont, 1999: 425–8; Major, 1999: 587).[11] For Lamont, the Eurosceptic banner offered an opportunity to project himself to a wider audience in the aftermath of his departure from government office. Notwithstanding his ministerial speeches in favour of ERM membership,[12] he now attempted a volte-face to attack the merits of ERM membership and the Treaty on European Union (Lamont, 1999: 448–60). But while his opinions had the intention of inflicting maximum damage on the government, particularly the Prime Minister, they were inevitably weakened by his own recent involvement as an architect of government policy. His views thus appeared to be formed more by a disgruntlement about his position outwith government than by a genuine criticism of government policy, as, for instance, Nigel Lawson's criticism of Thatcher had been.

The squabbling over Europe and the lack of cohesiveness within the Conservative Party were a heavy burden for John Major to bear. The Prime Minister commented that 'they were undermining everything we did' (Major, 1999: 608). Criticisms of government policy were obviously personal attacks on his leadership. As part of an effort to placate the Eurosceptics, government policy had increasingly become confrontational towards Europe. The Prime Minister himself had not forgiven Germany for its lack of support for sterling during the ERM crisis of 1992, and he was now less tolerant of the Franco-German alliance (see Chapter 8). This was certainly evident at the Corfu European Council of June 1994, when Major vetoed the candidacy of the Belgian Prime Minister Jean-Luc Dehaene for President of the Commission because his appointment had emerged from a Franco-German proposal (Major, 1999: 608) (see Box 9.2). For the British government, the preferred candidate had been its own Commissioner, Sir Leon Brittan, though when it became apparent that his candidacy lacked sufficient support among other member states, the government had advocated the Dutch Prime Minister, Ruud Lubbers, as a suitable choice.

The immediate effect of Major's veto of Dehaene's appointment was for a further (and extraordinary) European Council to be held in Brussels on 15 July 1994 with the sole purpose of resolving the election of the President of the Commission. At that meeting, agreement was reached on the appointment of the Luxembourg Prime Minister, Jacques Santer, as President of the Commission from January 1995.[13] One of the reasons for John Major's veto of the appointment of Dehaene was because of his own opposition to the private decision-making that had been demonstrated by the Franco-German alliance behind the appointment of the Belgian Prime Minister. But, more importantly, the adoption of a tough position at the European level satisfied the desires of the

---

BOX 9.2

Corfu European Council of 24–25 June 1994

The meeting was dominated by the failure of member states to agree on the appointment of the President of the European Commission. This was partly because the British
Prime Minister, John Major, blocked the candidacy of the Belgian Prime Minister, Jean-
Luc Dehaene. Although Major complained that Dehaene's appointment had arisen
from a Franco-German proposal, the blocking tactic had the benefit of appeasing the
growing tide of Eurosceptic support within the Conservative Party. The dispute over
the election of the President of the European Commission was finally resolved at the
Brussels European Council of July 1994, when member states agreed to the candidacy
of Jacques Santer.

Eurosceptics at home.[14] Moreover, the prominence of this European debate
– in which Britain was seen not to be losing – also meant that domestic difficulties and internal divisions, especially between Kenneth Clarke and Michael
Portillo, no longer appeared to dominate the agenda. The tactic of using foreign
policy issues as a means of shifting the focus away from contentious domestic
points had been used by Major (and other Prime Ministers) on many occasions.

Public gestures and tough talking at European meetings did little, however,
to appease Eurosceptic criticisms of government policy in the long term. By
1995 Major had had enough, announcing on 22 June that he would call a leadership election to take place on 4 July (Major, 1999: 608–47; Lamont, 1999:
434–47). For Major, this was an attempt to impose some form of authority on
the Conservative Party by challenging critics to 'put up, or shut up' (Major,
1999: 612). As a mark of the discontent that existed within the parliamentary
party, the Prime Minister had only a few days earlier faced a hostile meeting of
60 Conservative MPs from the Fresh Start Group (Stephens, 1996: 322–3;
Lamont, 1999: 433–4). The effect of this meeting was that it 'probably made
a leadership contest inevitable' (Lamont, 1999: 434).

The likelihood and eventual calling of the leadership contest produced a
great deal of discussion as to who would challenge the Prime Minister, with
Michael Portillo receiving a great deal of attention (Major, 1999: 624).[15] This
was primarily because Portillo was recognised as being hostile to EU policy,
having broken from the Cabinet agnostic line in May 1994 to stress that 'political or monetary union would mean giving up the government of this country'.[16] Portillo, however, did not stand, possibly remembering that although
Heseltine had been the first to challenge Thatcher, the prize of Prime Minister
went to Major. It was therefore extremely likely that Portillo had his eye firmly
fixed on the probability of a second round in the leadership contest, at which
stage he would advance himself as a candidate. This was certainly the view held
by Lamont from his discussions with Portillo. More importantly, it demonstrated the feeling within the upper echelons of government that Major's tenure
as Prime Minister was finished (Lamont, 1999: 438). Instead of Portillo putting

himself forward as a leadership candidate, the right-wing Welsh Secretary, John Redwood, resigned from the Cabinet to challenge Major.[17] Norman Lamont recollected that Redwood's decision spared him from standing: 'Now it was obvious Redwood was going to stand I concluded that there was no point in my thinking any longer about the matter' (Lamont, 1999: 438).

Despite being a Cabinet Minister, it was unlikely that Redwood would act as the galvanising force that Portillo could have offered. Redwood's own position within Cabinet actually suggested that he had little to lose from the leadership challenge; he had been an unsuccessful Welsh Secretary and it was possible that he would not survive the summer Cabinet reshuffle. As Major himself commented, 'he [Redwood] had nothing to lose' (Major, 1999: 621–2). Victory for Major was, however, likely, with the 4 July vote producing a convincing two-to-one majority for Major who obtained 218 votes. This result was partly influenced by the unwillingness of the supporters of Michael Portillo to vote for Redwood; there was a feeling among MPs that if John Redwood appeared to be too successful then his campaign would become unstoppable (Lamont, 1999: 443). The preferred outcome for many Conservative parliamentarians was consequently for an inconclusive first round of the election contest, at which stage Portillo could enter the second round of the leadership election. The achievement of such a balancing act was obviously extremely tricky, and it was inevitable that Major would fare the better considering the lack of outright support for Redwood. But despite Major's victory, Redwood had nonetheless achieved a notable level of support with 89 votes, and in the course of the campaign had emerged as the standard bearer for the right wing of the Conservative Party.[18] Although banished to the backbenches, Redwood and his fellow Eurosceptics could not be disregarded and in the months ahead he provided much of the intellectual input behind criticisms of government policy. It was consequently evident that there 'were many storms ahead' (Major, 1999: 443).

We can therefore see that despite Major's victory and the cementing of his position as leader of the Conservative Party, the prospects of the Conservative government had not altered.[19] 'My re-election ended the frenzy in the party, but not the conflict', reflected the Prime Minister (Major, 1999: 646). Lamont considered that 'between 1995 and 1997 the fortunes of the Conservative Party at first hardly moved at all and then plunged disastrously into defeat' (Lamont, 1999: 460). In this sense, Major's victory merely ensured that he would lead the Conservative Party to the next general election, and the likely loss of office. There was thus an enhancement of the Prime Minister's authority (especially in the short term), thereby allowing him to reshuffle the Cabinet. This included the promotion of Michael Heseltine to a broader 'firefighting role' as Deputy Prime Minister and Malcolm Rifkind's replacement of Douglas Hurd as Foreign Secretary. But such changes had little impact on voters or the wider unity of the Conservative Party. Major himself seemed unconvinced that his position was now secure, and did not set out to dominate policy. Instead, he continued to weave a path between the various wings of the Conservative Party. The same team was essentially still in power, despite a few changes of position. Some of these changes also portrayed a government that was more sympathetic to the Euro-sceptic position.[20] As a mark of the support obtained by Redwood in the leadership campaign and reflective of the need to resolve disputes within the Conservative Party on European issues, Major appointed a member of John Redwood's campaign team (Roger Knapman) to the government whip's office.[21] (Knapman was one of the organisers of the backbench rebellion against the Maastricht Treaty along with James Cran, who had subsequently become parliamentary private secretary to Sir Patrick Mayhew, the Northern Ireland Secretary.)

Crucially, however, the leadership election had not resolved the division over Europe within the Conservative Party.[22] Moreover, the overwhelming likelihood of defeat in the impending general election meant that many MPs were no longer concerned about party discipline or worried about threats of deselection. The party therefore became increasingly ungovernable. Major himself reflected that 'the European dispute was too deep-seated to be cut off at its source, and in due course the bitterness engendered by it was a primary cause of our party's overwhelming defeat in the 1997 general election' (Major, 1999: 646). Many of these tensions had arisen from the negotiation of the Maastricht Treaty and more specifically its provision for the creation of a single currency.

Ratifying Maastricht

Britain's exit from the ERM in September 1992 had created an extra difficulty in the government's attempt to ratify the Treaty on European Union, otherwise known as the Maastricht Treaty (see Box 9.3). It would be not until 2 August 1993 that Britain finally managed to ratify the treaty, some 19 months after it had been negotiated in December 1991. The intervening months were note-worthy for the deep divisions that emerged in the Conservative Party over the protracted negotiation of the treaty. Concern over the future direction of further European integration was not only evident in Britain; many other EU member states had been affected by a growing tide of Euroscepticism, caused not least by the exchange rate difficulties that have been detailed in Chapter 5. The Maastricht Treaty's convergence criteria for progression to monetary union also necessitated a tightening in the economic priorities of member states, causing a further source of tension among the electorate.

As noted in the previous chapter, the Danish referendum resulted in a degree of instability in the process of treaty ratification. In Britain the business of ratification was particularly tortuous, aided by Margaret Thatcher openly urging Conservative backbenchers to oppose the government and defeat the treaty (Major, 1999: 250 and 261). This certainly made the task of party management a more difficult one. Nevertheless, as Prime Minister, John Major was resolute that the process of ratification had to continue despite these setbacks. Along with other Cabinet colleagues, including Douglas Hurd[23] and Michael Heseltine,

BOX 9.3

Ratifying Maastricht

1992

7 Feb. The Treaty on European Union was formally signed at Maastricht by the EC Foreign and Finance Ministers.

7 May The first reading of the European Communities Bill in the House of Commons.

20–21 May The European Communities (Amendment) Bill passed the second reading in the House of Commons by 336 to 92.

2 June Danish referendum on Maastricht Treaty resulted in a 'no' vote of 50.7% to 49.3%.

3 June More than 100 Conservative MPs signed a House of Commons motion calling for a fresh start on Europe. John Major promised a further debate on the Maastricht Bill.

4 June In a House of Commons debate, Prime Minister Major announced that 'the ratification and implementation of the treaty is in our national interest'.

20 Sept. The Maastricht Treaty was narrowly passed in France by 51.04% to 48.95% – a difference of 539,410 votes.

1 Oct. UK government announced its decision to ratify the Maastricht Treaty and to bring the Bill back to Parliament in December, or early in the new year.

4 Nov. UK government won the paving debate, which allowed the Bill to proceed into the committee stage by 319 votes to 316.

5 Nov. Prime Minister announced that the European Communities Bill would not receive its third reading until after the second Danish referendum of May 1993.

1993

8 Mar. UK government was defeated on a Labour amendment to the Maastricht Bill concerning membership of the Council of Regions by 314 votes to 292, despite the fact that the government had a 20-seat majority in the House of Commons.

22 Mar. House of Commons rejected a call for a referendum on the Maastricht Treaty.

20 May House of Commons gave a third reading to the Maastricht Treaty Bill and the government secured a majority by 292 votes to 112.

24 May First reading in the House of Lords of the European Communities Bill.

7–8 June Second reading in the House of Lords with agreement reached without division.

22 June European Communities Bill reached the committee stage in the House of Lords.

20 July Third reading of the European Communities (Amendment) Bill in the House of Lords was secured by 141 votes to 29. This, therefore, completed the parliamentary stages of the Bill and it received royal assent that evening.

2 Aug. UK government formally ratified the Maastricht Treaty in Rome.

2 Sept. UK deposited its instrument of ratification of the Maastricht Treaty.

Major considered that the deal brokered at Maastricht provided the correct balance to ensure Britain's presence within the core of the Community while at the same time maintaining a degree of flexibility to preserve the national viewpoint. But apart from the merits of the Maastricht deal, any decision not to ratify the treaty had serious implications for Major's own personal authority and Britain's future position within the Community. He therefore announced that 'I have no intention of breaking the word of the British government.'[24] The Maastricht Treaty had been trumpeted as a triumph by Major and was central to his own authority; any decision to disown the treaty would certainly have weakened the remaining vestiges of his command. Secondly, any disavowing of the treaty would no doubt have wrecked Britain's reputation within the Community as a negotiating partner, thereby affecting 'Britain's future in Europe'.[25] In this context a question of trust would have henceforth hung over every decision or promise made by a British government. So while the issue of non-ratification was an objective of some Eurosceptic supporters, the government remained committed to the process of ratification.

Not all members of the Conservative Party agreed with this strategy. Prominent among this grouping were Bill Cash, James Cran, Teresa Gorman, Christopher Gill, Nicholas Budgen, Tony Marlow, Richard Shepherd, Teddy Taylor and John Wilkinson (Major, 1999: 353–8). The lack of sympathy for the Maastricht Treaty was represented by the 22 Tory MPs who voted against the Maastricht Treaty Bill on its second reading in May 1992, despite many of these MPs having supported the agreement brokered by Major at the Maastricht European Council. (Although often referred to in these terms, the proper name of the Maastricht Treaty Bill was the European Communities (Amendment) Bill.) This defection from the government was the biggest Conservative revolt on Europe since the initial debate on British entry, some 20 years previously. The difficulty that surrounded the ratification process was further evidenced a few months later when the government paving motion of 4 November 1992 was only carried by a majority of three votes (319 to 316).[26] Some 26 Conservative MPs had voted against the government, while another six abstained. The narrowness of this victory was especially worrying for the Major government. This was principally because many of the MPs who voted in favour of ratification had done so under the pretence that ratification would not be finalised until after the result of the second Danish referendum, which took place on 18 May 1993[27] and produced a 'yes' vote – much to Lamont's 'disappointment' (Lamont, 1999: 367). Delay was therefore firmly on the cards in light of the initial Danish 'no' vote.

The difficulties that Conservative Party managers had in marshalling a united line behind the government's objective of treaty ratification was made worse by the appearance of unity within the Labour Party. The Labour Party rightly considered Parliament's voting procedure for ratification a perfect opportunity to inflict maximum damage on the government, a point that was enhanced by the treaty having included an opt-out from the Social Chapter – this being an objective that Labour was firmly committed to (Stephens, 1996: 303–4). The effect of this was for the government to lose a vote by 324 to 316 on 22 July

1993.[28] This resulted in Major holding a vote of confidence the next day so as to take the process of ratification to the level of brinkmanship (Major, 1999: 383). This suicide option was not favoured by even the heartiest of Conservative Eurosceptics, who, despite their own views on the Maastricht Treaty, were not prepared to forgo their own Commons seats in favour of a widely predicted Labour victory. So, with the exception of one MP, the Eurosceptics had been silenced.

This silence nevertheless proved to be a false dawn. The party was still divided and Prime Minister Major had not imposed a commanding grip on the ship of state. The Eurosceptic camp included such notable MPs as Teddy Taylor and Bill Cash. In private, and increasingly in public, members of Major's own Cabinet would soon be adopting a Eurosceptic tone when briefing against government policy. Notable names included Cabinet Ministers such as Michael Portillo, John Redwood and Peter Lilley, while former Prime Minister Thatcher was ever more critical of government European policy, particularly with the publication of the second volume of her memoirs, *The Path to Power* (Thatcher, 1995: 602–6), which contained an epilogue that Major rightly considered 'could only be interpreted as an attack on my own policies' (Major, 1999: 613). Added to this the press adopted a hostile attitude to the EU, including *The Times*, the *Daily Telegraph* and *The Sun* (Major, 1999: 358–9, 587 and 611).

Satisfying EMU

From the foregoing information it is evident that a great many of the Conservative government's difficulties stemmed from disputes over European policies. Under this broad canopy sat a number of issues, including the extension of greater powers to the European Parliament and the future reform of the European Union. But despite the relative importance of these topics, particularly with regard to the accession of new member states, monetary union was the key question that focused the minds of Conservative MPs, of both a Eurosceptic and a Europhile persuasion. It was also the one question that the government, especially Prime Minister Major, found the most difficult to resolve. Major was himself quite pragmatic on the subject of monetary union, not wishing to rule out or rule in British participation, and his desire was to maximise the range of options available to him. As he himself commented: 'while my gut instincts were strongly opposed to a single currency, my assessment was that one day it would go ahead, and if it proved to be successful, an economic low-pressure system over the Continent would suck sterling into it. If our economic well-being demanded entry, as one day I thought it might, then in the end we would go in. That was my firm opinion' (Major, 1999: 272). This straddling of the centre ground was a regular procedure that the Prime Minister had followed when taking decisions on other policy matters. Monetary union was, however, a different issue to that of resolving an interdepartmental budgetary dispute and it was unlikely that compromising measures could bind the Conservative Party together.

An emphasis on unity had, in fact, been the key factor in determining the government's position at the Maastricht European Council of December 1991. In this sense the opt-out provision provided Major with the ability to make no formal commitment to EMU. The only other member state to hold a similar negotiating position was Denmark, which had brokered a special deal at the Edinburgh European Council of December 1992 (Seldon, 1997: 348–51). Ever the pragmatist, Major's own views on the validity and practicality of monetary union became increasingly sceptical after sterling's exit from the ERM in September 1992 (see Chapter 8). Nearly a year later the ERM faced collapse on 1–2 August 1993, when it was only saved by a widening of the fluctuation bands from 2.25% to 15%. In the midst of these developments, the policy that Major advocated was one of 'wait and see', receiving strong support from the Foreign Secretary, Douglas Hurd, who was agnostic towards the subject. This position certainly differed from Kenneth Clarke, who replaced Lamont as Chancellor in the 1993 Cabinet reshuffle, and was supportive of EMU.[29]

The issue of monetary union sat at the core of Conservative divisions over Europe, between those who considered that Britain could only maintain an active role in Europe by means of participation and those who regarded EMU as a real threat to the nation-state. Just as there were divisions in the parliamentary party, so too were there divisions in Cabinet, many of which spilled into the public domain. To this end, Prime Minister Major often tried to end the Cabinet 'speculation and debate' over the single currency (Major, 1999: 604). Within Cabinet, Michael Portillo, Peter Lilley, Michael Howard and John Redwood were all hostile to EMU, while Michael Heseltine and Kenneth Clarke wanted to ensure that the government gave proper consideration to this policy development. Between them sat pragmatists such as Gillian Shephard and Stephen Dorrell, who, although not being part of the sceptical camp, considered that there was little likelihood of the Conservative Party committing itself to the single currency, and that little benefit would come of it especially as such a decision would no doubt split the party. Outside government, Norman Tebbit and Margaret Thatcher demanded that sterling should not be scrapped.

As on previous occasions, the establishment of a British position on monetary union was fraught with the difficulty of creating a position to which all members of the Conservative Party could hold (Major, 1999: 138). In this light, the 'wait and see' approach followed the earlier hard ECU plan (Major, 1999: 150–1). For Major, the benefit of the 'wait and see' approach was firstly one of practical timing; there was no need to commit to a system that had yet to be established. As outlined in Chapter 7, the Maastricht Treaty had provided for a three-stage approach to monetary union. The first stage, involving the closer coordination of economic policies, had commenced in July 1990, while the second stage, involving the establishment of the European Monetary Institute – the predecessor of the European Central Bank – was scheduled to start in January 1994. Finally, Stage 3 was scheduled to commence in January 1997 or January 1999,[30] at which point a European System of Central Banks would be established to coordinate the interest rate policies of those countries wanting to

---

BOX 9.4

EMU convergence criteria

Four convergence criteria for progression to monetary union were set out in Article 109j and Protocol 6 of the Treaty on European Union (Maastricht Treaty):

1. A high degree of price stability, with an average rate of inflation of not more than 1.5% higher than that of the three best performing member states;

2. A sustainable financial position, including a budget deficit of not more than 3% of GDP and a public debt ratio not exceeding 60% of GDP;

3. Currency stability, with participation in the narrow bands of the ERM for two years without severe tension or devaluation;

4. Interest rate convergence, in which member states should have an average nominal long-term interest rate no more than 2% higher than that of the three best performers.

---

join a single currency. A start date of 1997 was only possible if a 'critical mass' of the member states achieved the convergence criteria – seven out of the 12 nations (see Box 9.4). If this were not possible then the third stage would commence in January 1999 for those nations who met the economic criteria, irrespective of how few in number.

For Major, and the government as a whole, the wait and see approach seemed the prudent choice, particularly in the aftermath of the ERM crisis.

> Envisaging that others would now seek to repeat the British experience outside the ERM, they [Major and Clarke] saw no reason to believe that the monetary union project was anything other than dead, ensuring that they would not have to try to sell the impossible to their backbenchers (Thompson, 1996: 206).

There were, in fact, grave doubts about the likelihood of the realisation of monetary union in all member states (Major, 1999: 585). The difficult economic conditions that beset member states in the early 1990s, evidenced by a downturn in growth and an increase in unemployment levels, made it more difficult for governments to adhere to the tough fiscal guidelines that were necessary to meet the convergence criteria for monetary union (the decisions for which were to be taken in March 1998 on the basis of economic performance over the previous year). In this context, in 1996 only Luxembourg and Ireland were certain to meet the convergence criteria,[31] with other states somewhat behind. (Italy had a public debt of 124% of GDP in January 1996, while Spain had a budget deficit of 6% of GDP.) Unsurprisingly, the support for monetary union among the EU electorate declined as governments undertook unpopular cuts in public expenditures so as to meet the convergence criteria. In Britain, both Eurosceptics and those of a more pragmatic viewpoint considered these developments as vindication of the government's lack of support for the single currency. More importantly, this situation increased the feeling in the Euro-sceptic camp that the time was now ripe for the government to firmly commit itself to a position of not joining EMU.

But just as France, Germany and the Benelux group had not been persuaded by opposition to monetary union in the late 1980s, so they remained support-ive of the objective of EMU, although 1997 was no longer regarded as a viable starting date for the single currency.[32] Such developments inevitably meant that Major's policy of 'wait and see' was subject to criticism at home and abroad. Many other European governments thought it duplicitous for Britain to take part in the discussions leading to monetary union, while at the same time offer-ing no evidence of a desire to take part in the project. At home, the Eurosceptics increasingly demanded that the Prime Minister moved from the middle ground to that of firmly stating that Britain would not take part in EMU (see Box 9.5). As

---

BOX 9.5

Arguments against EMU membership

1. Insufficient economic convergence of EU member states to establish a single currency.

2. Participation in monetary union would reduce the ability of national governments to have control over key aspects of the economy, thereby producing a loss of sovereignty.

3. Monetary union would accelerate pressure for the harmonisation of taxes and thereby possibly impact on the competitive advantage enjoyed by Britain by means of low levels of taxation.

4. A single currency would have certain economic costs because of the need to convert the British economy to the euro and these costs might outweigh any advantages of participating in monetary union.

5. Britain is strategically placed between the EU and the United States and a great deal of British trade is with non-EU countries.

6. Related to the above point is the consideration that the British economy is one of the largest in the world (within the top five) and consequently the country is per-fectly capable of maintaining its own currency as enjoyed by other nations that are not so prosperous. Despite its close links with the USA and participation in the North American Free Trade Agreement (NAFTA), Canada has not given up the Canadian dollar.

7. Monetary union would more than likely accelerate the cause of future European integration which would further erode national means of decision-making.

8. Other matters of policy are of greater importance, such as institutional reform and enlargement, and the EU should be attaching importance to them rather than concentrating on EMU.

on previous occasions, the intended outcome of creating a policy which all elements of the Conservative Party could support was soon proving to be worthless.

Just as the Prime Minister encountered pressure not to participate in EMU from Eurosceptics within the Conservative Party, it was also evident that many MPs considered that the government should be involved in EMU. In this context, the Europhiles, especially Kenneth Clarke and Michael Heseltine, told the Prime Minister that they were not prepared for the government to commit itself to not taking part in EMU. To be sure, this camp offered less trouble for Major, but equally they let him know that the option of British membership had to be maintained. Clarke regarded economic sovereignty to be an unrealistic objective and did not share the Eurosceptic viewpoint that Britain could remain unaffected by EMU.[33] Moreover, he also considered that the single currency would not necessitate political upheaval, and he did not share the belief of the Eurosceptics that EMU would result in the creation of a European superstate. The Chancellor thus considered that if Britain did not participate in EMU, it would nonetheless be affected by the single currency (see Box 9.6). Crucially, Kenneth Clarke was not alone in having this viewpoint, with the City and

---

BOX 9.6

Arguments in favour of EMU membership

1. Whilst a loss of sovereignty is obviously a concern to many opponents of EMU, this is not such a clear-cut argument. This is because there are many forces which have an impact on a national currency, and government does not have control over all of them, such as currency speculators.

2. While there would be economic costs in converting the British economy to the euro, there had of course been an earlier successful change through decimalisation.

3. Participation in a single currency would reduce the transaction costs between EU currencies. This would benefit business competitiveness as well as assisting travellers.

4. Business interests, such as the Confederation of British Industry, are supportive of Britain's involvement in the single currency. Non-participation might have an impact on levels of inward investment and this would more than likely lead to higher levels of unemployment.

5. Britain's non-participation in monetary union reduces the ability of government to exercise influence and leadership in the EU. Therefore, British participation in EMU would increase the nation's influence within the EU.

6. The EU accounts for the majority of British imports and exports and therefore the nation's economic interests are strongly focused on other EU member states.

7. The EU is the world's largest trading bloc and has a population and GDP that is greater than the USA. Future enlargement of the EU can only strengthen its international position and it is likely that the euro will emerge as a currency to equal the US dollar.

business groups being especially concerned about the economic and political considerations for Britain if the government was to rule out membership of the single currency.[34] A concern about economic competitiveness had been a long-standing worry of business groups, who considered that the economic and monetary policies pursued by the government did not reflect their interests. Such concerns had previously been evident over British participation in the ERM, while the City had provided the momentum behind the hard ECU plan (see Chapter 7).

Clarke was all too aware of these issues and was not prepared to accept revision of government policy in the light of Eurosceptic demands. These points were made clear in a speech to the European Movement in February 1995 (see Box 9.7),[35] and later emphasised during evidence to a House of Commons Treasury Select Committee.[36] It was not surprising that this public defiance in favour of maintaining the options open for progression to EMU further aggravated the Eurosceptic members of the Conservative Party. Moreover, the Chancellor also stressed in his speech to the European Movement that it would be 'quite possible to have monetary union without political union'.[37] This was a particularly important and controversial viewpoint because it watered down many of the Eurosceptics' concerns over the loss of sovereignty and therefore suggested that a Conservative government could happily participate in EMU without having to sign up to further political integration. While this position reflected the Chancellor's own beliefs, it further fanned the flames that surrounded the question of EMU within the Conservative Party. A strong reaction was partly the Chancellor's intended outcome as he had set out a public marker to the Conservative Party and also to the Prime Minister, who had unsuccessfully pressurised for a withdrawal of this section of the speech (Major, 1999: 604). In response to these developments the Prime Minister attempted to inject a degree of stability into the debate by reaffirming that the government would not decide on EMU until it had to.[38]

The Prime Minister's desire for balance and unity within the Conservative Party masked the fact that he too was becoming sceptical towards the reality of EMU. In this context he led a nationalistic campaign for the Conservative Party in the May 1994 European Parliament elections, thereby reflecting the Eurosceptic position. Helen Thompson notes that 'Major was now in the position of desperately trying to convince voters during the Euro-election campaign that his Cabinet was united, just as it was quite clear that the British government was out of step with its EU partners on the matter' (Thompson, 1996: 209). The fact of the matter was that the Eurosceptic position appeared to be gaining the ascendancy within the Conservative Party, evidenced by Michael Portillo (who was by then Defence Secretary) accusing Brussels of wanting to interfere on defence policy issues at the 1995 Conservative Party Conference.[39] This was despite the fact that Britain had been in the vanguard of the development of a European defence policy.[40]

The appearance of a shift towards a more sceptical tone was further confirmed when Malcolm Rifkind, in his first major speech as Foreign Secretary,

---

BOX 9.7

Paragraph extracts of speech by Chancellor of the Exchequer, Kenneth Clarke, to the European Movement Gala Dinner, 9 February 1995

12. The benefits to British business, and ultimately the living standards of the British people, from the European economy are immense. Thanks to the single market, British firms have direct access to over 370 million consumers in Europe. Our economic ties with Europe are deep-rooted. Over half of our exports are to Europe and 30 per cent of foreign investment into this country is from Europe. Both our trade and investment links have strengthened since we joined. And they are still strengthening.

Economic and Monetary Union

34. What are the potential benefits? By reducing an element of instability and removing the risk of competitive devaluations, a single currency could improve the efficiency of the single market. By providing an exchange rate certainty that, alas, the ERM did not deliver, a single currency could lead to stronger trade and investment links to the benefit of all. Monetary union could – and I emphasise could – secure low inflation and lower and more stable interest rates over the medium-term. We could all benefit from being part of a Europe-wide low-inflation zone. And, of course, a single currency within Europe would reduce the costs that businesses and tourists face every time they exchange money.

36. I entirely understand those who say that after the unhappy experience of our participation in the ERM they will need some persuading that a single currency is either feasible or desirable. The potential pitfalls of a single currency are well known . . .

37. A single currency would not work unless the participating countries were marching as one . . . At present they are out of step.

41. But, inadequate convergence is not the only risk. The framework for monetary policy is also unclear . . .

43. This combination of a lack of convergence and a lack of clarity about the detail convinces me that the exercise of our choice of whether or not to move to a single currency is unlikely to face us as a decision for this country for some time to come. But it would be folly for us to decide now one way or the other simply in response to the short-term political pressures of today . . .

Source: Chancellor's speech to European Movement Gala Dinner (London: HM Treasury, 9 February 1995)

---

stressed that henceforth the only objective for British policy would be the furtherance of the national interest.[41] A few months later, Rifkind announced at a press conference in Brussels on 29 January 1996 that the plans for monetary union by 1999 could collapse within a few weeks.[42] A cautious (sceptical) approach to the EU was mirrored in the negotiating position advanced by the

---

BOX 9.8

Florence European Council of 21–22 June 1996

Britain had adopted a policy of non-cooperation with the EU in May 1996 because of the implementation of a ban on the export of British beef in March 1996. The EU ban had been determined by the BSE crisis. During the four-week period when Britain had adopted a policy of non-cooperation the government had used its veto on more than 70 occasions. In the end a compromise was reached at the Florence European Council, when the government agreed to a more comprehensive slaughter programme of animals than had initially been suggested on 11 June.

---

government for the intergovernmental conference (IGC)[43] that commenced in March 1996.[44] The government specifically made clear that it did not want to give up its right of national veto to block future changes to the EU,[45] while it was also hostile to the introduction of qualified majority voting (QMV) in such policy areas as common foreign and security policy (CFSP), though this approach was strongly criticised by the former Foreign Secretary, Geoffrey Howe.[46] A tough negotiating position towards the EU was thereafter apparent in the government's policy of non-cooperation that emerged as a response to the ban on British beef (see Box 9.8).

Increasingly, the mood within the Conservative Party was that the forthcoming general election should be fought on a domestic basis, including the preservation of the pound. Such tactics appalled Kenneth Clarke and Michael Heseltine, who had been promoted to Deputy Prime Minister in the 1995 Cabinet reshuffle. Within Cabinet this strong alliance could tackle the Eurosceptic attacks from Portillo, Howard and Lilley. Outwith Cabinet, Heseltine had less freedom to defend this policy line as the position of Deputy Prime Minister meant that he had to mirror Major's position. The differences of opinion between Major and Clarke were especially apparent at the December 1995 Madrid European Council, with Major unwilling to appreciate the political will of Paris and Bonn to achieve EMU. Clarke disagreed with this view and informed the press that the odds were 60:40 in favour of EMU progressing,[47] a viewpoint that was confirmed by the summit communiqué which established the detail of the preparatory work necessary for the convergence criteria to be met. This specifically included the decision to call the new currency the euro and that the third stage of EMU would commence on 1 January 1999, with completion by 2002 when the new notes and coins would enter circulation. We can therefore see that just as the Conservative Party was split on EMU, so too was the Cabinet.

In an effort to establish party unity, Major became increasingly sympathetic to Eurosceptic desires for a referendum on the subject of EMU. As with previous policies on monetary union, the benefit of a referendum was that it would appease the Eurosceptics within the Conservative Party (Major, 1999: 687). Again, the decision would be put off by a government unwilling and unprepared to confront the subject. In this context, Major considered that any government embarking on such a policy would be wise to obtain the emphatic and specific endorsement of the electorate by means of a referendum on the single currency question (Major, 1999: 611). Some ministers were, however, unwilling to support a referendum, including Clarke and Heseltine, primarily because they considered such a decision should be taken solely by Parliament (Major, 1999: 275 and 688). Associated with this issue of the proper function of Parliament, there was concern that a referendum would be used as a protest vote against a wider range of government policies. A referendum on EMU would therefore become muddled with other issues, many of which could be of a domestic nature (see Chapter 11). Nevertheless, the desire for a referendum was growing all the time, with former ministers Nigel Lawson and Sir Norman Fowler adding their weight behind the issue,[48] while the Referendum Party led by Sir James Goldsmith had also pressurised for such an outcome.[49] There was thus a split of opinion within the Conservative Party, and moreover within Cabinet, as to the merits of a referendum on the single currency. In light of this division of opinion, Major found it impossible to persuade (in private) 'sufficient colleagues' of the merits of a referendum (Major, 1999: 688). This especially reflected the Prime Minister's inability to convince Heseltine and Clarke, rather than a majority of the Cabinet. Major was all too aware that Clarke would not (and could not) be pushed into accepting the referendum strategy and the Prime Minister more importantly acknowledged that Clarke would have resigned on this point.

Much has been written on John Major's lack of dominance within Cabinet, including his preference for consensus in policy-making (see Chapter 2). But that is not to say that he did not possess an acute political instinct. The Prime Minister was fully aware of the ways in which he could steer policy towards his own objectives, while presenting the outcome as Cabinet and government policy. This has been demonstrated by his handling of the Maastricht Treaty negotiations and was also mirrored by the way in which the referendum was eventually discussed at Cabinet level. As has been noted, John Major was fully aware of the positions taken by his colleagues on this topic, and he was also conscious that monetary union fell within Kenneth Clarke's portfolio as Chancellor. As such, the normal practice would have been for the Chancellor to discuss matters of a monetary nature within Cabinet. It was therefore somewhat surprising that it was the Agriculture Secretary, Douglas Hogg, who raised the option of a referendum on the single currency at a Cabinet meeting on 7 March 1996. Hogg was a junior member of the Cabinet who had little direct experience or knowledge of this matter. While Major suggests that the matter was 'unexpectedly raised' (Major, 1999: 688), it is more likely that the Prime Minister had pressurised Hogg into mentioning the referendum option so that it could be fully discussed at Cabinet level without a direct link back to him. The fact that Douglas Hogg's wife served as the head of the Prime Minister's policy unit also increased the likelihood of this; a strong link existed between the two individuals.

The outcome of the Cabinet discussion was that a majority emerged in favour of a referendum on the single currency. This included both the Eurosceptics, such as Michael Howard, Michael Forsyth and Peter Lilley, and some of the more moderate Europhiles, such as Tony Newton and Gillian Shephard. Somewhat predictably, Kenneth Clarke continued to oppose the strategy. Crucially, however, the concept of the referendum had now been discussed and supported by a meeting of the Cabinet. Prime Minister Major could thus legitimately promote this strategy as government policy, which he announced to Parliament on the afternoon of 7 March 1996. This was despite the opposition of Kenneth Clarke, Michael Heseltine and John Gummer who felt that they had been bounced into accepting the majority view (Major, 1999: 688).

The result of these developments was that on 3 April 1996 the Cabinet accepted the formula that there would be a general election commitment to have a referendum if and when a future Cabinet decided to take Britain into EMU, as well as after Parliament had given its support.[50] This was a move away from the Eurosceptics' desire to hold an independent referendum. Moreover, ministers could not establish independent views as in the 1975 referendum because this time there was the viewpoint that there would be collective Cabinet responsibility. The referendum would also not stretch to matters of other EU policy, but instead be limited to the question of a single currency. An undertaking to hold a referendum nevertheless reflected a further shift in government policy in a Eurosceptic direction, which was ever more at odds with business opinion, which wanted the government to have a strong commitment to Europe.[51]

John Major believed that the referendum commitment would reduce the divisions of opinion within the Conservative Party on the subject of monetary union. Therefore the government attempted to attach greater focus to the forthcoming general election and domestic issues, such as the sustainment of economic growth. But despite this desire, the issue of Britain's negotiating position towards the European Union did not fade away. This was the result of developments at both the domestic and EU levels. Domestically, the strong criticisms of EU policy that were advanced by the Referendum Party and the UK Independence Party meant that the issue of Europe did not stray far from the front pages of newspapers. It was particularly clear that the Referendum Party had moved from a desire for a referendum on the single currency to a more widespread denunciation of the European Union (Major, 1999: 705). Secondly, as the 1997 general election drew closer, discipline within the Conservative Party worsened. This was emphasised by the fact that only one week after Parliament was dissolved before the general election, more than 120 MPs declared their opposition to a single European currency.[52] At the EU level, the drive towards EMU continued unabated and thus British non-participation was ever more apparent. At the Dublin European Council of December 1996 agreement was reached on the legal status of the euro as a single currency and the setting of financial disciplines for the single currency (see Box 9.9).

BOX 9.9

Dublin European Council of 13 December 1996

The Dublin European Council reached agreement on the legal status of the euro and the stability and growth pact that would act as the discipline for the currency. This specifically meant that financial penalties would be applied to all member states that ran a budget deficit (negative growth) of up to 0.75%. It was also agreed that EU Finance Ministers would be able to exercise discretion in applying penalties if the GDP of a member state fell between 0.75% and 2%. Moreover, a member state would automatically be exempt from penalties if its GDP was at least 2% over one year, or in the event of a natural disaster.

Conclusion

John Major regarded the referendum commitment as a means of pacifying the Eurosceptic wing of the Conservative Party and thus as a way of stopping the issue of monetary union from dominating the government's agenda. From 1996 onwards the main focus of attention for the Prime Minister and his parliamentary colleagues was the forthcoming general election. A focus on domestic issues and the satisfying of MPs' interests had determined much of Britain's policy towards Europe, most recently evidenced by the IGC negotiations when the government was isolated on a number of issues, including the granting of powers to the European Parliament and reform of the European Court of Justice.[53] Such a strategy had not increased the chances of the Conservative Party winning the general election, and this was acknowledged both within and outwith government. There were many reasons for this prediction, not least the desire for change after nearly two decades of Conservative government. As John Major himself commented: 'there was deep national impatience with our party' (Major, 1999: 692). While the question of Britain's relations with Europe partly determined the public's lack of tolerance with the government, there was in essence no one definable reason for the 1997 election defeat.[54] To be sure, the behaviour of some Conservative MPs appalled the electorate, and financial, personal and sexual misbehaviour did not help the party's fortunes. The economic recession and pit closure programme of the 1990s that had caused such hardship for a great mass of the electorate was a further nail in the Conservative Party's coffin.[55] But instead of focusing on the core issue of economic recovery, the Conservative Party appeared to be more concerned with the government's negotiating position within the European Union.

The irony of this negotiating position was that while the government had often framed this strategy as being reflective of the national interest, it was increasingly questionable that this was so. After over 17 years of Conservative government, Britain remained adrift from Europe and was not at the 'heart of

Europe'[56] as Major had once predicted. Business, economic and political interests favoured constructive British engagement. But the government had faced isolation in the 1996–97 IGC and had advanced a set of policy proposals that were strongly reflective of the Eurosceptic point of view, and this did much to block progress for the future reform of the Union.[57] The Labour Party's victory in the general election of May 1997 helped to break the deadlock in the IGC negotiations,[58] resulting in a swift conclusion at the Amsterdam European Council of June 1997.[59] The new government offered a more constructive position on Europe, being backed by business leaders,[60] and evidenced by the acceptance of the Social Chapter. Crucially, however, Labour's victory had been substantial and Tony Blair did not suffer the lack of a parliamentary majority that Major had had to endure, but this did not necessarily mean that the new government would be able to resolve all policy matters, especially Britain's commitment to monetary union. As Chapter 10 makes clear, there are many similarities between the position adopted by the Labour government and the previous Conservative government.

Key points

- Whereas Britain's entry to the ERM was perceived by the public and Conservative MPs as a positive step to assist with obtaining lower interest rates, the pound's exit from the ERM assisted in creating a massive split within the Conservative Party. The possibility of a well-organised group of disloyal MPs causing significant damage to government objectives was accentuated by the government only having obtained a majority of 21 MPs in the April 1992 general election.

- From 1992 onwards a significant number of Conservative MPs were hostile to the government's policy, most notably on the issue of Europe. This meant that Prime Minister Major found it increasingly difficult to establish a policy that could bind the party together. In this sense there was an absence of a united policy from 1992 onwards, as splits and divisions eventually produced an ungovernable party that influenced the massive general election defeat in 1997.

- Division within the Conservative Party on the issue of Europe resulted in the government tending to pander to the interests of Eurosceptics by adopting an increasingly tough and hostile position when negotiating at the European level.

- An absence of cohesiveness within the party influenced the decision of John Major to have a leadership contest in 1995, and while he defeated his challenger, John Redwood, the winning margin was not overwhelming. This meant that Major's control and credibility as party leader was not fully restored and internal conflict continued.

- After Britain's exit from the ERM, Norman Lamont's position as Chancellor proved untenable, and while he stayed in office until 1993 his influence was severely limited. His successor, Kenneth Clarke, attempted to cultivate a more positive approach to Europe, but this proved difficult in light of internal party divisions. The net effect of this was that on monetary union the government adopted a 'wait and see' approach. The government was increasingly perceived to be an awkward partner within the EU and consequently the election of a new Labour government in 1997 was welcomed by European governments.

Questions

1. 'Instead of winning the 1992 general election, the Conservative Party would have been better off losing it.' Discuss.

2. In what ways did John Major's style of leadership differ from that of Margaret Thatcher?

3. Do you consider that the Major government's 'wait and see' approach to EMU was the correct strategy?

4. 'John Major was more concerned with maintaining unity within the Conservative Party than offering a constructive approach to Britain's role within the European Union.' Discuss.

5. To what extent did the 1995 Conservative Party leadership contest produce a convincing victory for John Major?

6. Why has European integration become such a contentious issue for the Conservative Party since 1979?

7. To what extent did the issue of monetary union sit at the core of Conservative divisions over Europe?

8. Why was John Major so keen to establish a commitment to hold a referendum to determine whether Britain should enter the single currency?

9. 'Unlike its predecessor, the Major government had no clear vision of Britain's role within the European Union.' Discuss.

10. 'Wrapped up in their own interests': is this a correct assessment of the Conservative government during the 1992–97 Parliament?

Further reading

Blair, Alasdair (2001) 'Understanding the Major Governments', *Contemporary British History*, Vol. 15, No. 1, Spring, pp. 115–22.

Lamont, Norman (1999) *In Office*, London: Little, Brown.

Major, John (1999) *The Autobiography*, London: HarperCollins, Chapters 23–6.

Stephens, Philip (1996) *Politics and the Pound*, London: Macmillan, Chapters 12–13.

Young, Hugo (1998) *This Blessed Plot: Britain and Europe from Churchill to Major*, Basingstoke: Macmillan, Chapter 11.

Notes

[1] Lamont rather cheekily referred to the ERM exit as 'Black or White Wednesday'.

[2] *The Independent*, 17 December 1994, p. 2.

[3] *The Guardian*, 13 April 1996, p. 13 and *The Times*, 13 April 1996, p. 9.

[4] *The Economist*, 20 April 1991, p. 34.

[5] *The Times*, 13 April 1996, p. 9.

[6] *The Independent*, 7 May 1994, p. 6.

[7] *The Independent*, 2 May 1996, p. 1.

[8] *Survey of Current Affairs*, Vol. 23, No. 1, London: HMSO, January 1993, pp. 9–13.

[9] The whipless eight were: Teresa Gorman, Christopher Gill, Nicholas Budgen, Tony Marlow, Richard Shepherd, Teddy Taylor, Michael Cartiss and John Wilkinson. Sir Richard Body, who resigned, joined them in support.

[10] *The Independent*, 18 January 1996.

[11] *Financial Times*, 12 October 1994, p. 10.

[12] Norman Lamont, 'British Objectives for Monetary Integration in Europe', speech at the Royal Institute for International Affairs, 30 May 1991, verbatim service VS00/91, and 'Britain and the Exchange Rate Mechanism', speech to the European Policy Forum, 10 July 1992. In the latter speech, Lamont remarked that 'the ERM is not an optional extra, an add-on to be jettisoned at the first hint of trouble. It is and will remain at the very centre of our macroeconomic strategy', para. 15.

[13] *The Independent*, 18 January 1995, p. 13.

[14] *Sunday Telegraph*, 26 June 1994, p. 1.

[15] *The Observer*, 2 July 1995, p. 23.

[16] *Financial Times*, 2 May 1994. Major, 1999: 587.

[17] *The Guardian*, 27 June 1995.

[18] *The Times*, 5 July 1995, p. 1.

[19] *The Times*, 5 July 1995, p. 16.

[20] *The Independent*, 6 July 1995, p. 3.

[21] *The Guardian*, 8 July 1995, p. 8.

[22] *The Times*, 5 July 1995, p. 5 and *The Independent*, 5 July 1995, p. 3.

[23] Douglas Hurd, 'The Maastricht Treaty and Closer European Union', speech to the Scottish Conservative Party Conference, 13 May 1993.

[24] *House of Commons Official Report*, 25 June 1992, cols. 381–2. Also Major, 1999: 362.

[25] John Major, Speech to the Conservative Party Conference, London: Conservative Central Office, 6 October 1992.

[26] *Survey of Current Affairs*, Vol. 22, No. 1, London: HMSO, November 1992, p. 482.

[27] *Survey of Current Affairs*, Vol. 23, No. 6, London: HMSO, June 1993, p. 133.

[28] *Survey of Current Affairs*, Vol. 23, No. 8, London: HMSO, August 1993, pp. 189–92.

[29] *Survey of Current Affairs*, Vol. 23, No. 6, London: HMSO, June 1993, p. 129.

[30] The 1997 and 1999 start dates for EMU had been inserted into the Maastricht Treaty at the request of France. See Major, 1999: 283.

[31] *The Independent*, 16 January 1996.

[32] *Progress Report on the Preparation of the Changeover to the Single European Currency*, submitted to the European Commission on 10 May 1995, Luxembourg: Office for Official Publications of the European Communities, 1995, p. 4.

[33] Interview in *The Daily Telegraph*, 4 March 1996.

[34] *The Independent*, 22 January 1996.

[35] Kenneth Clarke, *Chancellor's Speech to European Movement Gala Dinner*, London: HM Treasury, 9 February 1995. Also Major, 1999: 604.

[36] *The Times*, 2 May 1996.

[37] Kenneth Clarke, *Chancellor's Speech to European Movement Gala Dinner,* para. 47.

[38] *House of Commons Official Report,* 1 March 1995, col. 1068.

[39] Michael Portillo, *Speech to the Conservative Party Conference*, London: Conservative Central Office, 10 October 1995.

[40] *The Independent,* 12 October 1995, p. 14.

[41] Malcolm Rifkind, *Principles and Practice of British Foreign Policy*, speech to the Royal Institute for International Affairs, London: Foreign and Commonwealth Office, 21 September 1995.

[42] *The Times*, 30 January 1996.

[43] *Irish Times*, 19 July 1996, p. 2.

[44] *A Partnership of Nations: the British Approach to the Intergovernmental Conference 1996*, Cmd. 3181, March 1996. The Foreign Secretary, Malcolm Rifkind, set out the British line in the House of Commons on 12 March 1996. *House of Commons Official Report*, Vol. 273, cols. 785–9.

[45] *The Daily Telegraph*, 15 August 1996, p. 2 and *The Times*, 26 March 1997.

[46] *Financial Times*, 30 January 1995.

[47] *The Guardian*, 23 January 1996.

[48] Lawson's comments to the House of Commons Treasury Select Committee on 6 March 1996: *The Times*, 7 March 1996. Norman Fowler's views are recounted in *The Independent*, 9 March 1996.

[49] The Referendum Party was the successor of the European Foundation, which was an anti-European group established by Sir James Goldsmith in October 1993.

[50] *The Sunday Times*, 7 April 1996 and *The Independent*, 3–4 April 1996.

[51] *Financial Times*, 13 March 1997.

[52] *The Times*, 16 April 1997, p. 1.

[53] *Financial Times*, 5 August 1996, and *The European*, 6 September 1996.

[54] *The Times*, 3 May 1997, p. 41.

[55] For a review of John Major's record in office *The Guardian*, 3 May 1997, p. 4.

[56] John Major, 'The Evolution of Europe', speech to the Konrad Adenauer Foundation, 11 March 1991.

[57] *The Daily Telegraph*, 25 October 1996, p. 1, and *The Times*, 8 January 1997, p. 2.

[58] *The Observer*, 8 December 1996, and *The European*, 20 March 1997.

[59] *Financial Times*, 20 March 1997.

[60] *Financial Times*, 13 March 1997.

New Labour and monetary union: 1997–2001

CHAPTER 10

Objectives

- Establish the context of the economic and political environment in which the Labour Party was elected to office in May 1997.
- Examine whether the Labour government has offered a more positive approach to the EU.
- Review the implications of granting independence to the Bank of England.
- Highlight the extent to which the Labour government is united in its views on the euro.

Introduction

The analysis presented so far has demonstrated the difficulties encountered by successive Conservative governments in establishing a united and constructive position on the European Union. A divisiveness within government was particularly apparent during the 1992–97 premiership of John Major, resulting in Eurosceptic Members of Parliament pressurising for a commitment to a referendum on the single currency. Such a strategy was favourable to Prime Minister Major because he considered it would increase the cohesiveness of the Conservative Party, with the decision on EMU being put off to a later date. But while this approach had domestic political merits (in terms of uniting the Conservative Party), it failed to assist many of the wider interests of the electorate. This included the business community, which wanted the government to present a clear set of policy objectives on monetary union, including a commitment to membership. This objective was, however, beyond the reach of a Conservative Party that was beset by bitter and deep divisions, and which towards the end of the 1992–97 Parliament did not possess a big enough majority within Parliament to govern independently.

BOX 10.1

Labour Party manifesto pledges for 1997 general election

1. Match the inherited goal for low and stable inflation of 2.5% or less;
2. No increases in the basic or top rates of taxation for the life of the Parliament;
3. A long-term objective of starting income tax at 10 pence in the pound;
4. A commitment to work within the existing departmental spending ceilings for the first two years of government;
5. Immediately after entering office to undertake a comprehensive spending review.

In the midst of these events it was unsurprising that the Labour Party was elected to office in the 1997 general election. For months (if not years) before the election the Labour Party had acted as if it was in government, being both cohesive within Parliament and united behind the leader, Tony Blair. The effect of this state of affairs was that Labour's election to office was something of a formality, with the only doubt being the degree of victory. Of the factors that influenced Labour's election to office, the image of party unity, a commitment to cautious spending plans and the projection of economic competence were of importance (Margetts, 1997). This was based both on headline pledges in the 1997 general election, such as a commitment not to increase basic or top rates of income tax, and a promise to get 250,000 young unemployed people off benefit and back to work. The government additionally listed five key manifesto pledges for the election (see Box 10.1).

The economic strategy of the Labour Party was therefore aimed at both being elected to government and retaining power at the next general election (Moran and Alexander, 2000). The landslide 179-MP majority of May 1997 demonstrated Labour's aim of meeting the first objective, an outcome which was repeated by a 167 majority in the June 2001 general election.[1] This outcome was also influenced by the Conservative Party losing its reputation for economic competence after sterling's humiliating exit from the Exchange Rate Mechanism in September 1992. The subsequent economic difficulties that beset the nation during the 1992–97 Parliament additionally meant that the Conservative government had to increase taxation rates, the effect of which was for Labour to replace the Conservatives as the party of low taxation and economic competence.[2]

In the midst of these policy developments and manifesto commitments, the European Union was not perceived to be a dominant policy issue in the 1997 general election campaign, though the millionaire Sir James Goldsmith created a Referendum Party that called for a referendum on Britain's EU role. (In the 2001 general election campaign the issue of EU membership had a more prominent role, with the Conservative Party's central campaigning issue being hostility to EMU and a commitment to maintain the pound.) The Labour Party did, nevertheless, offer a more stable and committed approach to the EU, with Tony Blair later commenting that 'Britain has too often been an observer in

---

BOX 10.2

Biography of Tony (Anthony) Blair (1953–)

Elected leader of the Labour Party in 1994, having entered Parliament in 1983. Led the Labour Party to election victory in May 1997 and a historic second full term in June 2001. He has greatly strengthened the number of officials that staff No. 10 Downing Street and this is reflective of his power and influence within government. His style of government is to lead in the mould of Margaret Thatcher and rely less on the consensual style of John Major. One impact of this has been to decrease the importance of Cabinet as a method of decision-taking. While he has offered a more committed role to Britain's position within the EU, he has been more cautious towards Britain's membership of the euro. His decision to appoint Jack Straw as Foreign Secretary in June 2001 (replacing Robin Cook) was evidence of this downplaying of the euro, whilst it also further strengthened the Prime Minister's own control of foreign affairs.

Europe's development, not a player' (Blair, T., 2000). A commitment to leadership on the European stage by New Labour has, however, not been true for all areas of government policy-making. The government has attempted to take a leading role in those areas of EU policy-making that have impacted the least on the domestic political stage, while at the same time remaining hesitant on other policy areas. Of those areas where the government continues to remain adrift from the EU, the single currency is the most important. This chapter accordingly reviews the negotiating position of the Labour government on this subject, highlighting whether the Labour government led by Tony Blair has offered a greater commitment to the EU than its predecessors did.

Fresh hope?

In opposition the Labour Party committed itself to making foreign policy one of the 'four cornerstones' of its vision of a 'New Britain', with the government's intention being to take a leading role in the EU (Blair, T., 1996: viii). It had, for instance, supported the Social Chapter that John Major's Conservative government had opted out of at the December 1991 Maastricht European Council, while equally defending the importance of cultivating strong friendships with other European nations. To this end, in the first few months of office the Prime Minister (Tony Blair),[3] Foreign Secretary (Robin Cook)[4] and Chancellor of the Exchequer (Gordon Brown),[5] made similar statements calling for Britain to take a leading role within the EU (Hughes and Smith, 1998; Lawler, 2000). The government would therefore aim to influence decision-making from within, rather than from the margins (Young, 1998). To be sure, such statements had been made by previous governments, notably John Major's March 1991

BOX 10.3

Biography of Gordon Brown (1951–)

Appointed Chancellor of the Exchequer in May 1997, having been Shadow Chancellor since 1992. He is the architect of Labour's economic strategy and has a commanding influence over all aspects of government (not just taxation and public spending). Whilst committed to Britain's membership of the EU, he has been more cautious on the question of membership of the euro. His prudent approach, based on fulfilling the correct economic conditions to merit membership, was at odds with the more committed approach of Robin Cook. But the latter's move from the Foreign Office in June 2001 cemented Brown's grip on this policy area and ensured that any decision on the euro would be taken by him and Tony Blair. In other areas, he granted independence to the Bank of England and created a Monetary Policy Committee to oversee the setting of interest rates.

commitment for Britain to be at the 'heart of Europe'.[6] It was nevertheless significant that the three key politicians in government appeared to be united in their approach to the EU, contrasting with the public divisions between Margaret Thatcher and Nigel Lawson and John Major and Norman Lamont. That is not to say that there were no undercurrents of tension in the Blair–Brown–Cook relationship throughout the 1997–2001 Parliament, because there were. Robin Cook's advocation of the benefits of euro membership was in contrast to the more cautious approach of Gordon Brown (Rawnsley, 2001: 386). For instance, in Tokyo in September 1999 Cook spoke of the fact that the euro was 'providing a major stimulus to economic restructuring within the euro-zone' and that those countries participating in the euro-zone were obtaining 'real benefits of immediate relevance'.[7] By publicly noting the benefits of the single currency, and therefore essentially campaigning for Britain's entry to the system, Cook's more proactive approach was much to the annoyance of Brown, who while not sceptical of the single currency was certainly less enthusiastic. Cook's own views were, however, subservient to those of Brown. The Foreign Secretary's position within the Cabinet had been seriously weakened by the difficulties that hampered his early months at the FCO, such as the break-up of his marriage, and it was widely rumoured that he might lose his job in a Cabinet reshuffle. The retention of his post as Foreign Secretary therefore owed a lot to the personal support of the Prime Minister, though 'The upside for Blair was that the stature of Cook was diminished, and with it any capacity to cause trouble' (Rawnsley, 2001: 58).

But while divisions between Brown and Cook became more evident in the years after 1997, it was nevertheless the case that the Labour government as a whole was fundamentally committed to Britain playing a more proactive role within the EU. A change in British policy-making was reflected in both style and substance. In many respects the former was just as important as the latter because the previous Conservative administration had not just been out of step

---

BOX 10.4

Amsterdam European Council of 16–17 June 1997

The Amsterdam meeting brought to a close the intergovernmental conference negotiations that had started in March 1996. The purpose of those discussions was to plan the future developments of the EU. The IGC talks were nevertheless dominated by the refusal of the British government (led by John Major) to accept the granting of greater competencies to the EU. The election of the Labour Party to government in May 1997 produced a more positive approach to the EU and enabled the IGC to conclude its business at the Amsterdam European Council of June 1997. The resulting Treaty of Amsterdam had less ambitious objectives than the Maastricht Treaty. The main provisions of the Amsterdam Treaty were:

1. The treaty stipulated that policies on employment, consumer protection, human health protection and sustainable development were made formal EU objectives.

2. Policies dealing with asylum, immigration and visas were made subject to EU rules and procedures, though Britain, Denmark and Ireland were granted opt-outs. The Schengen Agreement providing for removal of border controls between EU member states was brought into the Community framework, while there was a strengthening of cooperation between national police forces.

3. The treaty made provision for the creation of a policy planning unit so as to improve the effectiveness of matters relating to foreign and defence policy, while cooperation with the WEU was increased. Finally, it was decided that a single commissioner would have responsibility for external relations.

4. As far as institutional matters were concerned, the treaty made provision for a downgrading of the cooperation procedure, while the co-decision procedure was altered to ensure that there was more of an equal status between the European Parliament and the Council of Ministers. There was also an increase in the number of areas that would be subject to qualified majority voting, while the Court of Auditors and the Committee of the Regions were given extra powers.

---

with its European colleagues on policy proposals, but had crucially reduced Britain's negotiating capital by means of a hostile tone to the European project. This had been reflected by such developments as the 1996 beef crisis and a foot-dragging approach to the 1996–97 intergovernmental conference (IGC). The new Labour government was therefore readily received by its EU partners,[8] ensuring that the IGC could reach a quick conclusion at the Amsterdam European Council of June 1997 (Box 10.4). At that meeting it was particularly noticeable that the Blair government seemed to present a vigorous and dynamic administration that was coveted by many of the other EU governments (of whom a majority were now led by centre-left administrations[9]).

The Amsterdam meeting was particularly noticeable for the government's signature of the Social Chapter, which not only brought Britain into a mainstream area of EU policy-making, but also got rid of a key ideological division between Britain and the EU. Thus British workers would be able to benefit from EU social legislation such as the Working Time Directive, though the government was careful to water down this piece of legislation when implementing it at the national level. While the Working Time Directive was adopted, its transposition into British law (the Working Time Regulations) produced a weaker set of rules than was applicable in other EU countries. The significance of this development was that it represented the balancing nature of the New Labour government, whereby the government had made an ideological commitment at the EU level, though limiting the impact at the national level (Blair, A., 2000).

The new government equally offered a more positive negotiating position on the single currency, Labour's policy on membership of the single currency having been outlined by the Chancellor of Exchequer, Gordon Brown, in a statement to the House of Commons in October 1997.[10] And while this statement acknowledged that a single currency would involve a significant pooling of economic sovereignty, it stressed that membership should take place if the economic benefits were clear and unambiguous. To this end the Chancellor established five economic tests for membership that would have to be met before any decision to join could be taken (see Box 10.5). But while the government committed itself to enter EMU if the economic conditions were right, it did so with the precondition that any decision on membership would need authorisation from the Cabinet and Parliament, and by means of a popular referendum. Thus, while the government set out a more positive stance on the single currency, it also established certain conditions that would have to be fulfilled to guarantee participation.

These conditions nevertheless held out the prospect of membership and contrasted with the approach taken by the Conservative Party. In opposition, its new leader, William Hague, outlined a different approach that replaced the previous 'when the time is right' formula that was advanced by John Major. The new strategy committed the Conservative Party to oppose British membership of the single currency for ten years,[11] with Hague stating that:

BOX 10.5

Labour government's five economic tests for EMU

1. Sustainable convergence between Britain and the economies of the single currency.
2. The new currency system should have enough flexibility to be able to cope with economic change.
3. Membership of the single currency should have a favourable impact on investment.
4. The financial service industry of Britain, especially the City of London, must benefit from the single currency.
5. The single currency must have a positive impact on employment within Britain.

the Conservative Party believes it is a mistake to commit this country in principle to joining a single currency. We oppose Britain joining a single currency for the lifetime of this Parliament, and we intend to campaign against British membership of the single currency at the next election.[12]

Hague's opposition to the single currency was subsequently confirmed by the report of the Policy Commission on the Pound Sterling, which he had set up in March 1999 to examine the implications of joining the euro.[13] Such opposition to the single currency was nevertheless opposed by senior Conservative MPs, particularly Kenneth Clarke and Michael Heseltine,[14] and was moreover proved to be a disastrous tactic in light of the inability of the Conservative Party to make any headway into Labour's majority in the 2001 election campaign.[15] Indeed, throughout the 2001 contest, the Conservatives were essentially a single-issue party campaigning against the euro.

A stable path?

The setting by the Labour government of economic conditions upon which membership would be based thus offered a more positive approach from the lack of details provided by the previous Conservative government. But, at the same time, an emphasis on economic conditions mirrored the policy of preceding Conservative governments. The prominence attached to economic factors for membership was thus representative of the stance taken by Margaret Thatcher towards participation in the Exchange Rate Mechanism (ERM), whereby the government would join when the 'time was right' (Chapter 5). In this context, the Labour government attempted to divorce the political factors associated with membership from the economic realities,[16] though the very strategy of making entry conditional on a series of economic tests was itself a highly political decision. The net effect of the setting of such economic tests was an appreciation that making a decision to join the single currency would be an unrealistic objective during the lifetime of the 1997 Parliament. Moreover, as the Chancellor of the Exchequer would determine the case for membership, Gordon Brown's ability to have full control over when Britain should enter the single currency was further cemented by this strategy. As Chapter 2 noted, Brown has been one of the most dominant Chancellors in recent years. 'One probably has to go back to Chamberlain in the 1930s, if not to Lloyd George before the First World War, to find a comparator wielding such a range and degree of power over policy' (Hennessy, 2000: 389).

From the government's perspective, one of the primary advantages of ruling out immediate entry to EMU and establishing a commitment in principle to the single currency was an awareness that while monetary union was scheduled to commence by 1999, it would be unlikely that the single currency would enter circulation until some time later. Therefore, there was an appreciation that non-commitment in the short term would not hinder British participation at a slightly later date when the entering into use of the single currency was itself likely to be delayed.

As far as the economic tests of membership were concerned, the question as to whether there was sufficient convergence between the British economy and those on the continent was not a new issue. As Chapter 5 highlighted, one of the main issues against British membership of the ERM in the mid-1980s was the lack of convergence between Britain's economic cycle and those on the continent. This was, for instance, determined by sterling's status as a petrocurrency causing it to be susceptible to oil price shocks, while other structural factors included the status of the UK housing market. And, as Chapter 7 made clear, the importance of convergence had been built into Article 109j(1) of the Maastricht Treaty. An emphasis on convergence was therefore reflective of the fact that EMU membership would mean that interest rates in Britain would not be determined solely on the basis of domestic economic conditions. On the contrary, interest rates would be set by the European Central Bank and if there was convergence between British and continental economies then the rates set by the ECB would be appropriate. However, if there was divergence between Britain and the continent, then the interest rates set by the ECB could either be too high or too low, the effect of which would be to create greater instability in the economy. Therefore, the government regarded it as essential that full and sustainable convergence should take place prior to membership. That this was not the case in the early part of the Parliament was emphasised by a 1997 Treasury report, which noted that the British economy was 'not convergent enough to commit to joining EMU in the first wave'.[17]

In the absence of economic conditions not being right for membership of the single currency, the government nevertheless put into place a strategy for membership. Central to this strategy was obviously a reduction in the degree of divergence between the British and continental economies through the creation of a more stable framework for determining monetary policy.[18] The first step to putting monetary policy on a stable basis was the Labour government's decision to give the Bank of England operational independence for setting interest rates, with the Bank of England Act 1998 giving operational responsibility to these arrangements.[19] Such a policy commitment was actually made by the new Chancellor, Gordon Brown, in a press statement on 6 May 1997,[20] though the genesis of this policy had first appeared in the Labour Party's general election manifesto. It specifically stressed that: 'We will reform the Bank of England to ensure that decision-making on monetary policy is more effective, open, accountable and free from short-term political manipulation.' The outcome of this decision was the creation of a Monetary Policy Committee (MPC)[21] to determine interest rates,[22] the minutes of which were to be published, thereby guaranteeing full transparency (see Box 10.6).[23]

As demonstrative of the power that Gordon Brown had within the Labour government, the decision on granting independence to the Bank of England had actually been taken outwith Cabinet in a meeting between the Chancellor and

---

BOX 10.6

Monetary Policy Committee

The Labour government's decision to grant the Bank of England operational respons-ibility for the setting of interest rates directly influenced the creation of the Monetary Policy Committee, which is the forum where decisions on interest rates are taken. The MPC comprises nine members, including the Governor of the Bank of England, the two Deputy Governors and six other members. Meetings of the MPC take place each month and decisions are based on one person, one vote, with the Governor of the Bank of England having the casting vote if there is not a majority decision. All decisions taken by the MPC are made public, including the voting intentions of its members. This level of transparency is considered to be an important means of injecting stability into the economy.

---

the Prime Minister, though Brown did not mention this policy to Blair until the day of the 1997 general election. Such a strategy was based on the belief that 'it would give Blair little time to consult others who might be cool about the idea' (Rawnsley, 2001: 31). On the day of the announcement the only other Cabinet Ministers to be informed of the policy change were Robin Cook and John Pre-scott (Hennessy, 1998: 7). The first that the Governor of the Bank of England knew about the policy was when he was informed by the Chancellor. Such a method of decision-making was, of course, reflective of Chancellor Brown's own desire to have full control of economic policy, demonstrating the extent to which Cabinet colleagues were not kept informed on important policy devel-opments (Stephens, 2001: 190). The outcome was therefore that 'The pattern of big decision-making in the Blair government – a duopoly, albeit an often volatile one, between Prime Minister and Chancellor – was set at the start' (Rawnsley, 2001: 34).

In examining this relationship it was also evident that Gordon Brown wanted to maintain a tight personal grip on the levers of economic policy, both by being less keen to consult his Cabinet colleagues and by remaining aloof from officials within the Treasury. As Chapter 2 noted, the Chancellor instead sought advice from his own policy advisers, particularly Ed Balls (Rawnsley, 2001: 34–5). The end product of this state of affairs was that Treasury officials were apparently outside the Chancellor's own policy-making circle, with Brown having a particularly poor working relationship with Terry Burns who was the Permanent Secretary at the Treasury (Rawnsley, 2001: 47–8). The reason for Brown's chosen method of decision-taking was that he jealously guarded his economic expertise and was conscious that the involvement of Treasury officials would lead to policy details being divulged to Prime Minister Blair. The significance of this was that it highlighted the fact that while the Blair–Brown relationship was the core upon which New Labour had been founded, it was nonetheless an extremely volatile one.

The granting of operational independence to the Bank of England altered the previous position of the Bank since its nationalisation under the Bank of England Act 1946, which provided the Bank with no statutory independence with respect to the direction of interest rate and exchange rate policy. In specific terms, Article 4(1) of the Bank of England Act 1946 stated that 'The Treasury may from time to time give such directions to the Bank as, after consultation with the Governor of the Bank, they think necessary in the public interest.'[24] In this context the Bank of England accepted Treasury control over policy, despite the fact that it was (and is) operationally and institutionally distinct from government (see Chapter 2). A direct linkage between the Treasury and the Bank was particularly noticeable during the 1980s when the Thatcher governments attached a great deal of emphasis to monetary policy. The net effect of this was that the subservient role of the Bank became even more noticeable at that time.

A change in the status of the Bank of England was thus based on the consideration that government involvement in the setting of British monetary policy had resulted in decisions being taken that were reflective of political interests rather than long-term economic benefits. This ability to make short-term changes based on political calculations was consequently regarded as a key point in devolving monetary policy to the Bank. As the House of Commons Treasury and Civil Service Committee emphasised: 'politicians may be tempted to sacrifice the longer term national interest and manipulate interest rates to secure short term economic, and therefore political, benefits'.[25] An independent Bank would be expected to pursue a more stable monetary policy whereby there would be a greater degree of consistency in the achievement of a low rate of inflation, as other short-term interests would be unlikely to cloud the judgement of its officials. This emphasis on market confidence in the pursuit of monetary policy was attractive to the Labour government because it removed any fear of Labour embarking on unstable economic policies. Brown was particularly aware of Labour's track record of economic (in)competence, such as Denis Healey's appeal to the International Monetary Fund (IMF) in 1976, and the new Chancellor accordingly wanted immediately to set the tone of Labour's economic strategy by reassuring the financial markets. The reform of the Bank of England also signalled Gordon Brown's own economic priorities, as it would 'offer more freedom to devote himself to the structural, social and employment reform that really engaged the new Chancellor' (Rawnsley, 2001: 32).

A desire to remove government interference from monetary policy had, in fact, been an objective held by previous Chancellors, including Nigel Lawson[26] and Norman Lamont. But Margaret Thatcher and John Major, in their capacity as Prime Ministers, opposed such an objective, considering that the setting of interest rates should be taken by government and that any deviation from this strategy would be an unacceptable loss of economic sovereignty. But as Chapter 2 demonstrated, such government interference had resulted in the British economy not having the same degree of stability to be found in other EU member states. The ERM crisis also demonstrated the extent to which monetary policy can be determined by internal and external factors that are out-with government control (see Chapter 8). Just as the newly created independence of the Bank of England was considered an important means of injecting stability into the domestic economy, and ergo increasing the preparedness of the country to participate in the single currency, the decision also marked a significant move towards the possible granting of economic control to the European Central Bank. In this context a reduction in the government's ability to interfere in domestic monetary policy thus meant that the further transfer of power to the European Central Bank would not be such an emotive decision. From the above information it is evident that the key power axis within the Labour government was between Gordon Brown and Tony Blair, with the former's influence being a particularly noticeable factor in the relationship.

Prepare and decide

The problem of adopting an approach that supported, but did not commit to, the single currency was that it still raised the question of Britain being isolated from the other countries that were committed to the single currency. This became more of a reality towards the end of 1997 when those countries that were committed to a single currency noted their intention to form an inner policy-making group.[27] For reasons of confidentiality in the setting of exchange rates and interest rates, it was advocated that a separate and informal forum was necessary.[28] This development resulted in Denmark, Greece, Sweden and Britain being left out in the cold, as none of the four countries was scheduled to be a first-wave entrant to monetary union (though Greece subsequently met the criteria and joined in 2001). Of the remaining countries, Denmark, like Britain, used its opt-out clause from the Maastricht Treaty and therefore chose not to be among the first-wave participants in EMU, with a referendum result in favour of entry being necessary for any change in this negotiating position. Sweden too was opposed to entry, though this was based on a December 1997 parliamentary decision that it would not join in the first wave. Somewhat reminiscent of the Conservative government of John Major, the Swedish government did not offer a concrete position on EMU, choosing instead to adopt a 'wait and see' approach.

At the heart of the Labour government's strategy towards monetary union in its first term of office from 1997 to 2001 was the Chancellor's October 1997 House of Commons statement ruling out Britain's participation in the single currency.[29] A decision by the new Labour administration to rule out Britain's membership of the single currency in the lifetime of the 1997–2001 Parliament had many strategic benefits (Rawnsley, 2001: 80). This included the granting of the government time to prepare the case for the single currency. Moreover, in the early years of the Labour government there was a lack of symmetry between Britain and other EU member states; the British economy was enjoying relatively fast economic growth when other EU nations were either in recession or experiencing far lower levels of growth. There was therefore a lack of convergence between Britain and other EU member states by the time the single currency was to be launched in 1999.

Having ruled out membership, the government's strategy was subsequently based on a 'prepare and decide' basis, and therefore contrasted with the 'wait and see' approach of the previous Conservative government. Thus the Treasury, and the Bank of England[30] in particular, established preparations for possible British entry. This included the Chancellor establishing in October 1997 five economic tests upon which the conditions for entry would be based (see Box 10.5). At the same time the government also started to give some thought to the practicalities of membership. This resulted in the publication of the first national changeover plan in February 1999,[31] with a revised second outline plan published in March 2000 (see Box 10.7).[32] This was in addition to a Business Advisory Group (BAG) set up in autumn 1997 to examine the practical implications of EMU.[33]

The setting of the economic tests for EMU membership was perceived by the government, and particularly the Chancellor, as a means of ensuring that the single currency question would be dominated by economic rather than political considerations. Nevertheless, some of the economic conditions were of a vague nature. Thus, whereas hard economic facts could be used to determine the degree of convergence, the other tests could be interpreted by the government in a number of ways. In this context, despite the fact that economic conditions were set to determine the case for Britain's participation in EMU, the fact of the matter was that the question as to whether a single currency would be of greater benefit than maintaining the pound was a highly political question. In essence, the setting of economic tests provided a degree of breathing space to the government on the single currency, whilst also helping to ensure that it did not become divided on the question.

Holding to a line that economic issues would be the determining factors in establishing Britain's case for membership of the single currency did, however, become an increasingly difficult task in the latter years of the 1997–2001 Parliament. The desire of Prime Minister Blair to play a front-line role in the EU,[34] evidenced by being a key player in the creation of a stronger European foreign policy, meant that participation in the euro was a central aspect of Britain's renaissance as a proactive and positive member of the EU (Bulmer, 2000).[35] The Prime Minister did, nevertheless, take care not to be too forthright on the subject, though on the occasion of the publication of the national changeover plan in February 1999 he announced that 'We have stated today that as a matter of principle Britain should join a single European currency.'[36] Blair's delivery of this upbeat assessment was in contrast to the Chancellor who was ever more sceptical on the merits of the single currency.[37]

The outcome was that the Chancellor's more cautious approach increasingly seemed to be at odds with the viewpoints of other more pro-European

---

BOX 10.7

British EMU changeover plan[38]

There are essentially four phases in the changeover process in Britain:

1. In the first instance, the government would have to make a decision to join the single currency and present a Referendum Bill to Parliament so as to hold a referendum.

2. Having taken a decision to join the single currency, and if the referendum legislation was passed by Parliament, then a referendum would have to be held on British membership of the single currency.

3. If a positive vote was recorded in favour of membership of the single currency, the government would have to inform the other EU member states who, in conjunction with Britain, would decide if the required conditions for joining the single currency had been met. In addition to this, the government would also have to present further legislation to Parliament, primarily with respect to the role of the Bank of England.

4. In the wake of the referendum vote, the government would have to increase the preparations for entry in the public and private sectors of the economy, as well as launching a national information campaign for businesses and individuals. At this time, the manufacture of euro notes and coins would also commence.

5. If Britain met the economic criteria for membership, then from the date when it joined the single currency the exchange rate between sterling and the euro would be irrevocably locked. At this stage, the financial markets would fully switch to the euro, while the use of the euro would increase throughout the economy despite the fact that euro notes and coins would not yet have been introduced. This would signify the start of the transition period.

6. The final element of the changeover plan would involve the introduction of euro notes and coins, with financial systems switching over to the euro and the withdrawal of sterling taking place. This would culminate in the total withdrawal of sterling, being fully replaced by the euro.

---

members of the Cabinet. This particularly applied to his relations with Robin Cook at the FCO and Stephen Byers at the DTI. While both Cook and Byers considered that the government should advocate a more positive approach on the single currency, the latter was more concerned about the practical implications that the government's uncertainty on the euro was having on British jobs rather than the wider issue of British engagement within the EU (Rawnsley, 2001: 386–7). Yet, as far as the Chancellor was concerned, the wisdom of a cautious approach was greatly influenced by the extent to which the Conservative Party was prepared to use the single currency as a political tool. For the Chancellor, who was also in charge of the 2001 Labour general election campaign, there appeared to be no sense in creating undue tension on the subject in the run-up to the election. Indeed, the Chancellor could argue that Labour's landslide victory in the 2001 campaign, and the Conservatives' over-emphasis on the euro, vindicated this strategy. It is therefore evident that the single currency was (and is) a key point of division between Blair and Brown. Whereas the Prime Minister had become convinced as to the importance of Britain's membership of the single currency, the Chancellor had become more sceptical, not least because Brown feared that membership would reduce his control over the economy (Rawnsley, 2001: 497).

In the wake of the June 2001 general election victory, Tony Blair undertook a sweeping reshuffle of ministerial posts within government. Of the changes that were made, the FCO had a complete changeover of ministerial staff, with the replacement of Robin Cook by Jack Straw being the most notable element of the reshuffle (Rawnsley, 2001: 507). As Chapter 2 notes, the significance of this change of Foreign Secretary was that it represented a desire by Tony Blair to advance a more cautious approach to the euro and one which followed a lead from Downing Street and the Treasury rather than the more pro-European instincts of the FCO. At the same time Blair also sought to bolster his own posi-tion by strengthening his ministerial team at the Cabinet Office (Rawnsley, 2001: 507–8). It was also noticeable that Cook's change of post to Leader of the House of Commons was the same move made by Sir Geoffrey Howe when Thatcher moved him out of the FCO. And, just like Thatcher, Prime Minister Blair offered a 'sweetener' to ease the transition, this being the continued use of the Foreign Secretary's official London residence. The government reshuffle was also noticeable for the replacement of the Europhile Stephen Byers by Patricia Hewitt at the Department of Trade and Industry (DTI).

The importance of these ministerial changes was that they resulted in the removal of two of the most pro-European Cabinet Ministers from key posts that had a significant input to the construction of Britain's position on mon-etary union (see Chapter 2). In the first instance, this was a means of shoring up the role of the Prime Minister on the question of euro membership at the expense of the FCO. Secondly, whereas Cook might have regarded Labour's landslide general election majority as a signal for advancing a more positive approach to the euro, the change in Foreign Secretary was a means of Blair

---

BOX 10.8

Biography of Robin Cook (1946–)

Foreign Secretary in the 1997–2001 Labour government and shadow Foreign Secretary 1994–97. Appointed leader of the House of Commons in the June 2001 Cabinet reshuffle, which was in essence a demotion in Cabinet rank. Intellectually bright, he was a committed pro-European throughout his tenure as Foreign Secretary and his enthusiastic support for the euro resulted in disagreements with the Chan-cellor, Gordon Brown.

ensuring that a more cautious tone was advanced by the more naturally Euro-sceptic Jack Straw. Finally, this meant that although Tony Blair had previously announced that a re-elected Labour government would decide within two years whether or not to hold a referendum,[39] the Prime Minister was not going to attempt to bounce the electorate into a decision at an early stage. Such a viewpoint takes account of the failure of Denmark to obtain a 'yes' vote on the euro in a referendum in 2000, and the 'no' vote recorded by Ireland in its 2001 referendum on the December 2000 Nice Treaty. Thus, in the wake of its historic election victory, the Labour government was clearly conscious that even if it fully supported the euro, there would be a strong likelihood that an early referendum on the question would not be endorsed by the electorate.[40] The net effect of this was that the government moved to a publicly more cautious approach towards the single currency at the Gothenburg European Council of June 2001.

Conclusion

The end product of these developments was that although the Labour government established a more positive approach to the EU, including the setting of economic criteria for membership of the single currency, there remained at the heart of government an undercurrent of tension on the extent to which a positive approach should be advanced. This was, of course, not a new state of affairs. Previous tension between Nigel Lawson and Margaret Thatcher on the question of Britain's entry to the ERM has been well documented (see Chapter 5). But whereas Lawson's influence was reduced by Thatcher's use of personal advisers such as Alan Walters, Brown had a massive influence on government. He was the main influence behind the transition of the Labour Party to credible economic governance, not least through the granting of independence to the Bank of England and the creation of the Monetary Policy Committee. Other aspects of Labour's economic strategy have, however, not been so positive. For instance, the government's insistence on maintaining tight spending plans for the first two years of the Parliament meant that the electorate did not notice the improvement in the public services that they had expected, a point which subsequently became apparent in the 2001 general election. Disgruntlement with the new government was, for instance, noticeable when Blair received a hostile reception to his appearance at the Women's Institute, while the government was severely panicked by the oil blockades of 2000 (Rawnsley, 2001: 159 and 395).

As far as the single currency was concerned, the lukewarm response of the Chancellor and the government as a whole has had a direct influence in increasing the value of sterling. As a result, the sheer strength of the pound has had a detrimental impact on many areas of the economy that have found it increasingly difficult to be competitive.[41] This is because the prices of British goods have become more expensive than those produced in other European countries, in some cases resulting in production being transferred out of Britain.[42] In this sense, the two factors of government uncertainty on the euro and an over-valued pound against the euro has had a knock-on impact on manufacturing capacity and the level of inward investment.[43] In many senses, it is this issue of jobs and prosperity that lies at the heart of any debate as to whether the single currency should or should not be adopted by Britain.

Key points

- The Labour government has adopted a more pro-European strategy than previous Conservative governments.

- By basing the case for membership of the euro on five economic tests the government attempted to dilute the political nature of the issue.

- During the 1997–2001 Parliament there appeared to be a division among government ministers on the question of the euro. The Foreign Secretary, Robin Cook, advocated a more positive approach than the Chancellor, Gordon Brown.

- In the wake of the re-election of the Labour Party in June 2001, Tony Blair undertook a government reshuffle. This resulted in Jack Straw replacing Robin Cook as Foreign Secretary. The implications of this are that Blair has attempted to advance a more cautious approach towards euro membership.

- The key decision-makers on the euro are the Chancellor and the Prime Minister.

Questions

1. Is there any evidence that the Labour government has advanced a more positive approach to European integration?

2. What factors influenced the decision to grant the Bank of England operational independence and to establish a Monetary Policy Committee to oversee the setting of interest rates?

3. Account for Gordon Brown's influence in determining Britain's negotiating position towards membership of the euro?

4. 'Vague': is this an accurate reflection of the five economic tests set to determine EMU membership?

5. 'Any referendum on the euro will produce a "no" vote.' Discuss.

6. 'Membership of the euro would cement Britain's position within the EU.' Discuss.

7. What was the significance of Jack Straw's replacement of Robin Cook as Foreign Secretary?

8. Compare the leadership styles of Margaret Thatcher, John Major and Tony Blair.

9. 'The Cabinet is no longer a mechanism for discussing key government policies.' Discuss.

10. 'The June 2001 Cabinet reshuffle reasserted the influence of Gordon Brown and Tony Blair over Britain's strategy towards participation in the single currency.' Discuss.

Further reading

Coates, David and Lawler, Peter (eds.) (2000) *New Labour in Power*, Manchester: Manchester University Press.

Rawnsley, Andrew (2001) *Servants of the People: The Inside Story of New Labour*, London: Penguin.

Seldon, Anthony (ed.) (2001) *The Blair Effect*, London: Little, Brown.

Young, Hugo (1998) *This Blessed Plot: Britain and Europe from Churchill to Major*, Basingstoke: Macmillan, Chapter 12.

Notes

[1] 'Election 2001', *The Observer*, 10 June 2001.

[2] One of the most significant developments in this process was the 1994 Labour Party Conference, when Tony Blair (in his first year as leader) set down a policy of responsibility, including the ending of the commitment to clause 4 of the party constitution. It had committed the party to the 'common ownership of the means of production, distribution and exchange'. *Financial Times*, 5 October 1994.

[3] See, for instance, Tony Blair's speech to the Party of European Socialists Congress, Malmö, 6 June 1997. Also Tony Blair, 'The Principles of a Modern British Foreign Policy', speech at the Lord Mayor's banquet, Guildhall, London, 1 November 1997. The Prime Minister stressed that 'we must end the isolation of the last 20 years and be a leading partner in Europe'.

[4] Mission statement by the Foreign and Commonwealth Office, 12 May 1997. Robin Cook had issued a mission statement with the aim of Britain being a 'leading player in a Europe of independent nation states'.

[5] Gordon Brown, 'Britain leading in Europe', speech at the Royal Institute of International Affairs, 17 July 1997.

[6] John Major, *The Evolution of Europe*, speech to the Konrad Adenauer Foundation, London: Conservative Political Centre, 11 March 1991. Also *The Economist*, 16 February 1991, p. 34 and 9 March 1991, pp. 27–8.

[7] *The Guardian*, 7 September 1999, p. 27.

[8] *Daily Telegraph*, 21 March 1998, p. 4.

[9] *The Guardian*, 15 September 1998, p. 19.

[10] 'Statement on EMU by the Chancellor of the Exchequer', HM Treasury Press Release, 126/97, 27 October 1997. See http://www.hm-treasury.gov.uk/press/1997/p.126_97.html

[11] *Financial Times*, 24 October 1997.

[12] William Hague, speech to CBI Conference, 10 November 1997.

[13] *The Times*, 1 March 1999, p. 8 and 23 September 1999, p. 13.

[14] *Financial Times*, 4 October 1999, p. 23 and *The Guardian*, 5 September 2000, p. 11.

[15] *The Times*, 19 March 1999, p. 2.

[16] *The Guardian*, 4 July 2000, p. 18.

[17] *UK Membership of the Single Currency: An Assessment of the Five Economic Tests*, London: HM Treasury, October 1997, point 1.29. See http://www.hm-treasury.gov.uk/pub/html/docs/emumem/main.html

[18] *United Kingdom Convergence Programme*, London: HM Treasury, December 1998. See http://www.hm-treasury.gov.uk/pub/html/docs/emucp/UKCP98.pdf

[19] *The Bank of England Act 1998*. See http://www.legislation.hmso.gov.uk/acts/acts1998/19980011.htm

[20] See http://www.hm-treasury.gov.uk/press/1997/p40_let.html

[21] See http://www.bankofengland.co.uk/mpc/index.htm. The creation of the Monetary Policy Committee reflected on earlier advice from the Treasury and Civil Service Select Committee. See 'The Role of the Bank of England', First Report, Vol. 1, *Treasury and Civil Service Committee*, House of Commons, Session 1993–94, para. 81.

[22] The decisions on interest rates can be consulted at http://www.bankofengland.co.uk/mpc/decisions.htm

[23] See http://www.bankofengland.co.uk/mpc/minutes.htm

[24] Cited from 'The Role of the Bank of England', First Report, Vol. 1, *Treasury and Civil Service Committee*, House of Commons, Session 1993–94, para. 14.

[25] Ibid., para. 23.

[26] Nigel Lawson noted the possibility of central bank 'independence' in his resignation speech to the House of Commons in October 1989.

[27] *The Guardian*, 2 December 1997, p. 2, and *Daily Telegraph*, 18 November 1997, p. 2.

[28] Article 103 of the Maastricht Treaty states that all discussions on economic policy should take place within Ecofin, though when a specific issue relating to the single currency arose, then only the members of the euro club would be able to vote.

[29] *House of Commons Official Report*, 27 October 1997, cols. 583–8.

[30] See Bank of England, *Practical Issues Arising from the Euro*, December 1999 Issue, Chapter 5 (http://www.bankofengland.co.uk/euro.eu9912ch5.pdf).

[31] See HM Treasury, *Outline National Changeover Plan*, February 1999 (http://www.euro.gov.uk/oncop.pdf), and Jill Sherman and Roland Watson, 'Britain could Switch to Euro in 40 Months', *The Times*, 21 February 1999, p. 11.

[32] See HM Treasury, *Second Outline National Changeover Plan*, March 2000 (http://www.euro.gov.uk/oncop2.pdf).

[33] The Business Advisory Group involved representatives from nearly 20 business and trade organisations, the Trades Union Congress and the Consumers' Association. See http://www.hm-treasury.gov.uk/pub/html/docs/emu/emubag.html

[34] *Financial Times*, 24 November 2000, p. 13.

[35] *Daily Telegraph*, 14 May 1999, p. 4.

[36] *House of Commons Official Report*, 23 February 1999, cols. 179–86.

[37] *Financial Times*, 29 October 1999, p. 3.

[38] HM Treasury, *Outline National Changeover Plan*, February 1999, p. 11.

[39] *The Guardian*, 8 February 2001, p. 1.

[40] *The Guardian*, 11 June 2001, p. 23. Also *The Guardian*, 8 February 2001, p. 10.

[41] *The Economist*, 12 June 1999, p. 27, and *The Observer*, 21 January 2001, p. 5.

[42] *The Guardian*, 4 August 2000, p. 21.

[43] *The Guardian*, 26 May 2000, p. 26; 1 July 2000, p. 24; and 29 September 2000, p. 30.

Assessment

CHAPTER 11

Conclusion

Objectives

- Understand the factors that influenced the creation of monetary union.
- Demonstrate the challenges that the euro poses to future European integration.
- Highlight the challenges surrounding Britain's relationship with the EU.
- Demonstrate the implications of a euro referendum.
- Provide an overview of the costs and benefits of the euro.

Introduction

This book has sought to explore British engagement in monetary union discussions within the European Union. One concern has been the manner in which successive governments have responded to developments at the European level. A second, and very much related, point has been the extent to which this response has been determined by domestic political circumstances. As Chapter 9 stressed, the government led by John Major in the 1992–97 Parliament was hampered by a divided parliamentary party. A third concern of the book has been an examination of the influence brought to bear on Britain's European monetary policy by key government departments, ministers, and outside pressure groups, such as the business lobby. This chapter takes a closer look at these issues and notes the implications of Britain's European policy. But prior to that discussion the chapter reviews some of the means by which we can analyse the causes of monetary union and outlines the implications of the single currency for future European integration.

The euro and European integration

Only months after member states had agreed on the monetary provisions of the Maastricht Treaty on European Union in December 1991, the timetable for the establishment of a single currency appeared to be in doubt. Increasing levels of unemployment caused by recession troubled EU member states. It accordingly seemed doubtful that there would be sufficient economic convergence between member states to permit monetary union to progress in line with the Maastricht timetable. Yet in the end the European Council announced in March 1998 that 11 member states were deemed to have met the convergence criteria, with Greece subsequently joining in 2001. By contrast, Britain, Denmark and Sweden refused to participate in the single currency. The net outcome of this situation was that all those member states that wished to participate in the single currency were able to do so.

In trying to understand the factors that influenced this eventual outcome, Chapter 3 outlined a number of different approaches that can be used (Verdun, 2000b). Of these approaches, one of the most commonly used is the neo-functionalist approach to monetary union. This approach is based on the works of key figures such as Ernst Haas, who considered that cooperation between states in areas of low politics would lead to spillover into areas of high politics (Haas, 1958). Integration might therefore follow a specific path. In this sense, integration in some areas would spillover into other areas. This would be shaped by the fact that solutions of a supranational nature might be sought as a means of finding a solution for a problem (Tranholm-Mikkelson, 1991). In a similar vein, the relative success of the Exchange Rate Mechanism (ERM) of the European Monetary System (EMS) was a further factor in advancing the cause of EMU. In the case of monetary union it is therefore possible to see that the single market programme acted as a catalyst for advancing further integration towards a single currency. This was because of the belief that to benefit fully from a single market a single currency would have to be established.

But while it is true that a single currency will bring benefits to the single market, it is nevertheless the case that this is not a cost-free exercise. Moreover, an efficient single market can exist without a single currency. In this sense the key factor is the extent to which the benefits of a single currency outweigh the costs involved. The question to be asked is therefore to what extent the costs of transition to a single currency, the absence of exchange rates and the presence of a single interest rate across all member states compare with the potential benefits of a single currency (Levitt and Lord, 2000: 241).

While the neo-functionalist approach provides some insight into possible reasons why EMU came about, it crucially does not give enough attention to the role of national governments in the integration process. As Chapter 3 noted, France attached emphasis to monetary union as a means of regaining some control over European monetary policy in the light of the dominance of the Deutschmark. By contrast, Germany perceived EMU as a means of binding the nation into Europe, while at the same time the single currency strongly reflected German concerns about the EU's institutional and mechanical workings, such as the convergence criteria (see Chapter 7). Italy was attracted to EMU in the light of its own difficulty in establishing a consistent and stable economic policy. For Italy the single currency was consequently perceived as a method of correcting a domestic political problem.

By focusing on the motivations of governments Andrew Moravcsik has provided a skilful means of understanding the role of states in the EU policy-making process. His view is that policy developments within the EU have come about through intergovernmental bargaining and that integration will only take place when sufficient domestic support exists for it and when the interests of member states are sufficiently convergent (Moravcsik, 1991; 1993). As far as EMU is concerned, Moravcsik therefore attaches prime importance to the intended nature of the Maastricht Treaty's outcome on monetary union, perceiving it to be the product of the negotiating desires of national governments. This does of course contrast with the neo-functionalist view of EMU, whereby the outcome is more the product of consequence than an intended series of bargains.

EMU can additionally be considered as a response to broader changes in the world economy. By focusing on the forces of interdependence and globalisation, this approach highlights the external factors that have impacted on monetary policy developments within the European Union. Attention is particularly attached to the role of the United States and the impact that its economic policies have had on the drive towards monetary union. In this sense, a motivating factor behind the desire of European member states to move towards monetary union has been a concern over the economic dominance of the United States and the impact that its policies have had. For instance, Kenneth Dyson has reflected that 'From 1978 onwards European monetary integration has been involved in the valiant effort to restore a measure of responsible international monetary leadership' (Dyson, 1994: 304). But while this approach rightly highlights the importance of external factors, it does not cast light on the role that member states and EU institutions have in the process and whether, for instance, they have the ability or the willingness to respond to such external circumstances.

The above-mentioned views clearly have an ability to shed some light on the reasons why monetary union came about. From such a brief assessment it is clear that all the approaches aim to provide an understanding of the factors that have been influential in advancing monetary policy and the reasons for the decisions taken. Yet, as Chapter 3 emphasised, a significant factor in propelling monetary union forward was a convergence of national interests and economic policies. The latter was, of course, developed through the ERM of the EMS.

In trying to galvanise our thinking on the factors that advanced the cause of monetary union, it is also important to focus on the implications that a single currency will have on the future of European integration. Chapter 4 has already highlighted some of the implications for those states not participating in monetary union, the so-called 'ins' and 'outs'. Because 11 member states initially qualified to participate in the single currency, the EU was not substantially divided between participating and non-participating states. Of those states not participating, only Greece committed itself to membership, which it subsequently obtained in 2001. The net effect of EMU membership is that there has arisen an 'insider–outsider' relationship (Levitt and Lord, 2000: 255). Central to this is the fact that non-EMU members are isolated from key meetings. This included the creation of the then Euro-11 Group (now Euro-12), which although not having a formal decision-making capability nevertheless remains an important forum for discussion (Dyson, 2000a).

A further difficulty that the establishment of the euro creates is in relation to the future enlargement of the EU. To be sure, for many applicant countries, the euro offers a source of economic stability, but it nevertheless significantly increases the hurdles to be jumped for obtaining membership of the EU. This is further compounded by the fact that those countries joining the EU will be obliged to adopt the single currency. Thus, 'There will be no more opt-outs after Denmark and the UK' (Levitt and Lord, 2000: 255). Those countries joining the EU will therefore have to engage in a swift process of transition towards the single currency, though during this period the new members will be able to participate in a revised version of the ERM (ERM 2) as a means of coordinating economic policies. Britain is, unsurprisingly, not a member of the ERM 2. For Britain, the existence of the euro, and the fact that no other opt-outs will be granted, has further highlighted its own isolated position and accentuated even more the need to engage in the EU.

The challenge of engagement

The information that has been presented in this book has demonstrated the extent to which successive British governments have responded in a half-hearted manner to developments at the European level. Whilst the focus of the book has been on monetary union, it is also true that Britain has found it hard to engage positively in many other EU policy areas (Forster and Blair, 2002). The former President of the European Commission, Roy Jenkins, has commented that 'the Single Market was the one European initiative in the whole post-war history of European initiatives of which the United Kingdom was an enthusiastic supporter'.[1]

What then are the reasons for this general lack of effective engagement by Britain in European policy-making? One point certainly concerns the manner in which negotiating policies are constructed within the British system of government. Chapter 2 indicated the role of the various government departments that have an input to the decision process. In general terms British proposals are often extremely skilful, but they are the product of a great deal of compromise and consultation at the domestic level. This has meant that when proposals are advanced at the European level they are sometimes developed to such an extent that they do not contain a great deal of flexibility (Bulmer and Burch, 1998). A consequence of this is that negotiators have less room to manoeuvre and Britain is therefore often presented as being 'awkward'.

A second point concerns the extent to which successive governments have attempted to construct negotiating alliances on individual topics, with a tendency to wipe the slate clean once the deal is done. This compartmentalised view of EU negotiations does not, however, reflect the ongoing nature of the negotiating process within the European Union. For instance, Mrs Thatcher's desire that the Governor of the Bank of England, Robin Leigh-Pemberton, should construct an alliance with the President of the Bundesbank, Karl-Otto Pöhl, in opposing the Delors Report did not take into account the poor relationship that Britain had with Germany at that time (see Chapter 6). That is not to say that individual alliances are not constructed on individual topics by other member states, because they are. However, many British governments have not been able to offer a positive approach to the EU in the same manner that other member states have.

A desire to play a leading role in the EU has been a particular concern of the Labour government that was elected in May 1997 and subsequently re-elected in June 2001. As Prime Minister, Tony Blair has been at the forefront of the move to establish closer relationships with all EU member states, and in particular France and Germany. One area where the government has actively engaged is the subject of Europe's common foreign and security policy (CFSP), directly leading to an Anglo-French initiative on this subject in December 1998. This in turn resulted in a commitment by the EU to establish a defence identity (Common European Security and Defence Policy (CESDP)) at the Nice Summit of December 2000.

Indeed, such was the desire of the Labour government to put forward a more positive tone and establish a consensus on the benefits of British membership of the EU that Prime Minister Blair actively supported the 'Britain in Europe' campaign when it was launched in October 1999.[2] As a cross-party group that included prominent Conservative pro-Europeans[3] such as Michael Heseltine and Kenneth Clarke, this initiative was reflective of Labour's desire for a more informed debate on the benefits of EU membership, though it quickly drew criticism from Eurosceptic quarters that included the 'Business for Sterling' campaign and the 'New Europe' movement.[4] But as a sign of the government's caution on the single currency, Tony Blair sidestepped the issue at the launch of the 'Britain in Europe' campaign.[5] Thus, the Labour government's apparent initial enthusiasm towards monetary union has gradually been replaced by a more cautious approach, while the 'Britain in Europe' campaign has moved into the shadows. What then are the reasons for this change in stance?

Irrespective of whether Britain's economy is sufficiently convergent with other member states so as to allow membership of the euro,[6] with sterling decreasing in value against the US dollar and moving towards the euro,[7] the primary reason for the adoption of a more careful approach to the single currency is the view of the electorate. It is certainly the case that the British electorate have not been exposed to a full debate on the nature of Britain's relationship with the EU and the implications of membership. By contrast, successive governments have promoted an image of negotiating deals producing winning outcomes for Britain. Margaret Thatcher considered the Single European Market to be a great success for British business, but did not emphasise that a whole range of legislation would now be dealt with at the European level. Yet, in essence, a massive transfer of sovereign decision-making had taken place. In a similar vein, John Major returned from the Maastricht European Council and pronounced that the outcome was 'game, set and match' for Britain, having obtained an opt-out from the single currency and the Social Chapter. Yet he was less quick to point out that the powers of the European Parliament had been dramatically increased, with its members thereafter having the ability to act as co-legislators with member states on certain policies. British governments have accordingly had a tendency to present EU negotiations in a 'win-win' format and consequently the public is not used to being presented with the reality that outcomes invariably do not reflect such a scenario.

A lack of informed debate on the nature of EU membership has therefore had the effect of distancing the electorate from this subject (Forster and Blair, 2002). This has moreover been further cemented by the complex nature of EU treaty language, the involvement of unfamiliar institutions and member states in the decision-making process, and the tendency of decisions to be taken in secret by ministers and officials behind closed doors. This state of affairs, compounded with evidence of corruption within the EU and the recent beef crisis, has had a definite impact on an increasing level of Euroscepticism within Britain. A recent survey suggested that slightly over half of the population – 50.3% – wanted either to leave the EU or reduce its powers.[8] The difficulty for the government is therefore that any referendum on the euro could produce a 'no' vote, with support for the euro registering at just 21% in 2001.[9]

Such scepticism is, nevertheless, not just confined to Britain. For instance, Denmark's September 2000 referendum on the euro resulted in a 'no' vote.[10] More significantly, this was despite a united campaign for a 'yes' vote from the major political parties and the press, something which would certainly not happen in a British referendum. Of course, a sceptical position is not uncommon in Denmark, with it having previously voted against the Maastricht Treaty in a May 1992 referendum (though a subsequent referendum produced a 'yes' vote). What was significant, however, was that the referendum held in Ireland in 2001 on the ratification of the December 2000 Nice Treaty also produced a 'no' vote. Whilst the result was not unexpected, it was nevertheless surprising because the Irish economy has profited substantially from EU membership. And as Chapter 8 noted, Ireland's 1992 vote on the ratification of the Maastricht Treaty had been a convincing 68.7% in favour. Within the British government, both 'no' votes were regarded by Gordon Brown as an endorsement of his more cautious approach on the question of membership of the euro.[11]

A notable factor has, however, been that whilst the level of scepticism among the electorate has increased, there has remained strong support among the business sector for British entry to the euro.[12] It is this division in opinions between the sceptical electorate and the more pro-European views of the business sector and the government which is the significant point. For instance, the Danish referendum did not just produce a 'no' vote against the euro, but moreover reflected wider concerns that the government was out of touch with the electorate.[13] In a similar vein, the record low turnout of 59% (13% less than 1997) in the June 2001 British general election was symbolic of the fact that many of the electorate felt isolated from government. In the case of the Labour government this isolation was further influenced by the degree to which Tony Blair has been a dominant Prime Minister (see Chapters 2 and 10). Many key decisions bypass Cabinet while Parliament's influence has been side-lined (Hennessy, 1998). An example of this is that Prime Minister's question time now takes place once a week for 30 minutes on a Wednesday rather than the previous 15-minute sessions on a Tuesday and Thursday.[14]

The outcome is that the government has a major job in attempting to re-establish contact with the electorate, which is a task that most governments of today face. The rioting which took place at the Gothenburg European Council in June 2001 was again symbolic of the unease that exists within many countries on the question of European integration and more broadly under the canopy of globalisation. In the face of this situation it is therefore more important than ever that government attempts to respond to the concerns of the electorate because otherwise they provide a breeding ground for extremist policies. A notable example of this was the significant proportion of the vote taken by the British National Party in certain constituencies in the 2001 general election, particularly in Oldham West where it took 16.4% of the vote.[15] But instead of taking the case of the euro and presenting it in an informed debate, the government has adopted an ever more cautious approach in the hope that the electorate will suddenly switch from a sceptical to a pro-European position.

When Britain previously had a referendum on the issue of Europe in 1975, a 'yes' vote was supported by nearly all of the business, media and political classes. This will certainly not be the case in the euro referendum. Prime Minister Tony Blair will obviously not wish to hold a referendum when the time does not look right. But having won a massive landslide in the 2001 general election, the problem that the government faces is that its popular support will be eroded if it does not deliver its promises on the domestic political agenda of education, crime and health. Possible concern over these issues could accordingly be used as a basis for voting in a euro referendum, with the referendum turned into a protest vote. The difficulty for the Prime Minister will be deciding when the best time for a referendum will be. In many senses the options appear to be never or sometime in the future. In the meantime the government needs to clarify the economic and political issues that surround the single currency.

The benefits of participation are tangible. First of all, they include a more efficient Single European Market, as trade and investment should not be interrupted by exchange rate adjustments. Secondly, a single currency would more than likely stimulate growth and employment by securing price stability and control public deficits, thereby assisting growth and employment. It is also likely that interest rates would be kept at a low level. A third benefit includes the elimination of transaction costs associated with the existence of different EU currencies. It is widely accepted that transaction costs amount to between 0.3% and 0.4% of the European Union's gross domestic product and the elimination of these costs by means of a single currency will result in substantial savings. Fourthly, a single currency would reflect the EU's position as the world's leading trading power and it is likely that the euro will become one of the world's main exchange and reserve currencies, equivalent to the US dollar and Japanese yen. Finally, a single currency would create enhanced joint monetary authority for member states. Although some sceptics consider that a single currency would take away national monetary authority, the fact of the matter is that few member states actually have independent control over monetary policy. Capital moves freely between nations irrespective of government views, as demonstrated by the 1992 ERM crisis. Those central banks participating in the single currency would consequently have a shared monetary authority over one of the world's strongest currencies.

Set against these positive points many sceptics are understandably unsure as to the likely success of the single currency and to what extent a single monetary policy would reflect the different economic conditions that could arise in different member states. Of course, this is an important point, but it is worthwhile to remember that successive British governments have put in place economic policies that have had a detrimental impact on certain areas of the economy. A single currency would reduce an important element of national control over monetary policy, but, as has already been pointed out in this book, the degree of control that governments can exercise is constrained by many external factors. At present such costs and benefits have not been clearly set out by the government in a public debate.

Of the reasons for this lack of clarity towards the single currency, the relationship between Prime Minister Blair and Chancellor Brown has been a key determining factor. This is because the two individuals at the heart of the Labour government have divergent views towards the single currency, with the Chancellor adopting the more sceptical approach. A lack of consensus on this issue has produced a disjointed European policy and one that has failed significantly to overcome the indecision towards the single currency that was such a feature of previous Conservative governments. Thus, whilst the Labour government has broadly sought to offer a more positive approach to the European Union by supporting the Social Chapter and by championing the development of a stronger European defence identity, it has failed to offer a similarly positive approach towards the single currency.

In examining Britain's engagement in European monetary discussions, a central feature has been the extent to which important policy debates have been dominated by key individuals. For instance, the tension that dominated the

Lawson–Thatcher relationship of the 1980s has been replaced by the Blair–Brown relationship of today. In many senses a highly charged debate on the question of euro membership is to be expected because of the very importance of the policy debate. But the fact of the matter is that short-term political objectives rather than long-term economic and political realities have dominated a great deal of British decision-making on monetary union. The outcome is therefore that Britain's relationship with the process of European integration has been one of the most difficult of all member states. In this sense the attitude of semi-detachment that dominated the response of policy-makers in the early years of the Community has proved to be a recurrent theme in Britain's relationship with the integration process.

Key points

The euro and European integration

- As with European integration in general, various approaches can be used to explain the path to monetary union. For instance, some approaches attach greater emphasis to key bargaining in intergovernmental conference negotiations, whilst others attach greater emphasis to more routine activity.

- One approach that has been used to help our understanding of why and how monetary union came about is the neo-functionalist approach to European integration. This approach attaches emphasis to states engaging in some form of international cooperation and relates to the work of Ernst Haas. Such an approach attached emphasis to states initially engaging in cooperation in areas of low politics, but through the process of cooperation there would occur a spillover of integration into other areas of high politics. In this context the development of the single market programme provided the impetus towards a single currency, as it became apparent that for the single market to be truly effective then there would have to be a single currency.

- Other approaches that attempt to cast some light on how and why monetary union reflected a particular outcome include the work of Andrew Moravcsik. He attaches prime importance to the role of governments in the process of European integration and considers that integration will only take place when the interests of member states are sufficiently convergent and when enough domestic support exists for the policy. Moravcsik particularly focuses on the bargaining in intergovernmental conferences and therefore the outcome of the Maastricht Treaty is the product of specific bargaining between states rather than through the spillover effect of neo-functionalism.

- Other approaches have attached emphasis to the broader changes that have taken place in the world economy. This specifically relates to the extent to which the USA has acted as a dominant force in the world economy and EU member states have sought to reduce this power and influence by means of creating a single currency to match the US dollar.

- Irrespective of the validity of the different approaches, a single currency will nevertheless have a dramatic impact on the future of European integration. For instance, there already exists a clear distinction between those states participating in the single currency and those who are not (the 'ins' and 'outs'). Moreover, the single currency has created a further discussion group for all participating states in the euro-zone and this important forum is further evidence of the distinctions emerging between participating and non-participating states.

- For those countries seeking to join the EU, the single currency does act as a further hurdle that they will have to jump.

- A single currency will strengthen the international position of the EU, as the euro will become one of the strongest currencies in the world.

Britain and European integration

- In the post-1945 period Britain was considerably weaker politically and economically than it had been before the war. Yet at the same time Britain's perspective was still different from that of other European states, such as Belgium, France, Germany, Italy, Luxembourg and the Netherlands. They not only faced a similar need to recover economic capacity, but also to establish a fresh means of bringing states closer together. This was motivated not least by the immediate fear of the Soviet Union as well as a desire to 'contain' any future German threat. This state of affairs directly influenced the creation of NATO as a means of establishing some form of collective security organisation and also pushed European states towards supranational cooperation that initially took the form of the European Coal and Steel Community (1952). Over time this has led to the establishment of the European Economic Community and European Atomic Energy Community (1957), their merger into the European Community (1967) and further transformation to European Union (1993).

- The British response to such developments was initially lukewarm. While it supported the move to create supranational institutions such as the ECSC and EEC, successive governments considered that Britain's interests were far wider than just Europe. Thus, the special relationship with the USA and the Empire (subsequently Commonwealth) were important factors in fashioning the minds of policy-makers. To be sure, Britain continued to be an economically and politically important power in the post-1945 period, but such strength quickly declined. Moreover, attempts to establish other organisations such as EFTA failed to provide sufficient stimulus to British economic competitiveness, while the debacle of the Suez crisis highlighted both Britain's strategic weakness and the weakness of the special relationship with the USA.

- Britain therefore sought entry to the Community only a few years after it had shown an unwillingness to take part in the talks that led to the establishment of the EEC. Some commentators have suggested that had Britain got involved in the Community from the beginning then she would have been a key player. Yet others have highlighted that the fact that British foreign trade and production of such commodities as steel greatly outstripped other European nations meant that its interests and needs were not directly centred on Europe.

- Britain eventually joined the Community in 1973 after its initial applications in 1961 and 1967 had failed, primarily because Charles de Gaulle considered that Britain would threaten France's dominant position within the Community. However, it was also true that initial British applications were motivated by the desire to redress the economic decline of the nation rather than as part of a genuine commitment to the Community. On a separate note, while many people consider that there were three different applications by Britain, this is not so. Instead, there were two, one in 1961 and one in 1967. The second application remained on the table and when Edward Heath was appointed Prime Minister he merely followed through on the previous Labour application, which had remained 'alive' since 1967.

- The 1970s proved to be a sluggish period for the development of the Community, with a general downturn in economic productivity influenced by the oil crisis. This meant that any initiatives to advance European integration further were generally unsuccessful, and this was certainly true of the 1970 Werner Report which had sought to establish monetary union within ten years.

- By contrast, the 1980s proved to be a far more dynamic period in European integration. The creation of the European Monetary System in 1979 certainly helped in this respect. At the same time this period also witnessed the further enlargement of the Community, with Greece (1981) and subsequently Portugal and Spain (1986) becoming members.

- Central to the move towards further European integration was the desire to create a single market, the initial report of which had been authored by a British member of the European Commission (Lord Cockfield). Britain was certainly supportive of the further development of economic cooperation and this sat well with the Thatcher government's domestic agenda of liberalising trade. But the commitment to the single market which was set down in the Single European Act (1987) also significantly strengthened the influence of the institutions of the Community and moved more areas of decision-making towards a qualified majority voting basis. Such changes did not sit as well with Britain, and Prime Minister Thatcher has reflected that she did not fully understand the implications of these integrative measures (deepening). But like all agreements at the Community level, this outcome was a compromise that reflected all interests, and in some senses a strengthening of the institutions and decision-making procedures was essential to ensure that some member states could not act as a blocking mechanism to the fulfilment of the single market objectives.

- In progressing towards the single market and further advancing the cause of European integration, the role of Jacques Delors as President of the European Commission was a key factor (1985–95). He proved to be instrumental in moving the interest of the Community into the area of social affairs and monetary policy. But attempts to strengthen social policy through the Social Charter (1989) and subsequent Social Chapter were not welcomed by Britain, which feared that such regulations over working conditions would reduce its economic competitiveness. Britain was similarly opposed to monetary union, though significantly the government did not fully appreciate the implications of initiatives in this policy area in the late 1980s.

- The net outcome was that British objectives increasingly appeared to be at odds with those of other member states from the late 1980s onwards and this certainly highlighted the view that it was an 'awkward' member of the Community. Thus, in the Maastricht Treaty on European Union, Britain secured an opt-out from a commitment to the single currency and was also not committed to implementing the Social Chapter. Throughout the 1990s Britain's reluctance to embrace developments at the European level did not significantly change, with the Conservative governments of John Major advancing a more Eurosceptical tone.

- The election of the Labour government in 1997 that was led by Tony Blair offered a more committed approach to Britain's membership of the EU and the Labour Party has not suffered from the same divisions over Europe that so greatly hampered John Major's ability to steer a coherent policy. On specific policies, such as security and defence, Labour has been a particularly committed EU member, while the government also accepted the Social Chapter. On the question of monetary union the government has nevertheless failed to offer a particularly committed approach, although it has certainly been more positive than the previous Conservative government.

Government decision-making

- In terms of the forces which shape British foreign policy, there have been some notable changes since Britain became a member of the Community. One of the most dramatic changes has been the extent to which European policy now dominates the workings of domestic government departments. Thus, from Agriculture to the Home Office, European affairs now play an important part of the daily policy-making process. The reach of European policy has thus widened significantly, with the consequent rules and regulations having to be interpreted by all government departments. One impact of this change has been that the traditional role of the Foreign and Commonwealth Office as the standard bearer of British European foreign policy has altered and some of its influence within government has been reduced as other departments have had to take up an interest in European matters. Yet on key issues, such as intergovernmental conference negotiations, the FCO does remain a force of power and influence.

- As far as the Treasury is concerned, the ERM and EMU have meant that it has had a stronger involvement in European policy developments. But, unlike the FCO, the Treasury has often advanced a more Eurosceptical position and this is not least because developments at the European level have threatened its overall commanding influence on domestic financial policy. Within government the Treasury is the most powerful government department, while the Chancellor is the second most powerful Cabinet Minister after the Prime Minister. In recent years, the power of the Chancellor has increased under Gordon Brown, though this is more because of his involvement in the wider aspects of government policy such as the welfare to work programme than because of an institutional strengthening of the Treasury. On the specific question of monetary union, Chancellor Brown occupies a near dominant position and essentially has a veto over whether Britain will take part in the single currency. This is the product of the Chancellor deciding whether Britain has fulfilled the five economic tests that were outlined in 1997. The likelihood of immediate entry remains uncertain, not least because of the increasingly cautious approach that Gordon Brown has adopted towards this subject.

- The other important government influence on monetary policy is, of course, the input from the Prime Minister. British Prime Ministers are often characterised as either being strong or weak, although the office of the Prime Minister invests its holder with a great deal of power and influence. In recent years Margaret Thatcher has been used as a typical example of a strong and dominant Prime Minister, while John Major had been portrayed as a weaker leader who favoured a more consensual style of decision-making. As Prime Minister, Tony Blair certainly fits into the dominant mould typified by Thatcher.

- Blair's own power flows from his position within the Labour government, as he has delivered what no other Labour leader has ever done before, namely, winning two successive full-term general election victories, and such results have clearly cemented his own position. This was evidenced by the significant reshuffle of Cabinet portfolios in June 2001 after the general election victory, when, for instance, Robin Cook was replaced by Jack Straw as Foreign Secretary. The end product has been to create a Cabinet that is far more 'Blairite' in its views. The other factors which have strengthened Tony Blair's command of government have been the institutional changes that have occurred since 1997. These have included a dramatic increase in the number of staff that serve in the Prime Minister's Office, resulting in a supporting office that is better staffed and equipped than that enjoyed by any previous Prime Minister. At the same time, Blair has also strengthened the Political Office in No. 10 Downing Street (it is paid for by Labour Party rather than public money), while he has also increased the size of the No. 10 Policy Unit. But, in addition to these organisational changes, Tony Blair has also rescheduled Prime Minister's question time from occurring twice a week (15 minutes on a Tuesday and Thursday) to a 30-minute session once a week on a Wednesday. Moreover, in terms of his operation of Cabinet government, the evidence again suggests that Blair operates a style of decision-making that is more akin to Margaret Thatcher, whereby Cabinet is not a key forum for decision-taking. Important decisions are instead taken among smaller groups of ministers and officials.

- The overall net effect of these changes is that the power of the Prime Minister has strengthened considerably under Tony Blair. At the same time, the factors that serve as a check on this authority, namely the effectiveness and robustness of Cabinet discussion and the role of Parliament, have severely weakened. The outcome is therefore an extremely powerful Prime Minister with few means of balancing this power. This state of affairs, combined with the prominence of the Prime Minister at important international summits (whose number has grown), have therefore elevated Tony Blair to the most powerful peacetime Prime Minister in living memory.

- As far as Britain's position on monetary union is concerned, the key decision to commit to the single currency will be taken by the Prime Minister and the Chancellor. Of course, a single currency will reduce the influence of domestic government in this particular area of policy but, as has been noted, there have occurred in recent years many significant changes to the British system of policy-making which have reduced the ability of Parliament and Cabinet to act as an effective check on the decision-making process.

Negotiating at the EU level

- Britain is often perceived as being awkward in its dealings with the EU. Yet, this is not a wholly just viewpoint. For instance, in terms of its record of implementation of EU legislation, Britain has one of the best records of all EU member states.

- One of the reasons why Britain is perceived to be awkward concerns the tendency for the government to advance rather rigid policy proposals in EU negotiations which do not always permit a great deal of flexibility for bargaining.

- In formulating EU negotiating positions, the British system of government has a highly efficient method of coordinating policy views at the domestic level, being centred on the Cabinet Office European Secretariat.

- To be successful in advancing viewpoints in EU negotiations it is important for government to establish good relations with other member states.

- The EU increasingly dominates the working practices of domestic government departments. This includes meetings of the European Council which take place on average two or three times each year, the regular meetings of the Council of Ministers (such as Agriculture, Finance, Foreign Affairs), and working group meetings. In addition, the increasing regularity of intergovernmental conference negotiations (Single European Act, Maastricht Treaty, Amsterdam Treaty, Treaty of Nice) provides another burden for government. The end product is that not only are government departments and ministers involved in the formulation of policy for EU negotiations, but they also have to ensure the effective implementation of EU legislation at the domestic level. Other areas of government, such as local and regional government and the devolved administrations in Wales, Scotland and Northern Ireland, are also affected by the EU.

Britain and EMU

- There are various costs and benefits associated with the single currency. The benefits include lower transaction costs and a stimulation to trade between EU member states. One of the main costs of the single currency is that national governments would no longer have the ability to determine interest rates. Instead, there would be a single interest rate covering all member states participating in the euro-zone.

- Having obtained an opt-out from participation in the single currency, Britain is in essence no nearer to participation. This is despite the fact that the Labour government has established economic criteria for membership and set out a national changeover plan.

- Whilst British non-participation in the euro has not appeared to be particularly costly in the early stages of the euro-zone, with, for instance, euro notes and coins being introduced on 1 January 2002, there are nevertheless some important implications of British policy. These include the cost to manufacturing industry which has witnessed a steady appreciation in the value of the pound, thereby making it more difficult for exporters to be competitive. This appears also to have had a negative impact on levels of inward investment. In a different vein, Britain has been isolated from meetings of those countries participating in the euro-zone, which, more generally, brings into question whether Britain can be a leading member of the EU and at the same time be absent from the euro-zone.

- Despite non-participation in the euro-zone, Britain will nonetheless be affected by the single currency. For instance, companies exporting to other euro-zone member states will have to trade in euros.

- In advancing the case for membership of the single currency, the British government is faced with an electorate that appears to be increasingly eurosceptic in its beliefs. The challenge for any government wishing to participate in the single currency is therefore to change the attitude of the electorate. There are many potent arguments for membership, not just the fact that it would make Britain more influential within the EU. Instead, the fact that participation in the euro-zone would more than likely reduce mortgage repayments is a particularly strong point to advance. A similarly important argument in favour of membership is that non-participation in the euro-zone has had a direct impact on increasing the value of the pound, which in turn has had a negative impact on jobs and manufacturing industry. Such points are salient ones that affect all individuals and are far away from political duelling among MPs as to whether membership is right or not.

Questions

1. To what extent is Britain an awkward partner in the EU?

2. Evaluate the arguments for and against British membership of the single currency.

3. Assess the impact that the EU has had on Britain.

4. Is it correct to view the single currency as a move too far in the process of European integration?

5. 'The history of Britain's engagement on monetary union is one of policy being primarily determined by a limited number of officials and ministers.' Discuss.

6. Why has the issue of European integration been such a divisive issue for the Conservative Party in recent years?

Further reading

Bulmer, Simon and Burch, Martin (1998) 'Organizing for Europe: Whitehall, the British State and European Union', *Public Administration*, Vol. 76, Winter, pp. 601–28.

Dyson, Kenneth (2000) *The Politics of the Euro-Zone: Stability or Breakdown?*, Oxford: Oxford University Press.

Eijffinger, Sylvester C. W. and De Haan, Jakob (2000) *European Monetary and Fiscal Policy*, Oxford: Oxford University Press.

Forster, Anthony and Blair, Alasdair (2002) *The Making of Britain's European Foreign Policy*, Harlow: Longman.

George, Stephen and Bache, Ian (2001) *Politics in the European Union*, Oxford: Oxford University Press, Chapters 1, 2 and 26.

Gros, Daniel and Thygesen, Niels (1998) *European Monetary Integration*, 2nd edn, Harlow: Longman.

Hennessy, Peter (1998) 'The Blair Style of Government: An Historical Perspective and an Interim Audit', *Government and Opposition*, Vol. 33, No. 1, Winter.

Hennessy, Peter (2000) 'The Blair Style and the Requirements of Twenty-First Century Premiership', *The Political Quarterly*, pp. 386–95.

Levitt, Malcolm and Lord, Christopher (2000) *The Political Economy of Monetary Union*, Basingstoke: Macmillan, Chapter 15.

Stephens, Philip (1996) *Politics and the Pound*, London: Macmillan.

Stephens, Philip (2001) 'The Treasury under Labour', in Anthony Seldon (ed.) *The Blair Effect*, London: Little, Brown.

Verdun, Amy (2000) 'Monetary Integration in Europe: Ideas and Evolution', in Maria Green Cowles and Michael Smith (eds.) *The State of the European Union*, Vol. 5: *Risks, Reform, Resistance, and Revival*, Oxford: Oxford University Press, pp. 91–109.

Wallace, Helen (1997) 'At Odds with Europe', *Political Studies*, Vol. 45, No. 4, pp. 677–88.

Notes

[1] Lord Jenkins, in House of Lords (1995–96), Vol. II – Evidence, HL86-I, Session 1995–96, Q. 306, p. 96.

[2] *Financial Times*, 17 June 1999, p. 10; *Financial Times*, 15 October 1999, p. 23; and *The Economist*, 16 October 1999, p. 33.

[3] *The Times*, 19 January 1998, p. 5.

[4] *The Times*, 15 October 1999, p. 1; *Financial Times*, 16 April 1999, p. 10; *The Sunday Telegraph*, 14 March 1999, p. 20; and *The Times*, 23 September 1999, p. 13.

[5] *The Times*, 15 October 1999, p. 6.

[6] *The Observer*, 21 January 2001, p. 5.

[7] *Financial Times*, 4 September 2000, p. 18.

[8] *Financial Times*, 30 November 1999, p. 1.

[9] *The Guardian*, 8 February 2001, p. 10, and *The Guardian*, 8 November 2000, p. 16.

[10] *The Guardian*, 30 September 2000, p. 5.

[11] *The Guardian*, 30 September 2000, p. 4.

[12] *The Times*, 12 April 1999, p. 2 and *The Observer*, 21 March 1999, p. 4.

[13] *Financial Times*, 2 October 2000, p. 23.

[14] *Daily Telegraph*, 19 February 1999, p. 10 and *Financial Times*, 19 March 1999, p. 6.

[15] *The Guardian*, 29 June 2001, p. 17.

Bibliography

Adams, J. J. (1990) 'The Exchange Rate Mechanism of the European Monetary System', *Bank of England Quarterly Bulletin*, Vol. 30, No. 4, pp. 479–81.

Aldcroft, Derek H. and Oliver, Michael J. (1998) *Exchange Rate Regimes in the Twentieth Century*, Cheltenham: Edward Elgar.

Apel, Emmanuel (1998) *European Monetary Integration: 1958–2002*, London: Routledge.

Artis, Michael (1990) 'The United Kingdom and the EMS', in Paul De Grauwe and Lucas Papademos (eds.) *The European Monetary System in the 1990's*, Harlow: Longman.

Artis, M. J. and Lewis, M. (1990) *Money in Britain: Monetary Policy, Innovation and Europe*, Hemel Hempstead: Philip Allan.

Baimbridge, Mark, et al. (2000) *The Impact of the Euro: Debating Britain's Future*, Basingstoke: Macmillan.

Baker, David, et al. (1993a) 'Whips or Scorpions? The Maastricht Vote and the Conservative Party', *Parliamentary Affairs*, Vol. 46, No. 2, pp. 147–66.

Baker, David, et al. (1993b) '1846 . . . 1906 . . . 1996? Conservative Splits and European Integration', *The Political Quarterly*, Vol. 64, No. 4, pp. 420–34.

Baker, David, et al. (1994) 'The Parliamentary Siege of Maastricht: Conservative Divisions and British Ratification', *Parliamentary Affairs*, Vol. 47, No. 1, pp. 37–60.

Balen, Malcolm (1994) *Kenneth Clarke*, London: Fourth Estate.

Bank of England (1992) 'The Maastricht Agreement on Economic and Monetary Union', *Bank of England Quarterly Bulletin*, Vol. 32, No. 1, pp. 64–8.

Barbour, Philippe (ed.) (1996) *The European Union Handbook*, London: Fitzroy Dearborn.

Barrell, Ray, Britton, Andrew and Pain, Nigel (1994) *When the Time was Right? The UK Experience of the ERM*, National Institute of Economic and Social Research, Discussion Paper No. 58, London: NIESR.

Beloff, Nora (1963) *The General Says No*, Harmondsworth: Penguin.

Bender, Brian (1991) 'Whitehall, Central Government and 1992', *Public Policy and Administration*, Vol. 6, No. 1, pp. 13–20.

Bethell-Jones, Richard (1999) *EMU: the Legal, I.T. and Practical Issue*, London: Sweet and Maxwell.

Blair, Alasdair (1998a) 'UK Policy Coordination during the 1990–91 Intergovernmental Conference', *Diplomacy and Statecraft*, Vol. 9, No. 2, pp. 160–83.

Blair, Alasdair (1998b) 'Swimming with the Tide? Britain and the Maastricht Treaty Negotiations on Common Foreign and Security Policy', *Contemporary British History*, Vol. 12, No. 4, Winter, pp. 87–102.

Blair, Alasdair (1999a) *Longman Companion to the European Union since 1945*, Harlow: Longman.

Blair, Alasdair (1999b) *Dealing with Europe: Britain and the Negotiation of the Maastricht Treaty*, Aldershot: Ashgate.

Blair, Alasdair (1999c) 'Negotiating Treaty Change: Britain and Maastricht', *Centre for the Study of Diplomacy*, University of Leicester, Discussion Paper No. 49.

Blair, Alasdair (2000) 'New Labour: New Social Policy', *Talking Politics*, Vol. 13, No. 1, pp. 4–8.

Blair, Alasdair (2001) 'Understanding the Major Governments', *Contemporary British History*, Vol. 15, No. 1, pp. 115–22.

Blair, Alasdair, Karsten, Luchien and Leopold, John (2001a) 'Britain and the Working Time Regulations', *Politics*, Vol. 21, No. 1, pp. 51–6.

Blair, Alasdair, Karsten, Luchien and Leopold, John (2001b) 'An Awkward Partner: Britain's Implementation of the Working Time Directive', *Time and Society*, Vol. 10, No. 1, pp. 63–76.

Blair, Tony (1996) *New Britain: My Vision of a Young Country*, London: Fourth Estate.

Blair, Tony (1997a) Speech to the Party of European Socialists Congress, Malmö, 6 June 1997.

Blair, Tony (1997b) 'The Principles of a Modern British Foreign Policy', speech at the Lord Mayor's banquet, Guildhall, London, 1 November.

Blair, Tony (2000) 'Committed to Europe, Reforming Europe', speech at Ghent City Hall, 23 February. See http://www.number-10.gov.uk/news.asp?NewsId=579& SectionId=32

Blaker, Peter (1974) 'Labour's "Renegotiation" Policy: A Conservative View', *World Today*, Vol. 30, No. 8, pp. 319–26.

Boardman, Robert (1973) 'What EEC Entry May Mean for Britain's Foreign Policy', *International Perspectives*, No. 2, pp. 7–11.

Britain in Europe (1999) *Britain and the Single Currency – The Business Case for Membership*, London: Britain in Europe.

British Invisibles Exports Council European Committee (1990) 'Stage 2 of Economic and Monetary Union', London: unpublished paper, 27 March.

Brittan, Leon (1994) *Europe: The Europe We Need*, London: Hamish Hamilton.

Brivati, Brian and Jones, Harriet (eds.) (1993) *From Reconstruction to Integration: Britain and Europe since 1945*, London: Leicester University Press.

Brivati, Brian and Heffernan, Richard (2000) *The Labour Party: A Centenary History*, Basingstoke: Macmillan.

Brown, George (1971) *In My Way*, London: Victor Gallancz.

Bullen, Roger and Pelly, M. E. (eds.) (1986) *Documents on British Policy Overseas*. Series II, Vol. I: *1950–1952*, London: HMSO.

Buller, Jim (2000) *National Statecraft and European Integration: The Conservative Government and the European Union, 1979–97*, London: Pinter.

Bullock, Alan (1983) *Ernest Bevin: Foreign Secretary*, London: Heinemann.

Bulmer, Simon (2000) 'European Policy: Fresh Start or False Dawn?', in David Coates and Peter Lawler (eds.) *New Labour in Power*, Manchester: Manchester University Press, pp. 240–53.

Bulmer, Simon and Burch, Martin (1998) 'Organizing for Europe: Whitehall, the British State and European Union', *Public Administration*, Vol. 76, Winter, pp. 601–28.

Bulmer, Simon and Burch, Martin (2000) 'The Europeanisation of British Central Government', in R. A. W. Rhodes, *Transforming British Government*, Vol. 1: *Changing Institutions*, Basingstoke: Macmillan, pp. 46–62.

Burch, Martin and Holliday, Ian (1996) *The British Cabinet System*, Hemel Hempstead: Prentice Hall/Harvester Wheatsheaf.

Burch, Martin and Holliday, Ian (2000) 'New Labour and the Machinery of Government', in David Coates and Peter Lawler (eds.) *New Labour in Power*, Manchester: Manchester University Press, pp. 65–79.

Busch, Andreas (1994) 'The Crisis in the EMS', *Government and Opposition*, Vol. 29, No. 1, pp. 80–96.

Butler, Sir Michael (1986) *Europe: More than a Continent*, London: William Heinemann.

Cameron, David R. (1992) 'The 1992 Initiative: Causes and Consequences', in Albert M. Sbragia (ed.) *Euro-Politics: Institutions and Policymaking in the New European Community*, Washington, D.C.: The Brookings Institution.

Campbell, John (1993) *Edward Heath*, London: Jonathan Cape.

Camps, Miriam (1965) *What Kind of Europe?*, London: Oxford University Press.

Camps, Miriam (1969) *European Unification in the Sixties: From the Veto to the Crisis*, Oxford: Oxford University Press.

Cash, William (1991) *Against a Federal Europe*, London: Duckworth.

Cecchini, Paolo, Catinat, Michel and Jacquemin, Alexis (1988) *The European Challenge: 1992: The Benefits of a Single Market*, Aldershot: Wildwood House.

Castle, Barbara (1984) *The Castle Diaries, 1964–70*, London: Weidenfeld and Nicolson.

Charlton, Michael (1993) *The Price of Victory*, London: BBC Publications.

Church, C. and Phinnemore, D. (1994) *European Union and European Community: A Handbook and Commentary on the Post-Maastricht Treaties*, Hemel Hempstead: Harvester Wheatsheaf.

Clark, Alan (1999) *The Tories: Conservatives and the Nation State 1922–97*, London: BCA.

Coates, David and Lawler, Peter (eds.) (2000) *New Labour in Power*, Manchester: Manchester University Press.

Cobham, David (1989) 'Strategies for Monetary Integration Revisited', *Journal of Common Market Studies*, Vol. 27, No. 3, pp. 203–18.

Coffey, Peter and Presley, John R. (1971) *European Monetary Integration*, Basingstoke: Macmillan.

Connolly, Bernard (1995) *The Rotten Heart of Europe: The Dirty War for Europe's Money*, London: Faber.

Cosgrove, Ken (1992) 'The Odd Man Out: The United Kingdom's Semidetached Relationship with Community Europe', *International Relations*, Vol. 11, No. 3, pp. 269–84.

Currie, David and Dicks, Geoffrey (1990) 'Options for ERM Entry', *Economic Outlook*, June, pp. 18–25.

Daniels, Philip (1998) 'From Hostility to "Constructive Engagement": The Europeanisation of the Labour Party', *West European Politics*, Vol. 21, No. 1, pp. 72–96.

Davies, Gavyn (1989) *Britain and the European Monetary Question*, Economic Study No. 1, London: Institute for Public Policy Research.

Davis, Richard (1997) 'The "Problem of de Gaulle": British Reactions to General de Gaulle's Veto of the UK Application to Join the Common Market', *Journal of Contemporary History*, Vol. 32, No. 4, pp. 453–64.

De Grauwe, Paul and Papademos, Lucas (eds.) (1990) *The European Monetary System in the 1990's*, Harlow: Longman.

De Grauwe, Paul (1994) 'Towards EMU without the EMS', *Economic Policy*, April, pp. 149–85.

Dell, Edmond (1995) *The Schuman Plan and the British Abdication of Leadership in Europe*, Oxford: Clarendon Press.

Denman, Roy (1996) *Missed Chances*, London: Cassell.

Dickie, John (1992) *Inside the Foreign Office*, London: Chapmans Publishers.

Dinan, Desmond (1999) *Ever Closer Union? An Introduction to European Integration*, 2nd edn, Basingstoke: Macmillan.

Dobson, Alan (1991) 'The Special Relationship and European Integration', *Diplomacy and Statecraft*, Vol. 2, No. 1, pp. 79–102.

Donoghue, Bernard and Jones, G. W. (1973) *Herbert Morrison: Portrait of a Politician*, London: Weidenfeld and Nicolson.

Duchène, François (1994) *Jean Monnet: The First Statesman of Interdependence*, London: W. W. Norton.

Dyson, Kenneth (1994) *Elusive Union: The Process of Economic and Monetary Union in Europe*, Harlow: Longman.

Dyson, Kenneth (2000a) *The Politics of the Euro-Zone: Stability or Breakdown?*, Oxford: Oxford University Press.

Dyson, Kenneth (2000b) 'Europeanization, Whitehall Culture and the Treasury as Institutional Veto Player: A Constructivist Approach to Economic and Monetary Union', *Public Administration*, Vol. 78, No. 4, pp. 897–914.

Dyson, Kenneth (2000c) 'EMU as Europeanization: Convergence, Diversity and Contingency', *Journal of Common Market Studies*, Vol. 38, No. 4, pp. 645–66.

Dyson, Kenneth and Featherstone, Kevin (1999) *The Road to Maastricht: Negotiating Economic and Monetary Union*, Oxford: Oxford University Press.

Eden, Sir Anthony (1960) *Full Circle*, London: Cassell.

Eijffinger, Sylvester C. W. and De Haan, Jakob (2000) *European Monetary and Fiscal Policy*, Oxford: Oxford University Press.

Ellison, James (2000) *Threatening Europe: Britain and the Creation of the European Community, 1955–58*, Basingstoke: Macmillan.

Emerson, Michael et al. (1992) *One Market, One Money. An Evaluation of the Potential Benefits and Costs of Forming an Economic and Monetary Union*, Oxford: Oxford University Press.

European Commission (1990) Committee for the Study of Economic and Monetary Union, *Report on Economic and Monetary Union in the European Community* (the Delors Report), Luxembourg: Office for Official Publications of the European Communities.

Forster, Anthony (1999) *Britain and the Maastricht Negotiations*, Basingstoke: Macmillan.

Forster, Anthony and Blair, Alasdair (2002) *The Making of Britain's European Foreign Policy*, Harlow: Longman.

Fratianni, Michele, Von Hagen, Jürgen and Waller, Christopher (1992) 'The Maastricht Way to EMU', *Essays in International Finance*, Department of Economics, Princeton University, No. 187.

Freeman, Vaughan (1999) *The Euro and the UK Automotive Industry*, London: Action Centre for Europe.

Geddes, Andrew (1994) 'Labour and the European Community 1973–93: pro-Europeanism, "Europeanisation" and their implications', *Contemporary Record*, Vol. 8, No. 2, pp. 370–80.

George, Stephen (1985) *Politics and Policy in the European Community*, Oxford: Clarendon Press.

George, Stephen (1992) *Britain and European Co-operation since 1945*, Oxford: Basil Blackwell.

George, Stephen (1998) *An Awkward Partner*, 3rd edn, Oxford: Oxford University Press.

George, Stephen and Bache, Ian (2001) *Politics in the European Union*, Oxford: Oxford University Press.

Giavazzi, F., Micossi, S. and Miller, M. (eds.) (1990) *The European Monetary System*, Cambridge: Cambridge University Press.

Gilmour, Ian (1992) *Dancing with Dogma*, London: Simon and Schuster.

Gladwyn, Lord (1966) *The European Idea*, London: Weidenfeld and Nicolson.

Goldsmith, James (1994) *The Trap*, Basingstoke: Macmillan.

Goldsmith, James (1995) *The Response*, Basingstoke: Macmillan.

Goodwin, Geoffrey (1972) 'British European Foreign Policy since 1945: The Long Odyssey to Europe', in Michael Leifer (ed.) *Constraints and Adjustments in British Foreign Policy*, London: George Allen and Unwin.

Gowland, D. A. and Turner, Arthur (2000a) *Britain and European Integration, 1945–1998: A Documentary History*, London: Routledge.

Gowland, D. A. and Turner, Arthur (2000b) *Reluctant Europeans: Britain and European Integration, 1945–1998*, Harlow: Longman.

Grahl, John (1997) *After Maastricht: A Guide to European Monetary Union*, London: Lawrence and Wishart.

Grant, Charles (1994) *Delors: Inside the House that Jacques Built*, London: Nicholas Brealey.

Grice, J. (1990) 'The UK Proposal for a European Monetary Fund and a "Hard ECU": Making Progress towards Economic and Monetary Union in Europe', *Treasury Bulletin*, Autumn, pp. 1–9.

Gros, Daniel (1989) 'Paradigms for the Monetary Union of Europe', *Journal of Common Market Studies*, Vol. 27, No. 3, pp. 218–30.

Gros, Daniel and Thygesen, Niels (1998) *European Monetary Integration* 2nd edn, Harlow: Longman.

Haas, Ernst (1958) *The Uniting of Europe: Political, Social and Economic Forces*, London: Stevens and Sons.

Harris, Kenneth (1988) *Thatcher*, London: Weidenfeld and Nicolson.

Heath, Edward (1998) *The Course of my Life*, London: Hodder and Stoughton.

Henderson, Nicholas (1994) *Mandarin: The Diaries of an Ambassador 1969–1982*, London: Weidenfeld and Nicolson.

Hennessy, Peter (1998) 'The Blair Style of Government: An Historical Perspective and an Interim Audit', *Government and Opposition*, Vol. 33, No. 1, Winter, pp. 3–20.

Hennessy, Peter (2000) 'The Blair Style and the Requirements of Twenty-First Century Premiership', *The Political Quarterly*, pp. 386–95.

Heseltine, Michael (1989) *The Challenge of Europe: Can Britain Win?*, London: Weidenfeld and Nicolson.

Higgins, Byron (1993) 'Was the ERM Crisis Inevitable?', *Federal Reserve Bank of Kansas City Economic Review*, Vol. 78, No. 4, pp. 27–40.

Hix, Simon (1999) *The Political System of the European Union*, Basingstoke: Macmillan.

HM Treasury (1988–89) 'Explanatory Memorandum on European Community Document: Report on Economic and Monetary Union in the European Community: Report of Committee for the Study of Economic and Monetary Union', May 1990, submitted to *Treasury and Civil Service Committee Fourth Report*, 'The Delors Report', HC341.

HM Treasury (1989) *An Evolutionary Approach to Economic and Monetary Union*, London: HM Treasury, November.

HM Treasury (1991) 'Economic and Monetary Union – Beyond Stage I. Possible Treaty Provisions and Statute for a European Monetary Fund', *Europe Documents*, No. 1682, 10 January.

HM Treasury (1991–92) 'Economic and Monetary Union: The Agreement at Maastricht', *Treasury Bulletin*, Vol. 3, Issue 1, London: HMSO.

Hogg, Sarah and Hill, Jonathan (1995) *Too Close to Call*, London: Little, Brown.

Holmes, Martin (1996) *The Eurosceptical Reader*, Basingstoke: Macmillan.

House of Lords (1989–90) Select Committee on the European Communities, *The Delors Committee Report*, Report HL3.

House of Lords (1989–90) Select Committee on the European Communities, *Economic and Monetary Union and Political Union*, Report HL88.

House of Lords (1995–96) Select Committee on the European Communities, *An EMU of 'Ins' and 'Outs'*, Vol. I – Report, HL86; Vol. II – Evidence, HL86-I.

Howe, Geoffrey (1990) 'Sovereignty and Interdependence: Britain's Place in the World', *International Affairs*, Vol. 66, No. 4, October, pp. 675–95.

Howe, Geoffrey (1994) *Conflict of Loyalty*, Basingstoke: Macmillan.

Hughes, Kirsty and Smith, Edward (1998) 'New Labour – New Europe', *International Affairs*, Vol. 74, No. 1, January 1998, pp. 93–103.

Ingham, Bernard (1991) *Kill the Messenger*, London: Fontana.

Jeffreys, Kevin (1993) *The Labour Party since 1945*, Basingstoke: Macmillan.

Jenkins, Roy (1978) 'European Monetary Union', lecture given at the European University Institute, Florence, 27 October 1977, reproduced in *Lloyds Bank Review*, Vol. 127, pp. 1–14.

Jenkins, Roy (1989) *European Diary, 1977–1981*, London: Collins.

Jenkins, Roy (1991) *A Life at the Centre*, Basingstoke: Macmillan.

Johnson, Christopher (ed.) (1991) *ECU: The Currency of Europe*, London: Euromoney Publication.

Johnson, Christopher (1996) *In with the Euro, Out with the Pound: The Single Currency for Britain*, London: Penguin.

Kassim, Hussein (2000) 'The United Kingdom', in Hussein Kassim, B. Guy Peters and Vincent Wright (eds.) *The National Co-ordination of EU Policy: The Domestic Level*, Oxford: Oxford University Press, pp. 22–53.

Kavanagh, Dennis (2000) *British Politics: Continuities and Change*, 4th edition, Oxford: Oxford University Press.

Kavanagh, Dennis (2001) 'The Cabinet and Prime Minister', in Bill Jones et al. (eds.) *Politics UK*, 4th edn, Harlow: Longman, pp. 409–36.

Keegan, William (1984) *Mrs Thatcher's Economic Experiment*, London: Allen Lane.

Kitzinger, U. W. (1967) *The Common Market and Community*, London: Routledge and Kegan Paul.

Kitzinger, U. W. (1968) *The Second Try: Labour and the EEC*, London: Pergamon Press.

Kitzinger, U. W. (1973) *Diplomacy and Persuasion*, London: Thames and Hudson.

Kloten, Norbert (1980) 'Germany's Monetary and Financial Policy and the European Community', in Wilfred L. Kohl and Giorgio Basevi (eds.) *West Germany: A European and Global Power*, Lexington: Lexington Books, D. C. Heath and Company.

Lamont, Norman (1995) *Sovereign Britain*, London: Duckworth.

Lamont, Norman (1999) *In Office*, London: Little, Brown.

Lawler, Peter (2000) 'New Labour's Foreign Policy', in David Coates and Peter Lawler (eds.) (2000) *New Labour in Power*, Manchester: Manchester University Press, pp. 281–99.

Lawson, Nigel (1992) *The View From No. 11*, London: Bantam Press.

Levitt, Malcolm and Lord, Christopher (2000) *The Political Economy of Monetary Union*, Basingstoke: Macmillan.

Lindberg, Leon (1963) *The Political Dynamics of European Integration*, Oxford: Oxford University Press.

Lipgens, Walter (1982) *A History of European Integration*, Vol. I: *1945–1947: The Formation of the European Unity Movement*, Oxford: Clarendon Press.

Lord, Christopher (1993) *British Entry to the European Community under the Heath Government, 1970–74*, London: Dartmouth.

Lord, Christopher (1996) *Britain and the Formation of the European Community, 1950–1952*, Aldershot: Dartmouth.

Louis, Jean-Victor (1988) 'Monetary Capacity in the Single European Act', *Common Market Law Review*, Vol. 25, pp. 9–34.

Louis, Jean-Victor (1989) 'A Monetary Union for Tomorrow', *Common Market Law Review*, Vol. 26, pp. 301–26.

Ludlow, N. Piers (1997) *Dealing with Britain: The Six and the First UK Application to the EEC*, Cambridge: Cambridge University Press.

Ludlow, P. (1982) *The Making of the European Monetary System: A Case Study of the Politics of the European Community*, London: Butterworth Scientific.

Ludlow, P. (1993) 'The UK Presidency: A View from Brussels', *Journal of Common Market Studies*, Vol. 31, No. 2, June, pp. 246–67.

Ludlow, P. (1998) 'The 1998 UK Presidency: A View from Brussels', *Journal of Common Market Studies*, Vol. 36, No. 4, June, pp. 573–83.

Lynch, Philip (1999) *The Politics of Nationhood: Sovereignty, Britishness and Conservative Politics*, Basingstoke: Macmillan.

McCormick, John (1999) *Understanding the European Union: A Concise Introduction*, Basingstoke: Macmillan.

Mcdonald, Frank and Zis, George (1989) 'The European Monetary System: Towards 1992 and Beyond', *Journal of Common Market Studies*, Vol. 27, No. 3, pp. 183–202.

Major, John (1999) *The Autobiography*, London: HarperCollins.

Margetts, Helen (1997) 'The 1997 British General Election: New Labour, New Britain?', *West European Politics*, Vol. 20, No. 4, pp. 180–91.

Marjolin, Robert et al. (1975) *Report of the Study Group Economic and Monetary Union 1980, 'Marjolin Report'*, Brussels: Commission of the European Communities.

Marsh, David (1993) *The Bundesbank: The Bank that Rules Europe*, London: Mandarin.

May, Alex (1999) *Britain and Europe since 1945*, Harlow: Longman.

Mayes, D. G. (1994) 'The European Monetary System', in Ali M. El-Agraa, *The Economics of the European Community*, London: Harvester Wheatsheaf.

Mayne, Richard and Pinder, John (1990) *Federal Union: The Pioneers*, Basingstoke: Macmillan.

Milward, Alan S. (1984) *The Reconstruction of Western Europe 1945–1951*, London: Methuen.

Minford, Patrick (1992) 'Why We Should Leave the ERM', *Economic Outlook*, February, pp. 31–4.

Monnet, Jean (1978) *Memoirs*, London: Collins.

Moon, Jeremy (1985) *European Integration in British Politics: A Study of Issue Change*, Aldershot: Gower.

Moran, Michael and Alexander, Elizabeth (2000) 'The Economic Policy of New Labour', in David Coates and Peter Lawler (eds.) *New Labour in Power*, Manchester: Manchester University Press, pp. 108–21.

Moravcsik, A. (1991) 'Negotiating the Single European Act: National Interests and Conventional Statecraft in the European Community', *International Organization*, Vol. 45, No. 1, pp. 19–56.

Moravcsik, A. (1993) 'Preferences and Power in the European Community: A Liberal Intergovernmentalist Approach', *Journal of Common Market Studies* Vol. 31, No. 4, pp. 473–524.

Northledge, F. S. (1974) *Descent from Power: British Foreign Policy, 1945–1973*, London: Allen and Unwin.

Nutting, Anthony (1960) *Europe Will Not Wait. A Warning and a Way Out*, London: Hollis and Carter.

O'Brien, Richard (1992) *Global Financial Integration: The End of Geography*, London: Pinter/RIIA.

Ohmae, Kenichi (1990) *The Borderless World: Power and Strategy in the Interlinked Economy*, New York: Harper Business.

O'Neill, Con and Hannay, David (2000) *Britain joins the European Community: Report on the Negotiations for UK Entry into the European Community, June 1970–January 1972*, Ilford: Frank Cass.

Padoa-Schioppa, Tommaso (1987) *Efficiency, Stability and Equity. A Strategy for the Evolution of the Economic System of the European Community*, Oxford: Oxford University Press.

Parkinson, Cecil (1992) *Right at the Centre*, London: Weidenfeld and Nicolson.

Peterson, John and Bomberg, Elizabeth (1999) *Decision-Making in the European Union*, Basingstoke: Macmillan.

Pipkorn, Jörn (1994) 'Legal Arrangements in the Treaty of Maastricht for the Effectiveness of the Economic and Monetary Union', *Common Market Law Review*, Vol. 31, pp. 263–91.

Porter, Dilwyn (1995) 'Downhill all the Way: Thirteen Tory Years 1951–64', in R. Coopley, S. Fielding and N. Tiratsoo (eds.) *The Wilson Governments 1964–1970*, London: Pinter.

Powell, Enoch (1971) *The Common Market – The Case Against*, London: Paperfonts.

Prior, James (1986) *A Balance of Power*, London: Hamish Hamilton.

Pryce, Roy (1973) *The Politics of the European Community*, London: Butterworth.

Rawnsley, Andrew (2001) *Servants of the People: The Inside Story of New Labour*, London: Penguin.

Redwood, John (1997) *Our Currency, Our Country: The Dangers of European Monetary Union*, London: Penguin Books.

Richards, Paul (1991) 'The UK Proposals for an Evolutionary Approach to Monetary Union', in Christopher Johnson (ed.) *ECU: The Currency of Europe*, London: Euromoney Publication, pp. 187–97.

Riddell, Peter (1983) *The Thatcher Government*, Oxford: Martin Robertson.

Ridley, Nicholas (1991) *My Style of Government: The Thatcher Years*, London: Hutchinson.

Rosamond, Ben (2000) *Theories of European Integration*, Basingstoke: Macmillan.

Sandholtz, Wayne (1993) 'Monetary Bargains: The Treaty on EMU', in Alan W. Cafruny and Glenda G. Rosenthal, *The State of the European Community*, Vol. 2, Harlow/Boulder: Longman/Lynne Rienner, pp. 125–42.

Scobie, H. M. (ed.) (1998) *European Monetary Union: The Way Forward*, London: Routledge.

Scott, Andrew (1986) 'Britain and the EMS: An Appraisal of the Report of the Treasury and Civil Service Committee', *Journal of Common Market Studies*, Vol. 24, No. 3, March, pp. 187–201.

Seldon, Anthony (1990) 'The Cabinet Office and Coordination 1979–87', *Public Administration*, Vol. 68, pp. 103–21.

Seldon, Anthony (1997) *Major: A Political Life*, London: Weidenfeld and Nicolson.

Seldon, Anthony and Ball, Stuart (eds.) (1994) *Conservative Century*, Oxford: Oxford University Press.

Sharp, Paul (1982) 'The Place of the European Community in the Foreign Policy of British Governments, 1961–1971', *Millennium: Journal of International Studies*, Vol. 11, No. 2, pp. 155–72.

Smith, Martin J. (1999) *The Core Executive in Britain*, Basingstoke: Macmillan.

Smith, Martin, Marsh, David and Richards, David (1993) 'Central Government Departments and the Policy Process', *Public Administration*, Vol. 71, pp. 567–94.

Spaak, Paul-Henri (1971) *The Continuing Battle. Memoirs of a European 1936–1966*, London: Weidenfeld and Nicolson.

Spicer, Michael (1992) *A Treaty Too Far: A New Policy for Europe*, London: Fourth Estate.

Stephens, Philip (1996) *Politics and the Pound*, London: Macmillan.

Stephens, Philip (2001) 'The Treasury under Labour', in Anthony Seldon (ed.) *The Blair Effect*, London: Little, Brown.

Szász, André (2000) *The Road to European Monetary Union*, Basingstoke: Macmillan.

Thain, Colin and Wright, Maurice (1995) *The Treasury and Whitehall: The Planning and Control of Public Expenditure, 1976–1993*, Oxford: Clarendon Press.

Thatcher, Margaret (1993) *The Downing Street Years*, London: HarperCollins.

Thatcher, Margaret (1995) *The Path to Power*, London: HarperCollins.

Thompson, Helen (1993) 'The UK and the Exchange Rate Mechanism 1978–90', in Brian Brivati and Harriet Jones (eds.) *From Reconstruction to Integration: Britain and Europe since 1945*, London: Leicester University Press, pp. 227–40.

Thompson, Helen (1996) *The British Conservative Government and the European Exchange Rate Mechanism, 1979–1994*, London: Pinter.

Tranholm-Mikkelsen, J. (1991) 'Neofunctionalism: Obstinate or Obsolete? A Reappraisal in Light of the New Dynamism of the European Community', *Millennium*, Vol. 20, pp. 1–22.

Tugendhat, Christopher (1987) *Making Sense of Europe*, Harmondsworth: Penguin.

Turner, John (2000) *The Tories and Europe*, Manchester: Manchester University Press.

Ungerer, Horst (1989) 'The European Monetary System and the International System', *Journal of Common Market Studies*, Vol. 27, No. 3, pp. 231–48.

United Kingdom (1989) *An Evolutionary Approach to Economic and Monetary Union*, London: HM Treasury.

United Kingdom (1997) *UK Membership of the Single Currency: An Assessment of the Five Economic Tests*, London: HM Treasury, October. http://www.hm-treasury.gov.uk/pub/html/docs/emumem/main.html

United Kingdom (1998) *United Kingdom Convergence Programme*, London: HM Treasury, December. http://www.hm-treasury.gov.uk/pub/html/docs/emucp/UKCP98.pdf

Uri, Pierre (ed.) (1968) *From Commonwealth to Common Market*, Harmondsworth: Penguin in association with the Atlantic Institute.

Urwin, Derek W. (1991) *The Community of Europe*, London: Longman.

Vaughan, Richard (1976) *Post-War Integration in Europe*, London: Edward Arnold.

Verdun, Amy (1999) 'The Role of the Delors Committee in the Creation of EMU: An Epistemic Community?', *Journal of European Public Policy*, Vol. 2, No. 2, pp. 308–28.

Verdun, Amy (2000a) *European Responses to Globalization and Financial Market Integration: Perceptions of Economic and Monetary Union in Britain, France and Germany*, Basingstoke: Macmillan.

Verdun, Amy (2000b) 'Monetary Integration in Europe: Ideas and Evolution', in Maria Green Cowles and Michael Smith (eds.) *The State of the European Union*, Vol. 5: *Risks, Reform, Resistance, and Revival*, Oxford: Oxford University Press, pp. 91–109.

Wallace, Helen (1997) 'At Odds with Europe', *Political Studies*, Vol. 45, No. 4, pp. 677–88.

Wallace, William (1975) *The Foreign Policy Process in Britain*, London: Royal Institute of International Affairs.

Walker, Peter (1991) *Staying Power: An Autobiography*, London: Bloomsbury.

Walters, Alan (1986) *Britain's Economic Renaissance*, Oxford: Oxford University Press.

Walters, Alan (1990) *Sterling in Danger*, London: Fontana.

Watson, Alison M. (1997) *Aspects of European Monetary Integration: The Politics of Convergence*, Basingstoke: Macmillan.

Werner, Pierre et al. (1970) 'Report to the Council and the Commission on the Realisation by Stages of Economic and Monetary Union in the Community' ('Werner Report'). *Bull. EC*, Supplement II.

Wilkes, George (ed.) (1997) *Britain's Failure to Enter the European Community 1961–63*, Ilford: Frank Cass.

Worre, Torben (1995) 'First No, then Yes: The Danish Referendums on the Maastricht Treaty 1992 and 1993', *Journal of Common Market Studies*, Vol. 33, Issue 2, June, pp. 235–57.

Young, Hugo (1993) *One of Us*, London: Pan Books.

Young, Hugo (1998) *This Blessed Plot: Britain and Europe from Churchill to Blair*, London: Papermac.

Young, John W. (1984) *Britain, France and the Unity of Europe*, London: Leicester University Press.

Young, John W. (2000) *Britain and European Unity, 1945–1999*, 2nd edn, Basingstoke: Macmillan.

Zurlinden, Mathias (1993) 'The Vulnerability of Pegged Exchange Rates: The British Pound in the ERM', *Federal Reserve Bank of St Louis Review*, Vol. 75, No. 5, September/October, pp. 41–56.

Internet addresses

Bank of England	http://www.bankofengland.co.uk
Bank of England: euro	http://www.bankofengland.co.uk/euro.htm
Bank of England: Practical Issues	http://www.bankofengland.co.uk/euro/piq.htm
Bank of England: practical preparations Q&A	http://www.bankofengland.co.uk/euro/qanda.htm
Department of Trade and Industry (DTI)	http://www.dti.gov.uk
HM Treasury	http://www.hm-treasury.gov.uk
HM Treasury: euro	http://www.euro.gov.uk
Prime Minister	http://www.number-10.gov.uk/
European Institutions (general)	http://europa.eu.int/index.htm
European Commission	http://europa.eu.int/comm/index_en.htm
European Parliament	http://www.europarl.eu.int
Economic and Financial Committee	http://europa.eu.int/comm/economy_finance/

Index